W9-AES-403

"PECULIAR INSTITUTIONS"

Books by ELAINE KENDALL

THE UPPER HAND

THE HAPPY MEDIOCRITY

"PECULIAR INSTITUTIONS"

An Informal History of the Seven Sister Colleges

by

Elaine Kendall

G. P. Putnam's Sons
New York

To the administrators, faculty, alumnae, students and trustees who shared the knowledge, recollection and opinion that fill this book. There were scores of them, and all were generous.

Contents

*Illustrations may be found
following pages 92 and 184.*

Prologue:
Beyond Mother's Knee

"COULD I have died a martyr in the cause, and thus ensured its success, I could have blessed the faggot and hugged the stake." The cause was state support for female education, the would-be St. Joan was Emma Willard, and the rhetorical standards of the 1820s were lofty and impassioned. The most militant feminists rarely scale such heights today. For one thing, dogged effort has finally reduced the supply of grand injustices, and for another, pejoration has deprived the movement of some dramatic images. Comparatively speaking, the rest of the struggle is a downhill run, leading straight to twenty-four-hour day care centers, revised and updated forms of marriage, free access to the executive suite and rows of Ms. on Senate office doors. As we glory in our headway, it's easy to forget that leverage comes with literacy, and literacy for women is a relative novelty.

Long before the Revolution, American males already had Harvard, Yale and Princeton, as well as a full range of other educational institutions—grammar schools, academies, seminaries and numerous smaller colleges. American girls had only their mother's knee. By 1818, the year that Emma Willard first introduced her *Plan for the Improvement of Female Education,* the gap was almost as wide as ever. Public schooling was a local option, whimsically interpreted. The towns could provide as much or as little as they wished, extending or restricting attendance as they saw fit. Ms. Willard presented her novel proposals to the New York state legislature, which dealt with the question by putting it repeatedly at the bottom of the agenda until the session was safely over. Lavish tributes to Mother's Knee filled the halls of Albany. In the opinion of the senators, it outshone not only our men's colleges, but also Oxford, Cambridge and Heidelberg as an institution of female edification. Despite the support of De Witt Clinton, John Adams and Thomas Jefferson, three more years went by before the Willard Seminary was actually under way, its building and grounds offered independently by the town of Troy. The academy still flourishes and claims to "mark the beginning of higher education for women in the United States." Since that is not precisely the same as being the first such school, and the rival contenders have either vanished or metamorphosed into other sorts of institutions entirely, there is no reason to dispute it. The Cavalier South did have a few early convents, including one at New Orleans that was established by an Ursuline order in 1727 and taught religion, needlework and something of what might be called "basic skills." Other religious groups, particularly the Moravians and Quakers, supported female seminaries during the eighteenth century, but these places did not really attempt to offer advanced education—a commodity for which there was little market in an era when girls were unwelcome in elementary schools. A few New England clergymen opened small academies for girls during the first decade of the nineteenth century, but these noble and well-intentioned efforts were ephemeral, never outlasting their founders. Until Emma Willard succeeded in extracting that bit of real estate from Troy, public and private support for such ventures were virtually nonexistent.

Some few ambitious and determined girls did succeed in learning to read and write in Colonial America, but hardly ever at public expense and certainly not in comfort. Their number was pitifully small, and those who gained more than the rudiments of literacy would hardly have crowded a saltbox parlor. The early Puritans apparently stretched St. Paul's dogma "I permit not a woman to teach" to mean that women should not be allowed to learn either. John Winthrop's *History of New England 1630–1649* tells what happened when a group of women met for what seems to have been a discussion of great issues. The town fathers decided that "though women might meet (some few together) to pray and edify one another; yet such a set assembly (as was then in practice at Boston) where sixty or more did meet every week, and one woman (in a prophetical way, by resolving questions of doctrine and expounding scripture) took upon her the whole exercise, was agreed to be disorderly, and without rule." Anne Hutchinson, the instigator of such a group, was banished by an inquisition that could have been conducted by Torquemada himself. She was branded a heretic and exiled to Rhode Island. Her persecutors trailed her there and eventually drove her to the hostile wilds of Long Island, where the entire Hutchinson family was murdered by Indians.

As the Puritan grip gradually relaxed, the image of a learned female improved infinitesimally. She was no longer regarded as a disorderly person or a heretic, but as a mere nuisance to her husband, family and friends. A sensible woman soon found ways to conceal her little store of knowledge or, if hints of it should accidentally slip out, to disparage or apologize for it. Abigail Adams, whose wistful letters show a continuing interest in women's education, described her own with a demurely rhymed disclaimer:

> The little learning I have gained
> Is all from simple nature drained.

In fact, the wife of John Adams was entirely self-educated. She disciplined herself to plod doggedly through works of ancient history whenever her household duties permitted, being careful to do so in the privacy of her boudoir. In her letters, she deplores the fact that it was still customary to "ridicule female learning" and, even in the "best families," to deny girls more than the barest rudiments. Matters had actually changed very little since the poet Anne Bradstreet described the Puritan attitude during the 1650s:

> For such despite they cast on female wits;
> If what I do proves well, it won't advance
> They'll say its stol'n, or else it was by chance.

The prevailing colonial feeling toward female education was so unanimously negative that it was not always thought necessary to mention it. Sometimes this turned out to be a boon. A few villages, in their haste to establish schools for boys, neglected to specify that only males would be admitted. From the beginning, they wrote their charters rather carelessly, using the loose generic term "children." This loophole was nearly always blocked as soon as the risks became apparent, but in the interim period of grace, girls were occasionally able to pick up a few crumbs of knowledge. They did so by sitting outside the schoolhouse or on its steps, eavesdropping on the boys' recitations. More rarely, girls were tolerated in the rear of the schoolhouse behind a curtain, in a kind of makeshift seraglio. This Levantine arrangement, however, was soon abandoned as inappropriate to the time and place, and the attendance requirements made unambiguous. New England winters and Cape Cod architecture being what they are, the amount of learning that one could acquire by these systems was necessarily scanty. Still, it was thought excessive. The female scholars in the yard and on the stairs seemed to suffer disproportionately from pleurisy and other respiratory ailments. Further proof of the Divine attitude toward the educating of women was not sought. Girls were excluded for their own good, as well as to ensure the future of the colonies.

After the Revolution the atmosphere in the New England states did become considerably more lenient. Here and there a town council might vote to allow girls inside the school building from five to seven in the morning, from six to eight at night or, in a few very liberal communities, during the few weeks in summer when the boys were at work in the fields or shipyards. This was a giant step forward and would have been epochal if teachers had always appeared at these awkward times. Unfortunately, the girls often had to muddle through on their own without benefit of faculty. The enlightened trend, moreover, was far from general. In 1792 the town of Wellesley, Massachusetts, voted "not to be at any expense for schooling girls," and similarly worded bylaws were quite usual throughout the Northern states until the 1820s. In the Southern colonies, where distances between the great estates delayed the beginnings of public schooling even longer, wealthy planters often imported tutors to instruct their sons in academic subjects. If they could afford the additional luxury, they might also engage singing and dancing masters for the daughters, who were not expected to share their brothers' more arduous lessons. In a pleasant little memoir of the South, *Colonial Days and Dames,* Anne Wharton, a descendant of Thomas Jefferson, noted that "very little from books was thought necessary for a girl. She was trained in domestic matters . . . the accomplishments of the day . . . to play upon the harpsichord or spinet, and to work impossible dragons and roses upon canvas."

Although the odds against a girl's gaining more than the sketchiest training during this era seem to have been overwhelming, there were some remarkable exceptions. The undiscouraged included Emma Willard herself; Catharine and Harriet Beecher, the clergyman's daughters who established an early academy at Hartford; and Mary Lyon, who founded the college that began in 1837 as Mount Holyoke Seminary. Usually, however, the tentative and halfhearted experiments permitted by the New England towns served only to give aid and comfort to the opposition. They seemed to show that the female mind was not inclined to scholarship and the female body was not strong enough to withstand exposure—*literal* exposure, in many cases—to it. By 1830 or so primary education had been grudgingly extended to girls almost everywhere, but it was almost impossible to find anyone who dared champion any further risks. Boston had actually opened a girls' high school in 1826 only to abolish it two years later. The closing notice mentioned the fact that the institution had been "an alarming success." Shaken, the town fathers did not allow another trial for twenty years. New Englanders have long memories, and the legend of poor Mistress Hopkins, the wife of Connecticut's colonial governor, was revived as a cautionary tale and repeated whenever the subject of female education was raised. She had, it seemed, gone mad from mental exertion. "If she had attended her household affairs and such things as belong to women," wrote John Winthrop, "and not gone out of her way and calling to meddle in such things as are proper for men, whose minds are stronger, etc., she had kept her wits." Widespread pity for Mistress Hopkins lasted for almost 200 years, a powerful deterrent to progress. The unfortunate lady became a standard text for countless sermons, achieving a sadly ironic immortality.

Having heard less about the awful consequences of study, the Middle Atlantic colonies seem to have been more willing to gamble, and the Dutch who settled New York tolerated girls in their primary schools from the very beginning. These were church-sponsored, and strict and total segregation was the rule. Smaller towns with only one building at their disposal specified:

"Boys and Girls should be separated as much as possible from each other." Girls again got the drafty back rows and the chilly corners. The good burghers of New Amsterdam took particular pains to guarantee that the thrifty mixing of the sexes did not encourage social evils. Their school rules spelled out the punishments to be used on those who "chase or throw at people's ducks or animals; run their hands through their hairs; buy candy; who throw their bread to dogs or cats; who spit in the drink of another or step on his dinner." These offenses were impartially dealt with by paddling, though there's no certain way of knowing whether "running the hands through the hairs" drew as many strokes as spitting in a classmate's drink.

In any case, the Dutch primary schools, even when coed, sound rather grim. In addition to the Bible and catechisms, boys and girls alike studied *Exquisite Proofs of Man's Misery, Last Wills* and *Hours of Death*. Most girls, after this taste of equality and the joys of erudition, left school before learning to write. Relatively few even stayed long enough to read, and the largest percentage, perhaps discouraged by the grisly offerings, never attended at all. The curriculum seemed expressly designed to produce the highest possible dropout rate. The girls could hardly be blamed for low motivation since they had an approved and tempting alternative. It was much easier and more pleasant to stay home and learn to cook, weave, spin, brew beer and tend children in the cheerful company of their sisters and friends. The boys must have envied them. Despite their apparent generosity, the Dutch settlers managed to achieve an even higher rate of female illiteracy than the adamant Puritans, and they accomplished it without discriminatory laws. The courthouse files of wills, deeds and marriages indicate 60 percent of New York women were unable to read or write during the colonial period. In New England, despite the obstacles, approximately 60 percent could at least sign their names.

The general lack of public schools, however, did not condemn all American female children to total ignorance. Fathers, especially clergyman fathers, would often drill their daughters in the Bible and sometimes teach them to read and do simple sums as well. Nothing that enhanced an understanding of the Scriptures could be entirely bad, and arithmetic was considered useful in case a woman were to find herself the sole support of her children. Brothers would sometimes lend or hand down their old schoolbooks, and fond uncles might help a favorite and clever niece with her sums. The boys' tutor was often amenable to a pretty sister's pleas for lessons.

For those girls not fortunate enough to be the daughters of foresighted New England parsons and wealthy tobacco and cotton factors, most colonial towns provided dame schools. These were open to boys as well as to girls of various ages. They offered a supplement to the curriculum at Mother's Knee, but only just. Because these schools were kept by women who had acquired their own learning by the haphazard ways and means available, the education they presented was motley at best, varying widely from one place to another. The solitary teacher could impart no more than she herself knew, and that rarely exceeded the alphabet, the shorter catechism, sewing, knitting, some numbers and perhaps a recipe for baked beans and brown bread. The actual academic function of these early American institutions seems to have been somewhat exaggerated and romanticized by historians. Dame schools were really no more than small businesses, managed by impoverished women who looked after neighborhood children and saw to it that idle little hands did not make work for the devil. The fees (tuition is too grand a word) were tiny, with threepence a week per child about par. That sum could hardly have paid for a single hornbook for the entire class. The dame school itself was an English idea, transplanted almost intact to the colonies. Several seem to have been under way by the end of the seventeenth century. A typical example was described by George Crabbe in rhymed couplets:

> When a deaf poor patient widow sits
> And awes some twenty infants as she knits
> Infants of humble, busy wives who pay
> Some trifling price for freedom through the day
> Her room is small, they cannot widely stray
> Her threshold high, they cannot run away. . . .

As early as 1682 the town of Springfield, Massachusetts, permitted Goodwife Mirick to establish one of these prototype day care centers, and the dame schools continued as the main fount

15

of female education for more than a century. We can be reasonably sure that they didn't violate the prevailing notions about female teaching and learning. Crabbe's poem was written in the 1780s, and there had been a few changes in the intervening century. With rare good luck, a child might get a competent schoolmistress like Miriam Wood of Dorchester, whose epitaph notes "that when she died, she scarcely left her mate" (the mate, of course, being an equal, not a consort), but often the "dame" seems to have been less than ideally qualified for her job. There were not many like Miriam Wood, and the New England court records are enlivened by reprimands to these women for their shortcomings. Some dozed through the day, others tippled, and there's one instance of a New Haven dame charged with "Prophane Swearing." In this last unhappy case, it was the small female pupil who was chastised, despite her plea that she had learned the offending phrases from her teacher.

As the country became more affluent, schoolkeeping gradually began to attract more ambitious types. Older girls were still being excluded from the town seminaries and, in many places, from the grammar schools as well. A great many people quickly realized that there was money to be made by teaching the children of the new middle class and that they could sell their services for far more than pennies. No special accreditation or qualification was required, and there was no competition from the state. Toward the end of the eighteenth century and at the beginning of the nineteenth, platoons of self-styled professors invaded American towns and cities, promising to instruct both sexes and all ages in every known art, science, air and grace. These projects were popularly known as adventure schools, a phrase that has a pleasant modern ring to it, suggesting open classrooms, free electives and individual attention. That, however, is deceptive. The people who ran such schools were usually adventurers in the original and not very admirable sense of the word: unscrupulous, self-serving and of doubtful origins and attainments. Many simply equipped themselves with false diplomas and titles from foreign universities and set up shop.

The schools continued to operate only as long as they turned a profit. When enrollment dropped, interest waned or fraud became obvious, the establishment would fold and the proprietors would move to another town for a fresh start. The newer

16

territories were particularly alluring to the worst of these entre-
preneurs since their reputations could neither precede nor
follow them there. A new name, a new prospectus, an ad in the
gazette, and they were in business again until scandal or mismanagement obliged them to move on. Such "schools" were not
devised for the particular benefit of girls, but because they were
independent commercial enterprises, no solvent person was
turned away. Thousands of young women did take advantage
of the new opportunity and were, in many cases, taken advantage of in return. For boys, the adventure schools were an alternative to the strict classicism and religiosity of the academies
and seminaries, but for girls, they were the only educational
possibility between the dame school and marriage.

There was little effort to devise a planned or coherent course
of study, though elaborately decorated certificates were awarded upon completion of a series of lessons. The scholar could
buy whatever he or she fancied from a mind-bending list. One
could take needlework at one place, languages at another,
dancing or "Uranology" at a third. It was a pompous era, and
no one was fonder of polysyllables than the professors. Uranology was sky watching, but it sounded impressive. There were
no minimum or maximum course requirements, though the
schoolmasters naturally made every effort to stock the same
subjects offered by the competition, in order to reduce the inci-
dence of school hopping.

By the end of the eighteenth century a prosperous New
Yorker had a choice of reading, writing, and arithmetic; Low
Dutch, English, French, Latin, Greek; merchant's accounts, algebra, logarithmetical and instrumental arithmetic, geometry,
trigonometry—plain or spherical—surveying, gauging, dialing,
mensuration of superficies and solids; astronomy, the calculation of and projection of the eclipses of the luminaries, planets
and places; the projection of the sphere upon the plane of any
circle; navigation, uses of charts and globes, geography; anatomy; and midwifery. That list is only partial but is representative
of the higher studies for sale during the Revolutionary era. The
catalogues were protean, but it's impossible to discover how
many of these courses were ever available at any given time.
The masters of such schools must certainly have left themselves
some outs comparable to those in contemporary college bul-

letins—"not given in the winter of 1779–80"; "offered only to groups of 10 or more"; "may be elected only by those who have fulfilled the prerequisites."

There was no dearth of students, but qualified students, especially females, were another matter. Few girls could have proceeded directly from knitting nightcaps in a dame school to "calculation and projection of the eclipses of the luminaries." At least one enterprising Pennsylvania teacher seems to have recognized the problem. He advertised that the rules of arithmetic would be "peculiarly adapted to the [female] sex so as to render them concise and familiar." A flourishing textbook industry quickly developed to serve the needs of lady scholars. A few of the more popular titles seem to indicate that girls were not always seizing their chance to learn navigation, gauging and spherical trig. In great demand, however, were *The Matrimonial Preceptor; The Compleat Housewife or Accomplish't Gentlewoman;* and *The Ladies' Friend, being a Treatise on the Virtues and Qualifications of the Fair Sex, so as to Render them most Agreeable to the Sensible Part of Mankind . . . to which is annexed, Real Beauty or the Art of Charming, by an Ingenious Poet.* All these appeared during the 1760s, and enjoyed what publishers call very respectable sales.

Such books promised to supplement classwork by spelling out "a Girl's duty to God and her Parents," instruction on how to make "the Choice of a Husband," and almost always included recipes and household hints. *The Matrimonial Preceptor* not only gave advice to spinsters and matrons on the capture, care and feeding of a husband, but also contained "a Thousand other Points, Essential to Husbands." The section designed to be read by husbands emphasized patience, understanding and tolerance. The several "elegant" authors of this anthology of essays rather surprisingly included Mr. Samuel Richardson, better known for *Clarissa,* Mr. Henry Fielding, famous for *Tom Jones,* as well as Alexander Pope, Ovid, and a mixed bag of other illustrious bellettrists. The publication notice promised a "Collection of Most Excellent Examples Relating to the Married State," among which were *The Folly of Precipatate Matches, The Brutality of Husbands* and *The Duties of a Good Wife,* titles designed to prepare romantic girls for the inevitable moment. The witty and satirical tone of Richardson, Fielding and Pope's other work is largely missing in *The Matrimonial Preceptor,* and Ovid has been drastically edited. Marriage was presented as a solemn economic necessity, a fate that only extraordinary cleverness could make endurable. As with the rules of arithmetic, peculiar adaptions seem to have been indicated.

Many of the adventure schools hedged the risks by functioning as a combination store and educational institution, selling fancy work, "very good orange oyl," sweetmeats, sewing notions, painted china and candles along with lessons in dancing, foreign language, geography, penmanship and spelling. Usually they were mama and papa affairs, with the wife instructing girls in "curious works" and the husband concentrating on "higher studies." Curious works covered a great deal of ground—the making of artificial fruits and flowers, the "raising of paste," enameling, japanning, quilting, fancy embroidery and, in at least one recorded case, "flowering on catgut," an intriguing accomplishment that has passed into total oblivion, leaving neither surviving practitioners nor well-preserved examples.

The adventure schools advertised heavily in newspapers and journals of the period, often in terms indicating that teaching was not an especially prestigious profession. One Thomas Carroll took several columns in a May, 1765, issue of the New York *Mercury* to announce a curriculum that would have taxed the entire faculty of Harvard and then proceeded to explain that "he was not under the necessity of coming here to teach, he had views of living more happy, but some unforeseen and unexpected events have happened since his arrival here . . . ," thus reducing this Renaissance paragon to schoolkeeping and his lady to French knots and samplers.

While they lasted, adventure schools attempted to offer something for everyone, including adults, and came in all forms, sizes and price ranges. They met anywhere and everywhere: "at the Back of Mrs. Benson's Brew-House," in rented halls, in borrowed parlors, at inns and, from time to time, in barns or open fields. The adventurer was usually available for private lessons as well, making house calls "with the utmost discretion," especially in the case of questionable studies like dancing or French verbs. The entire classroom paraphernalia usually fitted easily into a carpetbag. In comparison to the pittance

19

paid to the keepers of dame schools, the tuition charged by these teachers must have seemed astronomically high—a shilling an hour for language classes and whatever the traffic would stand for the more recondite specialties. Fees were negotiable, and the socially prominent often received favorable rates in the hope that they would lend cachet and attract a wider clientele.

The pretentious and empty promises of the adventure schools eventually aroused considerable criticism. Americans may not yet have appreciated the value of female education, but they seem always to have known the value of a dollar. It was not long before the public realized that flowering on catgut was not so useful an accomplishment for their daughters as ciphering or reading. The schoolmasters were obliged to devote more attention to practical subjects and eliminate many of the patent absurdities. The field was gradually cleared of the more marginal operators.

Penmanship classes, often separate enterprises, flourished everywhere from the 1750s on, and one John Wingfield of New York promised to teach the art within three months for a flat fee of $5. Wingfield's ads were grimly pragmatic, stressing the importance of a fine hand for those who could so easily fall into the "Melancholy State of Widowhood." For want of this" (skill), ran Wingfield's notice in the New York *Gazette*, "how often do we see women, when they are left to shift for themselves (in the MSOW), obliged to leave their Business to the Management of others; sometimes to their great Loss, and Sometimes to their utter Ruin." "Business," "Loss" and "Ruin" seem to have been the operative words, and the penmanship schools were thronged. As a testament to their newly acquire proficiency, graduates were awarded diplomas decorated by fancifully penned flora and fauna, suitable for framing. Swans, which lent themselves easily to Spencerian flourishes and curves, seem to have been a particular favorite. The study of arithmetic was also urged, as were reading and grammar. It quickly became obvious that literacy could increase earning power—or at least, *saving* power, and while America was still a very long way from accepting the notion that a woman might *choose* to support herself, people did acknowledge that there were some cases when she might have no option.

Certain religious groups, particularly the Moravians and the

Quakers, had always eschewed frippery and pioneered in the more realistic education of women. Friends schools were organized as soon as the size and prosperity of the settlements permitted them. This training emphasized housewifery but did include the fundamentals of literacy. Many of the earliest eighteenth-century Quaker primary schools were coeducational, though access to them was limited to the immediate community. Because these were concentrated in the Philadelphia area, girls born in Pennsylvania had a much better chance of acquiring some education than their contemporaries elsewhere. The Moravians, who also settled in the Southeastern states, quickly recognized the general lack of facilities in the rest of the colonies and offered boarding arrangements in a few of their schools. The student body soon included intrepid and homesick girls from New England and even the West Indies. These institutions were purposeful and rather solemn, the antithesis of superficiality. The Moravians insisted on communal household chores as well as domestic skills, and in the eighteenth century these obligations could be onerous; dusting, sweeping, spinning, carding and weaving came before embroidery and hemstitching. These homely lessons were enlivened by rhymes celebrating the pleasure of honest work. Examples survive in the seminary archives and supply a hint of the uplifting atmosphere.

> I've spun seven cuts, dear companions allow
> That I am yet little, and know not right how:
> . . . Mine twenty and four, which I finished with joy,
> And my hands and my feet did willing employ.

Though the teaching sisters in these sectarian schools seem to have been kind and patient, the life was rigorous and strictly ordered, a distinct and not always popular alternative to pleasant afternoons with easygoing adventure masters. In an era when education for women was still widely regarded as a luxury for the upper classes, the appeal of the pioneering religious seminaries tended to be somewhat narrow. If a family happened to be sufficiently well off to think of educating their girls, the tendency was to make fine ladies of them. As a result, there were many young women who could trill their way through "Greensleeves" but never heard of the composer's other activities, who could model a passable wax apple but couldn't read a recipe, who had memorized the language of flowers but had only the vaguest grasp of the English grammar. There seemed to be no middle ground between the austerities of the religious schools and the hollow frivolities offered by commercial ventures. Alternatives did not really exist until the 1820s, when the first tentative attempts were made to found independent academies and seminaries.

Catharine and Harriet Beecher, who were among the first to open a school designed to bridge this gulf, believed almost as strongly as the Moravians in the importance of domestic economy. They were, however, obliged by public demand to include a long list of dainty accomplishments in their Hartford curriculum. Many girls continued to regard the new secular seminaries as they had the adventure schools—like rival shops where they could browse or buy at will, dropping in and out at any time they chose. To the despair of the well-intentioned founders, few students ever stayed to complete the course at any one place. Parents judged a school as if it were a buffet table, evaluating it by the number and variety of subjects displayed. In writing later of the difficult beginnings of the Hartford Seminary, Catharine Beecher said that "all was perpetual haste, imperfection, irregularity, and the merely mechanical commitment of words to memory, without any chance for imparting clear and connected ideas in a single branch of knowledge. The review of those days is like the memory of a troubled and distracting dream."

Public opinion about the education of girls continued to be sharply, if never clearly, divided until after the Civil War. Those who pioneered in the field were at the mercy of ambitious and ambivalent parents, confused and unevenly prepared students and constantly shifting attitudes. In sudden and disconcerting switches the "friends" of women's education often turned out to be less than wholehearted in their advocacy. Benjamin Rush, whose *Thoughts upon Female Education*, written in 1787, influenced and inspired Emma Willard, Mary Lyon and the Beecher sisters, later admitted that his thoughtful considerations had finally left him "not enthusiastical upon the subject." Even at his best, Rush sounds no more than tepid. "Our ladies should be qualified to a certain degree by a peculiar and suitable education," he wrote, "to concur in instructing their sons in the principles of liberty and government." During her long editorship of *Godey's Lady's Book*, Sarah Josepha Hale welcomed every new female seminary and academy but faithfully reminded her readers that the sanctity of the home came first. "On what does social well-being rest but in our homes?" "Oh, Spare our homes" was a constant refrain, this chorus coming from the September, 1856, issue. *Godey's* reflects the pervasive nineteenth-century fear that the educated woman was a threat to the established and symbiotic pattern of American family life.

The totally ignorant woman, on the other hand, was something of an embarrassment to the new nation. The country was inundated by visiting European journalists during this period, and they invariably commented on the dullness of our social life and the disappointing vacuity of the sweet-faced girls and handsome matrons they met. Though Americans themselves seemed to feel safer with a bore than with a bluestocking, they were forced to give the matter some worried thought. "If all our girls become philosophers," the critics asked, "who will darn our stocking and cook the meals?" It was widely, if somewhat irrationally, assumed that a maiden who had learned Continental stitchery on fine lawn might heave to and sew up a shirt if necessary, but few men believed that a woman who had once tasted the heady delights of Shakespeare's plays would ever have dinner ready on time—or at all.

The founders of female seminaries were obliged to cater to this unease by modifying their plans and their pronouncements accordingly. The solid academic subjects were so generally thought irrelevant for "housewives and helpmeets" that it was usually necessary to disguise them as something more palatable. The Beechers taught their girls chemistry at Hartford but were careful to assure parents and prospective husbands that its principles were applicable in the kitchen. The study of mathematics could be justified by its usefulness in running a household. Eventually, the educators grew more daring, recommending geology as a means toward understanding the Deluge and other Biblical mysteries and suggesting geography and even history as suitable because these studies would "enlarge women's sphere of thought, rendering them more interesting as companions to men of science." There is, however, little evidence that many converts were made to this extreme point of view. The average nineteenth-century American man was not at all keen on chat with an interesting companion, preferring a wife like the one in the popular jingle

> who never learnt the art of schooling
> untainted with the itch of ruling.

The cliché of the period was "woman's sphere." The phrase was so frequently repeated that it acquired actual physical qualities. Woman's Sphere—the nineteenth-century woman was fixed and sealed within it like a model ship inside a bottle. To tamper with the arrangement was to risk ruining a complex and fragile structure that had been painstakingly assembled over the course of two centuries. Just one ill-considered jolt might make matchwood of the entire apparatus.

In 1812 the anonymous author of *Sketches of the History, Genius, and Disposition of the Fair Sex* wrote that women are "born for a life of uniformity and dependence. Were it in your power to give them genius, it would almost always be a useless and very often a dangerous present. It would, in general, make them regret the station which Providence has assigned them, or have recourse to unjustifiable ways to get from it." The writer identified himself only as a "friend of the sex"—not actually specifying which one.

This century's feminists may rage at such quotes and revel in them, but the nineteenth-century educators were forced to live with this attitude and work within and around it. In order to gain any public or private support for women's secondary schools, they had to prove that a woman would not desert her husband and children as soon as she could write a legible sentence or recite a theorem. That fear was genuine, though few had any specific idea of where the women would flee or how they would survive in exile. The consequences of female education were unknown and threatening, and anything could happen. In their heads some Americans may have felt that women deserved equal opportunities, but in their hearts they weren't ready to take the chance. The old arguments resurfaced time and time again. What about St. Paul's injunction? What about the sanctity of the home? What about the health of the future mothers of the race? What about supper?

The advocates became consummate politicians, theologians, hygienists and, when necessary, apologists. "It is desirable," wrote Mary Lyon in 1836 of her Mount Holyoke Female Seminary project, "that the plans relating to the subject should not seem to originate with us but with benevolent *gentlemen*. If the object should excite attention there is danger that many good men will fear the effect on society of so much female influence and what they will call female greatness." New and subtle counterarguments were presented with great delicacy. God had entrusted the tender minds of children to women; therefore, women were morally obliged to teach. The home would be a holier place if the chatelaine understood religious principles and could explain them. The founders of Abbot Academy proclaimed: "To form the mortal mind to habits suited to an immortal being, and to instill principles of conduct and form the character for an immortal destiny, shall be subordinate to no other care." All that harping on immortality went down smoothly in the evangelistic atmosphere of the 1820s. A thick coating of religion was applied to every new educational venture. The parents of prospective students were assured that their daughters not only would study religion in class, but would have twice-daily periods of silent meditation, frequent revival meetings, compulsory chapel services and a Sunday that included all these. When one reads the early seminary catalogues, it's hard to see where secular studies could have fitted in at all. To the religious guarantees were appended promises of careful attention to health. The educators lost no time in adding the new science of calisthenics to their curricula. They had the medical records of their students compared to those of the public at large and published the gratifying results in newspapers and magazines. Domestic work was also to be required of girls who attended the new seminaries, partly for economy's sake, but mainly so that they would not forget their ultimate destiny.

All this was calming and persuasive, but nothing was as effective as simple economics. By the 1830s most states had begun a program of primary public education. As the West followed suit, the need for teachers became acute and desperate. Men were not attracted to the profession because the pay was wretched, the living conditions lonely and the status of a schoolmaster negligible, if not downright laughable. St. Paul was revised, updated and finally reversed. He had not, after all, envisioned the one-room schoolhouses of the American prairie, the wages of $3 a month or the practice of boarding around.

Within an astonishingly short time, fears for female health subsided. The first women teachers proved amazingly durable, able to withstand every rigor of frontier life. In a letter to her former headmistress one alumna of the Hartford Seminary described accommodations out West:

> I board where there are eight children and the parents, and only two rooms in the house. I must do as the family do about washing, as there is but one basin, and no place to go to wash but out the door. I have not enjoyed the luxury of either lamp or candle, their only light being a cup of grease with a rag for a wick. Evening is my only time to write, but this kind of light makes such a disagreeable smoke and smell, I cannot bear it, and do without light, except the fire. I occupy a room with three of the children and a niece who boards here. The other room serves as a kitchen, parlor, and bedroom for the rest of the family. . . .

Other graduates were every bit as stoical, if no more comfortable.

> I board with a physician, and the house has only two rooms. One serves as kitchen, eating, and sitting room; the other, where I lodge, serves also as the doctor's office, and there is no time, night or day, when I am not liable to interruption. My school embraces both sexes, and all ages from five to seventeen, and not one can read intelligibly. They have no idea of the proprieties of the schoolroom or of study. My furniture consists now of benches, a single board put up against the side of the room for a writing desk, a few bricks for andirons, and a stick of wood for shovel and tongs.

These letters were collected by Catharine Beecher in her book *True Remedy*, which advanced the cause of women's education by showing the worthwhile uses to which it could be put. Delighted with the early returns, several states quickly set up committees to consider training women teachers on a larger scale. Their findings were favorable, though couched in oddly ambiguous language. New York's group reported that women seemed to be "endued with peculiar faculties" for the occupation. "While man's nature is rough, stern, impatient, ambitious, hers is gentle, tender, enduring, unaspiring." That was most encouraging, but the gentlemen also generously acknowledged that "the habits of female teachers are better and their morals purer; they are much more apt to be content with, and continue in, the occupation of teaching." A Michigan commission announced in 1842:

> An elementary school, where the rudiments of an English education only are taught, such as reading, spelling, writing, and the outlines barely of geography, arithmetic, and grammar, requires a female of practical common sense with amiable and winning manners, a patient spirit, and a tolerable knowledge of the springs of human action. A female thus qualified, carrying with her into the schoolroom the gentle influences of her sex, will do more to inculcate right morals and prepare the youthful intellect for the severer discipline of its after years, than the most accomplished and learned male teacher.

Far from objecting to these rather condescending statements, the founders of the struggling seminaries were happy to hear them. Even the miserable wages offered to teachers could be regarded as an advantage since they provided the single most affective argument for more female academies. "But where are we to raise such an army of teachers as are required for this great work?" asked Catharine Beecher in the same book that contained the letters from her ex-student. "Not from the sex which finds it so much more honorable, easy, and lucrative, to enter the many roads to wealth and honor open in this land. It is WOMAN who is to come at this emergency, and meet the demand—woman, whom experience and testimony have shown to be the best, as well as the cheapest guardian and teacher of childhood, in the school as well as the nursery." Teaching became a woman's profession, by default and by ra-

27

tionalization. Clergymen and theologians suddenly had nothing but praise for women teachers. God must have meant them to teach because he made them so good at it. They would work for half or a third of the salary demanded by a man. What, after all, was a schoolroom but an extension of the home, woman's natural sphere? And if females had to have schools of their own to prepare them for this holy mission, then so be it. Future American generations must not be allowed to suffer for want of instruction when a Troy, Hartford or Mount Holyoke girl asked no more than a "safe escort" to the boondocks and $3 a month. Only the bold requested the additional luxury of a new-fangled oil lamp.

I
The Operative Word

FIVE years ago it was possible to mention the Seven Sisters almost anywhere in the temperate zone and expect instant recognition, if not always total recall. Beyond the Mississippi and south of the Potomac, the response may have been somewhat slower, but it was still gratifyingly predictable. "Seven Sisters," however, seems to have been merely a catchphrase that first surfaced in the late 1920s, the inspiration of an unsung reporter in an unspecified city room. In 1915 Smith, Mount Holyoke, Vassar and Wellesley had informally organized themselves into a Four College Conference, which was to meet for the purpose of discussing matters of common interest and concern. Bryn Mawr joined the group in 1925, and Barnard and Radcliffe were added in 1926. That made a Seven College Conference of nice, manageable proportions, and no additions were thought necessary or desirable, even though there were those who felt that some might be indicated. Seven it was, and seven it remained, and the representatives busied themselves with plans for presenting their achievements and their needs to the public. It was hoped that philanthropists who had been donating portfolios of skyrocketing stocks and bonds to men's colleges could be persuaded to sign over some certificates to the women's schools. (Optimism was rampant.) The members of the conference were labled the Big Seven, which suggests that size may have had something to do with inclusion. Big Seven, however, was neither particularly flattering nor especially apt, and it soon gave way to the more memorable and appropriate Seven Sisters.

The Eastern women's colleges have long had an international reputation, and though the stereotypes varied from one place to another, all seven shared in the general luster. Even if the girls of the Golden West often preferred to stay within sound of the surf and the South exported comparatively few of its belles, the Celestial Seven continued to come out ahead. Each of them had a maharani or two, as well as a sprinkling of contessas, honorables and other impressive exotics listed inconspicuously in the back of the catalogue, under "Foreign Countries." American Presidents could usually be counted on to send nieces, if not always their daughters, and by 1900 the Seven had a near monopoly on social cachet. Intellectual preeminence had been there from the very beginning.

Alumnae were handed an image with their freshman registration forms, and with minimal upkeep it could be made to last for a lifetime. Radcliffe was academically rigorous; Bryn Mawr, intense; Smith, athletic; Barnard, sophisticated; Wellesley, blond and literary; Vassar, radical; and Mount Holyoke refreshingly wholesome. The frequent and often flagrant exceptions only seemed to reinforce the prevailing notions. Now, of course, the aura has become diffuse and somewhat vague. "Seven Sisters" sounds embarrassingly quaint, and the colleges have quietly dropped the phrase and renamed themselves the Seven College Conference. Not only is that more contemporary and businesslike, but it neatly covers the question of brothers-in-law, marriages and liaisons. The Seven are still on speaking terms, but the old intimacy has disappeared. Vassar is now fully coeducational; Bryn Mawr has become a coordinate college with Haverford; Barnard is a Columbia quadrangle; Radcliffe is the name of a dormitory; and only Smith, Mount Holyoke and Wellesley remain, in the carefully chosen phrase, "colleges predominantly for the education of women."

Since 1970 "predominantly" has been the operative word in all news bulletins and press releases. After the Vassar decision, and once Yale, Princeton and Dartmouth voted to admit women, the continued existence of separate colleges became highly doubtful. Duplicate institutions had long been considered slightly eccentric by the rest of the country, but once the Ivy League became coed they seemed bizarre. All the contraindications, overgrown and bypassed for a century, were simultaneously exposed. Adjectives like "archaic," "artificial," "unnatural," "unconstitutional," "wasteful" and "doomed" were flung toward Massachusetts, resulting in a number of direct hits. There were administrative shake-ups, faculty defections and, most depressing of all, significantly fewer requests for catalogues. It no longer mattered even to the oldest alumnae which had actually been the first women's college in America. The urgent question in 1970 was which would be the last.

From a distance, the turmoil at Smith, Wellesley and Mount Holyoke resembled the last frantic round of musical chairs. The debates, meetings, referenda and tensions on those three campuses were constant, passionate and time-consuming. Should they or shouldn't they? If they did yield, would the world continue to respect them, or would they slip from first-rate women's colleges to second- or third-rate coeducational schools? Could they compete with the ex-men's institutions for the brightest young men, or would they only get the weak, the dim, the myopic and the stoop-shouldered? Outside pressures exacerbated the internal agonies. The women's liberation movement, at its most strident in 1970 and '71, demanded instant reorganization of all sexist institutions, and its spokespeople insisted that the Great Leap Forward could never take place until sex ceased to be a factor in admission. Many trustees and administrators were disturbed and intimidated by these tirades, and some were persuaded that the college endowments would shrivel away, unreplenished by those who saw no further reason to perpetuate an anachronism. What sort of faculty or student body could an anachronism lure and keep? The proponents of coeducation outlined their grimmest visions. The fate of old maids, one Shakespearean scholar reminded his colleagues, is to lead apes in hell. The separate women's colleges had outlived their purpose, which was to provide an education for women during the dark ages in which females were not admitted to other institutions of higher learning. Once this deplorable state of affairs was corrected, women's colleges could have no further justification, and any attempt to infuse life into them after the enlightenment of 1970 made no more sense than to build dirigibles to compete with 747s.

Then, toward the end of 1971 and all through 1972, the early returns from the coeds at Yale and Princeton began to drift back. The first transfer requests turned up in the registrars' offices. The Ivy League colleges, it seemed, remained sexist establishments run by and for the benefit of males. Women were tolerated but, in some sad cases, just barely. The squash courts and the highest campus offices remained male bastions. Professors, particularly the oldest and most distinguished, continued to address their classes as "gentlemen." Nothing much had been done about the plumbing in the older buildings. Undergraduate girls were finding that they had to compete not only *with* boys, but *for* boys, and the two forms of competition often seemed mutually exclusive.

During the same hectic season the women's liberation movement reexamined the colleges and began to temper its judgment. The evidence was reviewed, and a reprieve was granted, provided that the institutions made some effort to rehabilitate themselves. Demeaning and archaic parietal regulations were abandoned, catalogues rewritten, courses in "women's studies" quickly devised, and arrangements made to salt the campuses with male exchange students. High school seniors appeared at Mount Holyoke, Smith and Wellesley for interviews, sounding positive and delivering new lines. "Literally dozens of them used the same words," a Mount Holyoke official said. "'I don't want to be a second-class citizen at a men's college.' It was a complete reversal. Applications for '71 and '72 were not only up seven percent, but we were getting fewer whose first choices were Yale or Princeton. We actually had excellent candidates who applied only to the women's colleges, just as in the old days." It seemed obvious that such schools were needed— despite the recent changes or perhaps because of them. At Mount Holyoke's last referendum in November, 1971, the vote was 85 percent against full coeducation. The count at Smith and Wellesley was somewhat less definitive, but no banns were published at either place. Instead, the idea of a women's college has been almost completely redefined. All three colleges have men on campus, as both day students and residents, and participate in a variety of exchange programs. The only favor they still withhold is granting the BA degree to men, and under the circumstances that's merely a technicality.

At the moment equivocation seems to be comfortable. "Those who want coeducation can find it here," said a Smith professor. "Those who don't can escape it. Of course we're on the fence, but right now the fence is a good spot. Vassar panicked, and now they're just a small coed school in the Hudson Valley." There is, of course, a double standard. When an all-male college decides to admit women, it is immediately deluged with applications from the strongest candidates. When a women's college goes coeducational, however, it may be presented to somewhat underqualified high school boys as an easy acceptance. "Vassar was the safe choice for Exeter in 1970," said a member of that class. "They took almost every male who applied." The football captains, the hockey stars and the National Merit Scholars continue to go elsewhere. The women's college contemplating coeducation must come to terms with the fact that there's going to be a long and somewhat bumpy transition period with dissatisfaction all around. "I asked a group of our male exchange students if they'd like to stay on and receive our degree," said president David Truman of Mount Holyoke, "and although every one of them thought that this was a great place, they admitted that they preferred to have their BA from Wesleyan or Dartmouth or wherever they had come from. That was just one of the incidents that convinced me that going coed would mean a compromise in standards. Even if we attracted some good male students, we'd risk losing them to the competition."

The détente between the women's liberation movement and the women's colleges may be only temporary, but it has been undeniably invigorating and Smith and Wellesley celebrated their 1975 centennials more or less intact. Options for the second century, however, remain open. The mood at Mount Holyoke, the most venerable of the trio, seems to have become considerably more relaxed after that last reassuring vote, though its officials admit that a great deal depends on Amherst.

"If Amherst ever becomes coeducational, the whole debate will be renewed," said one dean. "When that happens, the odds are that we will go along. We can't permit ourselves to become a refuge." That all-male college, perfectly situated almost equidistant from both Smith and Mount Holyoke, at the apex of a neat Connecticut Valley triangle, had always been a great boon to the two women's schools and had enabled them to beg the question of full coeducation on the grounds that young men were readily accessible and more than eager for companionship. In November, 1974, however, Amherst finally voted to admit women transfers at once. The new class that enters in 1976 will be mixed, and Amherst will expand from its present size of 1,300 to 1,500, a "fair" proportion of which will be female. Before the cheering that greeted this announcement had quite died away, a Radcliffe-Harvard student who happened to be visiting on that epochal weekend submitted the first application. Neither Mount Holyoke nor Smith has quite come to terms with this shattering news, though they are pondering its implications on every level. A coed Amherst is bound to have a profound effect on their present status, though by October, 1975, no changes had yet been announced.

II
The Founders: Teacher

A "REFUGE" for girls reluctant or unfit to confront the world was never the idea, not even in 1837, when Mary Lyon first announced her plans for a "Peculiar Institution," especially designed for the higher education of women. The avowed intention of this new venture was to enable women to *enter* the world, not to withdraw from it. Separate facilities were expedient and necessary because no real alternative existed or seemed imminent, at least in the Northeast. (Oberlin College in Ohio admitted a few women during the 1830s, but only in a special, limited and even somewhat exploitive sense. Female students there were relegated to a substandard "collegiate department" and expected to make themselves useful by performing domestic chores for the men, whose more demanding curriculum didn't allow them time to clear the tables, tidy the residence halls or mend their clothes.)

With the exception of Mary Lyon, who was a teacher, the pioneers in women's higher education were an assorted, improbable and often inadvertent lot. The others—Matthew Vassar, Sophia Smith, Henry Durant of Wellesley, Joseph Taylor of Bryn Mawr, Annie Nathan of Barnard and the small Cambridge group who arranged for certain Harvard professors to teach women after hours—were perhaps the most unlikely collection of people ever to create a set of closely related institutions.

Unfortunately, the legend of Mary Lyon's heroic efforts to get Mount Holyoke under way, though inspiring, is somewhat short on glamor or mystery. There have always been a few Holyoke alumni in every generation who might have preferred that their college had been established by a more fiery personage, someone who would have chained herself to lampposts for women's rights, or lain down across the Springfield trolley tracks, or even been touched by a faint hint of scandal. Though

35

there is nothing really wrong with having a founder as exemplary as Mary Lyon, a college so immaculately conceived does tend to acquire an unshakably pristine image. "This is a marvelous school," said a member of the class of 1974, "and very avant-garde, but no one thinks of us that way. It's so unfair, when we were the only women's college to have real revolution in 1970. A radical group held a building for two days. There was even a fire, but everyone thinks it all happened somewhere else."

That, obviously, is a clear case of the Mary Lyon mystique, still vigorous at 138. The founder was modest, dedicated and personally beloved even by those who considered the higher education of women both misguided and perilous. She was even quite witty, in a gentle and inoffensive Victorian way. Mary Lyon was no mere philanthropist or benefactor, but the entire creative force behind the college and its hardworking principal until her early death in 1847. Her first biographer and great admirer, Professor and eventual President of Amherst Edward Hitchcock, titled his life of Mary Lyon *The Power of Christian Benevolence*. He varnished his subject with so heavy a coating of sanctity that her real qualities have been obscured. Hitchcock meant well, but neither Miss Lyon nor Mount Holyoke has ever fully recovered from his treatment. Subsequent writers have gone to considerable trouble to deemphasize her piety and bring her character into focus, but it has been an uphill job. She was an original, vital and extraordinary woman, and none of the other founders resembled her in the least, though they freely borrowed many of her advanced ideas.

Mary Lyon's own education was acquired by the haphazard ways and means available to a New England child in the years just after the American Revolution. The district primary school serving her corner of Massachusetts seems to have been more liberal than some and actually permitted little girls inside. After exhausting the limited possibilities of Buckland, Mary Lyon boarded with families in larger towns, helping with the housework in return for her keep and a chance to continue her training. By the time she was twenty she was earning seventy-five cents a week as a teacher, saving as much as she could and hoping to continue her own studies at one of the few recently opened female seminaries. Mary Lyon attended two or three

different such schools before she found herself at the Reverend
Joseph Emerson's Academy in Byfield, Massachusetts. Emerson had begun this school after working out a plan for the education of his fiancée. He wanted a wife who would be neither a
"slave" nor a "toy," and having succeeded nicely with one
young lady, he enlarged his sphere of operations and took in a
few dozen others. It was a very personal sort of school, and
advanced for its time and place. "Be not frightened of the
sound of Philosophy! Metaphysics! Speculation! Human Reason! Logic! Theory! System! Disputation! They can never harm
you so long as you keep clear of error and sin," he wrote. This
enlightened man died after his novel school had been open for
only a few years, and there was no way of carrying on without
him.

Saddened, impressed and thoroughly convinced that the
education of women would always be a short-lived and sporadic
phenomenon unless similar schools were financially endowed,
Mary Lyon began her long crusade to collect funds to establish
a permanent institution, one that would outlast its founders.
She had apparently learned Politics! from the Reverend Mr.
Emerson as well as Metaphysics! Theory! and System! because
she decided at once that the venture should avoid any taint of
feminism. Though the Mount Holyoke seminary was to be of a
very different order from those already in existence, she deliberately avoided calling her project a college. That word would
have terrified and alienated the "benevolent gentlemen" she so
desperately needed. "Seminary," with its familiar connotations
of spiritual uplift and ladylike accomplishment, was Miss Lyon's
concession to her era, and it gave her a twenty-five-year head
start.

Women's rights were a very sensitive subject in the 1830s and
there was a great deal of free-floating anxiety about what would
happen if ever the future wives and mothers of America were
to taste the heady pleasures of real learning. Most men seemed
content with wives that were either slaves, toys, or, best of all,
some delightful combination of the two. A few ephemeral
academies tucked inconspicuously away in the Berkshire hills
didn't pose much of a threat, but a large, centrally located, permanently endowed institution was something else again. There
were fears that it would draw the daughters of New England

like a giant magnet, pulling them away from hearth and home and undermining the very foundations of society. The only chance of ever establishing such a place (precisely the sort that Mary Lyon had in mind) was to present it as a male idea. The sweet smile, the prim bonnet and the ruffled fichu effectively camouflaged a gentle but single-minded feminist. "My heart has so yearned," she wrote, "over the adult female youth in the common walks of life, that it has sometimes seemed as if there were a fire shut up in my bones."

Mary Lyon judiciously kept the fire damped in public, and little by pathetically little she assembled the necessary funds. There were few single large gifts, but simply a slow accretion of tiny contributions, the smallest of which was six cents and the largest rarely more than a few hundred dollars, subscribed by a whole village. Miss Lyon traveled up and down the countryside, talking softly and reasonably to sewing circles, missionary societies and town meetings, graciously accepting whatever she was given. One ladies' group promised her feathers for eventual pillows; another donated scraps for quilts. She thanked them and persisted. In 1834 the Massachusetts General Association of Congregational Churches voted a rather belated endorsement of "Christian education among women." A state charter was immediately applied for and granted. The campaign, now sanctioned by the two bodies that counted most, was intensified. On October 3, 1836, as Mount Holyoke's cornerstone was finally laid, Mary Lyon sounded considerably less restrained than usual: "The stones and brick and mortar speak a language which vibrates through my very soul. Surely the Lord hath remembered our low estate."

Additional funds, however, did not exactly pour into the seminary coffers, and Miss Lyon's fund-raising tours became longer and more arduous. She was criticized for traveling by stagecoach and train without an escort, and the green velvet bag with which she took up her collections became an over-familiar and not always welcome sight. The perfect Victorian lady began to lose patience and occasionally showed it. "My heart is sick; my soul pained with this empty gentility, this genteel nothingness," she said, adding that the Catholic Church was considerably more energetic about providing money for educating teachers than New England Protestants seemed to be. The Catholics, she said, were happy "to prepare the females of our land, and through them the children and youth of the coming generation, to lend their aid in converting this nation to the Church of Rome." That statement, however, does not seem to have galvanized many New Englanders into generosity. All it did was to plant the idea in some already confused and suspicious minds that Miss Lyon was trying to create a "Protestant nunnery." As construction advanced and bills mounted, Miss Lyon began to publicize her educational theories, and there was considerable objection to those, especially to her novel idea of keeping tuition costs down by having students share household chores. That notion, in an era when any sort of advanced education for women was the luxury of the very rich, seemed both radical and repulsive to many. "Servile labor" was one of the kinder phrases applied to it. It was widely assumed that no gentlewoman would ever attend Mount Holyoke. "She wishes to consider us as neither servants nor boarders, but daughters," wrote one of the early students, but the public at large was hard to convince. Mary Lyon did her best to assure potential supporters that the housework would be discontinued if it became too onerous and promised that it was merely a temporary economy, but the system continued to arouse serious misgivings in parents and students alike. Miss Lyon was strongly urged to abandon the domestic chores entirely or at least revise her sensible program and have the girls grow grapes or raise silkworms instead. (These were two ladylike activities that had recently become very fashionable, and it was thought that they might be profitable as well.) The founder of Mount Holyoke, however, remained adamant, and there were no mulberry bushes in South Hadley when the college finally opened, nor any trellised vineyards either.

Incoming students were tested for proficiency in grammar, modern geography, American history and arithmetic. They were also expected to have familiarized themselves with *Watts on the Mind*, a rather forbidding theological treatise far less penetrable than it sounds. One year's room, board and tuition at the new seminary were to cost $64, a mere fraction of the sum that prosperous fathers had been spending on china painting lessons, French tutoring or dancing masters for their daughters. The advantages of the new venture became suddenly and dramatically apparent to canny New Englanders, and the seminary was overbooked from the very beginning. At the end of the first year Mary Lyon was somewhat surprised to discover that the school had actually turned a rather sizable profit. She promptly reduced the yearly rates to $60, which left just the right amount of money for operating expenses with no embarrassing surplus. Objections to the domestic duties began to wane, and Mary Lyon noted with considerable satisfaction (and some of her old tact): "The vivacity and apparent vigor of our young ladies near the close of the winter term of twenty weeks, and at the examination, was noticed as unusual by gentlemen of discrimination." In the 1830s that was what counted, but even so, almost seventy-five years would elapse before the next great experiment.

III
The Founders: Brewer

MATTHEW VASSAR was a found to pique the most jaded imagination. A pious Poughkeepsie brewer, he fixed his vision of immortality on a hospital, though from time to time he thought of endowing a library, a boys' school, an orphanage and, briefly, a home for indigent females in which they would be trained as domestic servants. Each of these causes bloomed for a while in his affections but quickly faded. Off-season, he spoke glumly of giving the bulk of his fortune to the Baptist Church, a safe solution, but one which depressed him. In rare surges of family feeling he would sometimes talk of leaving his entire estate to his nephews, Matthew, and Guy. The younger men naturally thought this a plendid notion, far superior to any their uncle had previously considered, and encouraged him heartily. Their bounding enthusiasm, however, aroused certain misgivings in the old gentleman's mind, and he decided against this arrangement almost as soon as he had mentioned it. Nepotic relationships, cordial until then, suddenly became acutely strained.

During most of Vassar's long and uneventful life he showed so little interest in women that some of his closest associates were unaware that he was even married. Like many self-made men of his time, he had succeeded wonderfully without any higher learning whatever. He was fond of proclaiming that fact and proud of it. Childless, narrow-minded, provincial and somewhat misogynistic, he was the last man anyone would have expected to found a women's college. The shadowy Mrs. Vassar, to whom he remained bound in wedlock for fifty years, neither inspired nor encouraged his ultimate project. In fact, there's no evidence that she ever even visited it. One wouldn't have to be a disinherited nephew to suspect coercion when this particular uncle abruptly announced, at the age of sixty-three, that he was leaving hundreds of thousands for the higher education of females. The decision seemed totally outlandish, coming as it did from a man who turned apoplectic whenever the sensitive subject of women's rights and possible suffrage arose. Matthew and Guy were convinced that so astonishing a change of heart could never have happened without an agent provocateur, and they were right.

In the mid-1850s an obscure schoolmaster named Milo P. Jewett appeared in Poughkeepsie and inquired about properties that might be suitable for an academy. There weren't many. The only one that seemed at all appropriate was owned by the senior Matthew Vassar and had been recently vacated by the untimely death of his schoolteacher-niece, Miss Lydia Booth. Jewett put a down payment on the building at once, even though it was far more modest than the colonnaded establishment he claimed to have left behind in Marion, Alabama. That, he told Mr. Vassar, had been one of the largest and finest female institutes in the world, but growing tensions in the South had made terrible inroads on his enrollment. Mr. Jewett had originally been from Vermont, and by 1855 or so Southern planters were no longer sending their daughters to Yankee schoolmasters with abolitionist leanings. The Hudson Valley seemed a safer place to a man of Jewett's convictions, and he left Alabama abruptly.

Once Jewett met Matthew Vassar, he was convinced that Providence had led him to Poughkeepsie. The friendship quickly deepened in the Baptist Church, where Jewett found many opportunities to discuss theology with his new acquaintance. One topic they both found especially stimulating was what Jewett called "the duty of the rich man to use his property for the glory of God." At that time the hospital project was Vassar's current favorite, and he lost no time in asking Jewett's sage advice about it. As a disinterested and impartial observer, Jewett could be refreshingly candid. The hospital idea did not seem at all wise to him. Quite the contrary. "Great hospitals," said Jewett, "are for great cities," and not for insignificant towns like Poughkeepsie. He could hardly imagine a "more unwise use of money." Jewett's feelings were so forcefully phrased that they teetered on the very edge of passion. "Indeed," he said, "I think you may as well throw it in the Hudson River." "Mr. Vassar expressed great surprise at this unexpected disapproval of his plans," Jewett wrote later, but shortly "became dissatisfied with the provisions of his will."

The proposed hospital soon joined the growing collection of discarded beneficiaries, and Jewett immediately proceeded to elaborate on his alternative plan. He just happened to have some pertinent material in writing. One of these documents was called "Facts and Reflections Respecting the Founding of a College for Young Ladies." The facts may have been a bit shaky, but the reflections showed evidence of careful research into the nature of Matthew Vassar. Jewett knew his man. "From its towers lifted to the sky, it will reflect the luster of your munificence so long as the sun shall shine in the heavens." That made heady reading for a country brewer who had been thinking about an infirmary. The present, Jewett emphasized, is the time for action, "at least as far as to making a final testamentary arrangement on the subject." The sooner Vassar acted, the better. No one knew what would happen to the stock market in case of civil war. Jewett himself, growing no younger, was burning to realize his dream at once. In return for the new will, Jewett offered Vassar nothing less than immortality. "To you, Providence offers the high privilege, the peculiar honor, of actually establishing and putting into operation the first grand permanent endowed female college ever opened in the United States."

By building such a college, Vassar would have a monument to himself beyond his most elaborate fantasies—"More lasting than the pyramids," Jewett said. Vassar was dazzled, transformed by these words from an ordinary prosperous brewer into the Poughkeepsie Pharaoh. He liked the role immediately and fancied himself perfectly cast. This brilliant newcomer understood him far better than his unimaginative and self-seeking nephews or his dreary wife ever had. He would, of course, be a benevolent pharaoh, a pioneer educator and uplifter of half of humanity, a great emancipator at least on par with the President of the United States. Vassar tried out his new concept of himself in his private diary: "The Founder of Vassar College and President Lincoln—two noble emancipationists, one of women."

Jewett, of course, had his own dream of glory, and it was much more explicit, if slightly less grandiose, than Matthew

Vassar's. He wanted only to be president of the "first grand permanant endowed female college." Purveying trivial airs and graces to planters' daughters, though profitable, had never really fulfilled him, and although he had already invested in the little Poughkeepsie schoolhouse, he considered the teaching of tots far beneath his abilities—a waste of his Dartmouth BA and his advanced degree in divinity. During the long and steamy Alabama afternoons, Jewett must have envisioned another sort of women's academy altogether. He had, in fact, become obsessed with it. In this glorious and hypothetical institution, graceful young ladies would bend their pretty heads over logarithm tables and study the sermons of Jonathan Edwards. From time to time they would lift their eyes heavenward to note the position of the stars in their courses, perceiving the faint but unmistakable music of the spheres. They would be ennobled and transported far beyond the mundane realm of French knots and china painting, and so would Milo P. Jewett, their mentor and guide on this marvelous journey of the spirit.

Jewett assured Matthew Vassar that it all could be done for $400,000, the estimated size of Vassar's personal fortune. During the following months Vassar's enthusiasm for the college plan advanced and receded like the tides. He was tempted, but he saw objections, risks and hazards. The old man was vain and susceptible, but he hadn't become rich by being either gullible or impulsive. Moreover, the nephews objected strenuously to the college idea and to Jewett himself, whom they called "an incubus" and worse. Vassar wavered and reneged, but finally he acceded to Jewett's demands, bravely destroying all former wills and allocating not only the basic $400,000 to the women's college project but the rest of his estate as well. It was a total and unqualified triumph for Milo P. Jewett, except for one small thing. Vassar had written a *will*, which meant that he would have to die before the college could get under way. Jewett would have preferred a gift. A gift, in fact, was what he had in mind all along. Though Matthew Vassar was considerably older than Jewett, the brewer was sturdy, rosy and, from all outward appearances, nowhere near the end that preoccupied him. Jewett, on the other hand, was frail, thin and white-haired. He had to have his college at once if he were to be in fit condition to lead it. An *eventual* college, fifteen or even twenty years in the future, would be worse than none.

Jewett's persuasive powers, already somewhat taxed, were now stretched to the utmost. He changed his tactics and marshaled a whole new set of arguments. If civil war came, the male population would be decimated. Young women, deprived of husbands and fathers, would have to support themselves. A fate worse than death awaited those who lacked education and marketable skills. A *will* could be contested by the spiteful nephews, but an outright *gift* could not. Moreover, if Vassar gave the money at once, he could personally oversee the construction and make sure that the funds were well spent. Jewett urged the childless Vassar to think of the happiness to be derived from hearing students hail him as "friend and benefactor" blessing him daily for their salvation. Vassar weighed the possibilities, balancing the delightful against the disturbing. He couldn't imagine himself alive and well without his money. Presiding over its disbursement wasn't the same thing as having it in the bank. There was a world of difference between the Late Matthew Vassar, Philanthropist and Uplifter of Half the Human Race, and Matthew Vassar, Esquire, doling out every one of his dollars to carpenters, bricklayers, teachers and janitors.

The nephews sensed a certain weakening of resolve at this point and intensified their anti-Jewett campaign. The old man changed his mind again. There would be no college. The young Matthew Vassar gleefully relayed the news to Jewett, diabolically choosing Sunday morning at the Baptist Church as the most appropriate time and place for the announcement.

Distraught and incredulous, the would-be president of Vassar Female College composed his masterpiece of rhetoric. "Oh, what a fall was there, my countryman! Your advisors have razed your magnificent 120 gun ship down to a barge. You give up your coach and six for a wheelbarrow! Your monument which would have been more enduring than the Pyramids is given up for a pine slab at the head of your grave." Jewett signed his four-page letter "with a heavy heart and trembling hand" and sent it over by messenger.

Vassar, whose resistance had been weakened by years of constant importuning, capitulated for the third time. He apologized to Jewett, cursed his nephews and promised to turn over the necessary funds at once. He and Jewett signed an agreement in the office of a local lawyer, and plans for the college proceeded. There was an awkward moment later on when Vassar discovered that he would have to turn over the money to a board of trustees. He had not, it seemed, entirely realized what trustees did or what they were for, assuming that he would have full and sole control over the disposition of his gift. "Why," he said, "it is not necessary for me to give up my money into the hands of the trustees, is it?" Assured that it was customary, Vassar reluctantly made over the sum, and Jewett "ran to the post office."

At that safe juncture Jewett relaxed his vigilance. It had been a long grind, and he was utterly exhausted. He told Matthew Vassar that he was going to Europe in order to investigate the state of women's education abroad and set sail. Pressed for his findings, Jewett said that they could "not be imprinted upon paper, but would be transferred by spiritual photography to the minds and hearts and lives of future generations." He had a delightful time.

Intrigue began as soon as Jewett was safely incommunicado on the North Atlantic. Matthew Vassar immediately began receiving urgent advisory letters from another ex-New Englander turned Southern schoolmaster, a man named Charles A. Raymond. Though this man's academic credentials were not as impeccable as Jewett's, in all other respects the two were weirdly and eerily similar. Vassar was deeply impressed. The stalwart brewer seems to have had a fatal weakness for refugee schoolmasters, and Raymond's suggestions grew steadily bolder. There were a few things that Raymond would change if it were *his* college. He would, for instance, prefer to see a women's *university*. There was surely enough money? And land? Matthew Vassar introduced Raymond and Jewett by transatlantic mail, and soon the two of them were corresponding with each other and quarreling bitterly. The founder remained in the middle, buffeted by letters and pleas from both men, who were competing furiously for his favor.

Jewett returned from Europe four months sooner than he had planned. The struggle for the mind and heart of Matthew Vassar could not be conducted from a distance, and Jewett had every reason to think he was losing. Raymond had supplanted him. Desperation made Jewett injudicious, and he wrote a peevish letter to six of the trustees, which he concluded with the statement that "Mr. Vassar grows more fickle and childish every day." That was the end of Jewett. The letter was shown to Mr. Vassar, who reacted with appropriate emotion. Jewett's resignation was requested, and Charles A. Raymond was informed of the contretemps. He instantly offered to serve in Jewett's place. That, however, was not to be. The trustees wanted nothing more to do with Southern schoolmasters. Instead, they quickly chose one of their own number to be head of Vassar Female College. This man's name was John Howard Raymond, and he was ultimately installed in office after he had proved that he was no relation whatever to Charles A. and that the names were the merest and most peculiar coincidence.

IV
The Founders: Spinster

AFTER Mary Lyon, the founders of the Seven proceed in a descending spiral of unlikelihood, with Sophia Smith perhaps the most enigmatic of the entire group. Fortunately, the college named for her managed to erase most traces of her eccentric personality early in its history, and the Smith image has evolved independently of its odd benefactor. She is justly remembered as "the first woman to have willed a fortune towards a college for her sex"—a true epitaph, but one that seems to have been written with someone else in mind: the Sophia Smith that *should* have been.

Miss Smith was an unworldly Massachusetts spinster of few ambitions, no pretensions and an assortment of afflictions. Although all her brothers and sisters were remarkable in one way or another, Sophia was shy, plain, deaf and, as she grew older, increasingly suspicious and melancholy. The family was prosperous by the standards of the time, but the males were almost pathologically miserly. The Smiths carried respectable New England frugality to unpopular and unprecedented extremes. Sophia Smith's bachelor brother Austin, for whom she kept house, was fond of boasting that he had neither offered nor given away "a meal of victuals" in his entire lifetime. He charged each of his sisters a shilling in fare to ride in the family carriage, and he wore the same suit for twenty years. Being a consistent sort of person, Austin Smith attempted to convince the town fathers that they should run the village of Hatfield as parsimoniously as he managed his own home. The municipal extravagance he thought most absurd and unnecessary was free general education, and he is known to have introduced a resolution that would have forbidden the public schools to offer any instruction beyond reading, writing and arithmetic. He didn't really believe that most youngsters deserved even that but was grudgingly willing to make allowances for the changing times.

However, when Hatfield considered the ultimate folly of building a high school, Austin Smith left town in a fury. He went to New York to increase his fortune, attracted there not only for business reasons, but because he had heard nothing about taxation for advanced education from that direction. He did astonishingly well in the city and was able to save almost every penny he earned. His neighbors in the small village of Hatfield had sometimes been able to humiliate him into small expenditures, but New York was pleasantly anonymous. It suited him perfectly. Austin Smith knew no one, joined nothing and was apparently content with his narrow and solitary life. The money accumulated without hindrance, until he suddenly became seriously ill and died before drafting a final will. Like many misers, he had been a compulsive testator, convinced that no beneficiary, public or private, would ever treat his money with the proper respect. He might decide on a legatee but on further consideration would destroy the document and begin looking for someone less likely to fritter away his fortune.

Will making filled his empty evenings and was his only diversion, but since notarizing the various rough versions would have cost money, Austin didn't bother. As a result of this attitude, his timid and bewildered sister Sophia unexpectedly inherited all his money, an eventuality for which she was totally unprepared, since the living Austin had been anything but generous to her.

To the astonishment of the community of Hatfield, which had always assumed that Sophia shared her brother's notions of economy, she built the grandest mansion in town, making sure that it contained every luxurious feature that her late brother had most loathed and abominated. Sophia Smith put in mirrors, bay windows, marble mantels, black walnut furniture and a grand piano. That last would have been something of a curiosity in any Hatfeld household, but it was particularly conspicuous in the home of the deaf and lonely Miss Smith and caused considerable comment and speculation. Uncaring (and probably unhearing), Miss Smith moved into this magnificent edifice with a maid and lived there for three uneasy years, worrying constantly about how best to dispose of the balance of Austin's fortune. She had tried, but she had been unable to dissipate more than a fraction of it. The Smith family tradition died hard, and none of the usual expenditures of the wealthy seemed to have occurred to her. The church would have been a natural choice for so religious a woman, but since Austin had publicly vowed, "The Lord won't get a cent of my money," Sophia hesitated. Perhaps building and furnishing the house had temporarily satisfied her need for revenge on her brother.

In any case, after much soul-searching and agonizing, she came to favor the idea of endowing a school for deaf-mutes. Within weeks after she came to this difficult decision, however, another and more purposeful philanthropist preempted her plan and broke ground for exactly the sort of institution she had in mind. Since there were only a few hundred deaf-mutes in the entire Commonwealth of Massachusetts, a second school seemed redundant, though she considered it anyway, abandoning the idea only after every single deaf-mute had been counted and she was forced to accept the fact that there simply weren't enough to go around.

Her pastor, John Greene, a young and eager Amherst graduate, tried valiantly to interest her in Mount Holyoke Seminary. Mary Lyon had actually been a distant relative of the Smiths, and the Reverend Mr. Greene naturally thought that the seminary just over the mountain would be a logical choice. It was nearby, flourishing and, by 1870 or so, considered a great asset to the neighborhood. Moreover, John Greene's charming and intelligent wife had been educated there, and both he and Mrs. Greene agreed that no more worthy cause existed. Since Sophia Smith stubbornly refused to take the ten-mile trip to South Hadley even to see the place, a delegation of Mount Holyoke teachers came to call on her. On that occasion she abruptly became more deaf than ever, convincing the ambassadors that further visits would serve no purpose. They left without ever really stating their case, positive that Miss Smith would enter the next world with her wealth undiminished by so much as the price of a cup of tea.

The Reverend Mr. Greene himself finally conceded defeat and proposed a plan he thought almost as worthwhile. Amherst College, he was sure, would be able to make excellent use of a bequest. It was just as conveniently located, and the training of ministers was a completely accepted necessity, not a risky experiment like the higher education of women.

Miss Smith, however, rejected the Amherst proposal out of hand. She had never been to the town of Amherst either and would not think of going there. She had always believed that Amherst professors were a subversive group secretly bent on controlling central Massachusetts, and she was not about to offer them either aid or comfort. Nothing that the Greenes could do or say persuaded her otherwise. It was a fixed idea. If there were a few exceptions, like her agreeable young pastor, they only served to prove the rule.

Though the burden of Austin's money was growing more and more intolerable every day, Sophia Smith could not bring herself to deposit it at either of the two most logical and deserving places. The Reverend Mr. Greene was a patient and sympathetic man, but he had already spent a disproportionate amount of his time shouting about money to his parishioner, slighting his other pastoral duties and neglecting his growing family. A gift to Amherst or Mount Holyoke would not benefit him, except perhaps spiritually, and he was already in an advanced state of grace. John Greene tried to resign as Sophia Smith's financial counselor, but she wouldn't allow that either. An estate advisory service was considered an important part of a nineteenth-century minister's duty, and he was reminded of that fact whenever he spoke of other responsibilities. Their relationship cooled considerably, but the demands on his time continued.

As a compromise, Miss Smith eventually agreed to consider some alternative proposals if the Reverend Mr. Greene would write them out in detail. Since he had already invested three whole years in futile conversations with this quixotic woman, he seems to have felt that there was little to lose by putting his suggestions on paper. At least he would be spared the high-decibel bellowing sessions. His letters were polite, but terse. He now addressed Miss Smith as "Madam" and tried another approach entirely. "One of the finest opportunities ever offered a person in this world is now offered to you in another enterprise. You may become to all time a Benefactress to the race. I refer to the endowment of a Womans' College." (Mount Holyoke was still technically a seminary, and Miss Smith seems to have been happily unaware of Matthew Vassar's magnificent enterprise off in the Hudson Valley.) "You can now, by a codicil to your will, appropriate the sum designed for a deaf mute institution to this object and have your name attached to the first Woman's College in New England." (The Reverend Mr. Greene, of course, knew all about Vassar, but he didn't consider Poughkeepsie New England.) "I remember that such an idea was very pleasing to you some years ago. But then it seemed to be an experiment. But it is no longer to be so regarded. Somebody will very soon endow in this state of woman's college. I wish that the honor might be yours." "It seems to me," continued John Greene, "that I can see the hand of God in prompting Mr. Clarke to endow the institution for Deaf Mutes that you might do this nobler and wider-reaching work for the women of New England."

As the letter indicates, the idea was one that Sophia Smith had previously examined without exactly entertaining—entertainment of any kind not being a Smith family tradition. It had never really appealed to her, but the Reverend Mr. Greene was hoping that the passage of time had dimmed her hostility and increased her desperation. He freshened up the proposal and presented it as attractively as he could. He was still intensely interested in women's education, and though both Greenes would have preferred that Holyoke be the recipient of any funds, they realized that Miss Smith's vanity could be served only by a charity bearing her own name. She was still antisocial and excruciatingly shy, but wealth had long since relieved her of her earlier modesty. The Greenes reasoned that since Mount Holyoke already had a name, it would have to be another place altogether. They wondered why they hadn't perceived this obvious fact before. They foresaw one potential problem, but the chance had to be taken. Miss Smith's college and Mount Holyoke would be a mere ten miles apart and could eventually find themselves in competition for students, faculty members and even prestige.

They kept their misgivings to themselves, however, and the second time around, Sophia Smith seemed more receptive to the thought of a college, though she did create a few difficulties and insist on certain conditions. One important proviso was that no Amherst professors be consulted about anything whatever. Another was that all students be housed in one-story cottages because Miss Smith believed that stairs were damaging to the female reproductive system. And of course, the place was to be called Sophia Smith College. At the suggestion that it be just plain *Smith,* she grew furious and threatened to withdraw all support. She would have much preferred the town of Hatfield to Northampton as a site but gave in when it was pointed out to her that land was higher, drier and cheaper in Northampton and that the college would have more room to expand. Ample space would be necessary if no buildings were to exceed a single story. After these matters were all arranged to her near satisfaction, she signed the will. The women's college idea had one great point in its favor all along. Nothing, absolutely nothing, could have been further from her brother Austin's desire.

V
The Founders: Evangelist

WHEN the main hall of Wellesley College was finally completed in 1875, astonished reporters, overcome by its magnificence, called it "a palace" and "a fairyland." The project had taken four years, but it had been conducted with such discretion that no one was prepared for the sudden materialization of a brick structure 480 feet long, 80 feet high, and even further extended by a pair of 166-foot wings at the sides. Though the basic design was a double Latin cross, so many embellishments had been added that the fundamental shape was hard to find. The building was an anthology of architectural styles through the ages, with towers, bays, spires, pavilions and verandas projecting from every elevation. Urbane representatives of *Harper's New Monthly Magazine* and the *Atlantic,* sent out to cover the routine opening of a new female seminary, found themselves gasping like backwoods plowboys, and their dispatches showed it. Bracing themselves for an anticlimax, they were guided inside, where they found a four-story central hall roofed with glass. Sunshine streamed down to a ground-floor conservatory filled with jungle plants and surrounded by arches, in each of which stood a life-sized classical statue, blindingly white and chastely draped. The whole glorious fantasy was set in a lavishly landscaped park and situated so that it would be reflected in Lake Waban. On fair and breezy days there seemed to be multiple castles in constant motion. The rest of the time the vision merely shimmered. Wellesley immediately made every other New England college look like a textile mill.

There was considerable worried speculation about the influence of all that gorgeousness on tender young female minds, and a great deal of simple bafflement. Although it was immediately announced that Wellesley students would be expected to share in domestic chores just as at Mount Holyoke and that the religious requirements at the new seminary would be much more stringent, the public was only slightly reassured, and people continued to wonder what sort of institution the founder really had in mind. There were inevitable comparisons to the Garden of Eden, the last days of Pompeii and the Taj Mahal. Being New Englanders, the neighbors naturally feared the worst.

The college building, however, was no more or less florid than the man who made it possible. Had Henry Durant been born a century later, there would have been a large vocabulary by which to explain him, but in his own pre-Freudian era there was only a limited choice. "Flamboyant," "prodigal," "unsavory" and "scurrilous" turn up often in accounts of his early life. So does "brilliant," but it's almost always modified by one of the other adjectives. Durant began his career as an attorney, but not quite the sort that Victorian Boston understood or approved. He became quickly notorious as a criminal lawyer, and his services were much in demand by grand larcenists, embezzlers and even murderers. Henry Durant accepted cases that no other Boylston Street barrister would touch, and he usually won them by tactics to which his colleagues would not stoop. Though his practice was lucrative, it wasn't quite respectable, and Durant made little public effort to compensate. He was not, for example, either a pillar of the Unitarian Church or a great benefactor of Harvard, and his behavior outside the courtroom seems to have been every bit as abrasive, inconsistent and theatrical as his manner inside it.

In addition to his legal work, Durant had many business investments (conflict of interest did not yet exist), and his personal fortune accumulated at a most un-Bostonian rate. Eventually, he began to indulge a latent aesthetic passion and filled his house and grounds with job lots of books, paintings, sculpture and specimen shrubs from all over the world. His taste in these areas seems to have run to the recondite, the lushly naturalistic and the frankly bizarre. Even the plants he assiduously collected violated prevailing Boston standards. His hothouses included exotica like night-blooming cereus, passionflowers, succulents of various sorts and other intemperate species. The women of Needham, in fact, would often avert their eyes from some of the glories of the Durant garden, finding them obscurely disturbing.

Before settling on the law, Durant had attempted to be a

poet, and even at the height of his extraordinary career, he would often lapse into youthful romanticism, jotting verses in the margins of his briefs and filling his summations with quatrains and couplets, mixing his own work with examples from the classics. This evidence of another and gentler side to his personality, however, only seemed to make Durant less comprehensible to his contemporaries. There was simply no place in nineteenth-century Boston for a newly rich underworld mouthpiece with such unorthodox enthusiasms, and Henry and Pauline Durant spent much of their time alone in their West Needham summer house, adding to their collections and enjoying them in privacy. By all accounts, they seem to have been a happy and compatible couple, despite the fact that Pauline was deeply devout and Henry, at best, was merely tolerant of religion.

When their infant daughter died, Pauline Durant begged and pleaded with her husband to "submit his will to God," but his biographers report that he merely said, "Pauline, you must take your medicine in your way and I must take mine in mine." His way was to lavish all his affection on his two-year-old son and to devote even more time and energy to his various flourishing enterprises. He gradually bought up much of the land that adjoined the country house and dreamed of the day when his son would be grown and grandchildren would marvel at the glorious surroundings that he had so imaginatively created for them.

When this only son died of diphtheria at the age of eight, the effect on Henry Durant was cataclysmic. During the boy's illness the father had vowed that he "would henceforth live for God," whether or not his child recovered. There is no way of knowing how he would have interpreted that promise if the story had ended happily, but upon the child's death, Durant immediately renounced his career and abruptly resigned from the bar. He then burned all the books, pictures and objects of art that he considered unsuitable for a servant of the Lord, even throwing some of his most carefully nurtured plants on the pyre. It was a massive bonfire, and it smoldered for days.

These outlandish gestures did nothing to enhance Durant's already strained social relationships, and there seems to have been collective relief when the couple moved away to New

York. There Henry Durant attended to business and the Bible, apparently having convinced himself that commerce was more acceptable in the sight of God than the law. During the 1860s he did spectacularly well in the manufacture of engines and other war materiel for the Union Army. Every one of his evenings was now spent poring over Scripture, and he was soon devoting all his spare time to evangelism, speaking at prayer meetings and religious revivals up and down the Eastern seaboard. The hypnotic presence that had made him such a power in the courtroom worked equally well in church, and he became something of a superstar, drawing large and emotional crowds wherever he spoke. He swayed congregations as he had once influenced juries and was personally credited with hundreds of conversions. Strong men wept and women swooned at these gatherings, and news of them quickly reached Massachusetts. There his former legal colleagues discussed his radical change of heart and direction with great skepticism. One Boston attorney cynically commented: "He himself held that he was 'converted.' His early period was spent as a sharp, unscrupulous lawyer in Boston, a man of masterful powers but not deeply respected. . . . The striking and sudden contrast caused many to count his later life insincere." (It should, of course, be remembered that proper Bostonians "have" their religion the way they are said to "have" their hats, and faith is not considered something to be suddenly acquired in middle age.)

Although the Durants continued to spend their summers on their suburban Boston property, they found that they had even more time to themselves than before. The narrow society that couldn't quite absorb a freethinking criminal lawyer found a hellfire-and-brimstone entrepreneur no more to its liking. In solitude, Henry Durant wandered over the hillside property that he had bought for his dead son and began to consider suitable memorials. He knew that the land would have to be used for "God's Work," but the perfect vocation remained a problem. Though Durant was sure that God would approve a strictly religious boys' preparatory school, the New England woods were already well filled with those. Pauline Durant thought that a girls' school might be less redundant, but that alone seemed rather too modest. Durant then proceeded to plan an orphanage as well as two schools, hypothesizing an entire holy community in which youngsters of all ages, both sexes and all economic classes would be taught Gospel according to evangelical methods. It was a grand program, but the Durants eventually agreed that it might be impractical and overly ambitious. Eventually they narrowed the proposal down to a more manageable project, definitely deciding on an institution for the higher education of girls, a still uncrowded field in which there was more than enough room for something startlingly original.

Throughout the convolutions of his life Durant had remained a showman, and he proceeded to design a college that would satisfy the various facets of his complex personality. The similarities between Wellesley and the Taj Mahal were neither entirely accidental nor wholly in the eye of the beholder.

Once Durant had made up his mind to establish a seminary to train women as teachers "upon sound Christian principles," he moved quickly. Mary Lyon, Matthew Vassar and Sophia Smith, the vacillating spinster from Hatfield, had all got off to a running start, and Henry Durant was determined that his college would overtake the entire field. By 1870 Durant had appointed a board of trustees, acquired the official incorporation from the Commonwealth of Massachusetts and set aside $600,000 in liquid assets. He had also drafted his primary stipulation: "It is required that every Trustee, teacher and officer shall be a member of an Evangelical Church, and that the study of the Holy Scripture shall be pursued by every student throughout the entire college course under the direction of the faculty." A solid religious base was no novelty in New England colleges, and diligent attention to Scripture was taken for granted everywhere, but evangelism of the stand-up-and-confess kind was something else again, a far cry from the restrained usage that had become the norm. This was, after all, 1870, not 1630, and Puritan religious fervor had cooled considerably. Durant's blatant zeal was considered in poor taste, just as his pictures, his books and his indecorous plants had been.

Dressed in his most conservative country tweeds, his white hair flowing in the wind, Durant set out each day to make sure that every brick in his college would be godly. He forbade loud talking, profanity and fighting among his laboring force and even went so far as to build a dormitory for them in which the rules were as strict as those in a theological seminary. Bricklayers and carpenters who couldn't live like monks were discharged on the spot, and replacements sent out from the city. On the day the cornerstone was laid, Henry and Pauline optimistically presented each surprised workman with a Bible as a memento of the occasion. No other spectators had been asked to the ceremony, which took place without any of the traditional publicity that accompanies such events. A last, specially inscribed Bible was sealed into a tin box, inserted into the cornerstone and mortared over.

Building the college hall took considerably longer than expected partly because the Durants were such perfectionists, but also because there was so much turnover among the laborers. Competent craftsmen of sufficiently high moral principles weren't easy to find, and Durant was often obliged to discharge entire crews for violations of his rules. Regulated dormitory life for the duration of the job did not appeal to the men, and dozens deserted when they heard the conditions. Wellesley was a long trip from Boston for a day's work, and there were few overnight accommodations to be had in the vicinity of the project. Durant was a meticulous superintendent, as fanatic about joists and beams as he was about cursing and fighting, though toward the end of 1874 impatience obliged him to relent. By then, eager to see the college done, he was ignoring loud talking and even closing his eyes to the occasional rum bottle on the premises.

Absolutely everything that went into that massive structure was selected and tested by the Durants. They bathed at the washstands, sat in the chairs, read by the lights, poured from the pitchers and even walked dozens of sample stairways before settling on the ideal height for the risers. There were to be autographed portraits of notable poets in the Great Hall, and the Durants made sure that the signatures were legible. Longfellow, Bryant and Tennyson came through beautifully, but a few minor figures sent in hasty scrawls, and the untidiest were returned for revision. Durant's quixotic religious convictions did not demand austerity, and the college had an elevator, a steam heat and humidity system and gaslight throughout. There was only one obvious omission, but it seemed as striking and capricious as any of the inclusions. Henry Durant forbade any portrait or statue of himself in the building. Visitors who asked why there was no likeness of the founder were answered curtly. "This is God's College," Durant would say. "I am not in the monument business." (Long after his death a building was dedicated to Durant, but in deference to his commandment it's called merely Founder's Hall.)

Durant was thoroughly and happily involved in the education business and went about researching and developing a curriculum with the same single-mindedness that he had spent on the furnishings and accessories. He visited all the institutions that admitted women and cross-examined them assiduously. He found a strength here and a weakness there, admirable features and serious flaws wherever he looked. He soon concluded that the academic system would have to be custom-made, like everything else at Wellesley, to his precise and particular specifications. His college was to have an entirely female administration and faculty, despite the difficulty of finding an adequate number of well-trained women for the posts. "Women can do the work," he said. "I give them the chance." In order to collect this faculty, Durant ranged far afield, raiding Oberlin, Vassar and Mount Holyoke for newly minted graduates, often returning again and again to persuade the reluctant.

"Doing the work" was just a part of the job at Wellesley, and the best academic credentials alone were no guarantee of employment. There was also the matter of faith, and that narrowed an already small pool. Only the saved could teach at Durant's college, and many young women who could fulfill the academic requirements failed the rigorous spiritual examinations that Durant conducted and were not considered. Proof of a lifetime of regular church attendance did not satisfy him. Prospective instructors were expected to take on Bible classes in addition to their specialties, and there were no exceptions. A faculty was finally assembled, but there were several entire departments without a degree among them, though every teacher was in a demonstrable state of grace.

"Mr. Durant rules the college," wrote a member of the class of 1879, "from the amount of Latin we shall read to the kind of meat that we shall have for dinner." Prayers, of course, were his particular dominion, and Sunday his favorite time to inspect his handiwork. After the rising bell at seven, there was breakfast at seven forty-five, silent time at nine thirty, Bible class at nine forty-five, church services at ten thirty, dinner at one, another church service at four thirty, prayer meeting at seven thirty and a reprise of silent time at nine before bedtime at nine thirty. (Weekdays were a comparative relief. There was no four thirty church service, and the evening prayer meeting was optional.) Durant could appear at any moment and demand to know if a particular student believed herself saved. No matter what her answer, he would usually stop for long enough to reinforce her spiritual state with a mini-sermon. "All this," said a woman who had been in the class of 1881, "was the tonic positiveness of a reformer; a very pillar of fire to those who were willing to be led." Students unprepared to meet their founder on his weekly rounds soon learned which of the hundreds of unusual plants and trees offered the best chance of shelter and would scatter like dryads at the sound of Henry Durant's unmistakable voice. Even as a very old man he could be heard in the farthest reaches of the garden, and those who had been at Wellesley during its first decade never forgot their encounters with him. Later classes could never quite imagine what those years had been like since there were no graven images anywhere to remind them of his physical appearance, nor even a Durant Hall to perpetuate his name.

VI
The Founders: Plotters

THE other colleges began with characters—Radcliffe started as a plot. At first those responsible for organizing the Society for the Collegiate Instruction of Women seem to have worked almost surreptitiously. By 1879 the issue of higher education for women had some eloquent advocates, but few people in Cambridge, Massachusetts, seem to have considered having such a facility in that particular town. There was already a university there, and it was generally considered perfect as it stood, everything a reasonable citizen could desire. Adulterating it was unthinkable, and a separate and independent institution for women would, it was thought, quickly turn into a distraction, a hazard or worse. One might as well talk of opening a Protestant chapel in Vatican City. Even the most enthusiastic supporters of female colleges quickly realized that anything in the least conspicuous would be strenuously opposed and possibly doomed. Under the circumstances, the society did a most sensible thing. They decided on an invisible college, with shadow students, a closet faculty and neither an actual name nor a specific location. A residence hall, with young women entering, leaving, eating and sleeping in the vicinity of the square was never even suggested. At a slight risk of vulgarity, one could compare the experiment to a floating dice game. The only people who knew where to find it were the players themselves, and even they could not always be sure.

The society was to meet as small groups in private houses, with moonlighting Harvard instructors lecturing behind closed doors. Neither a formal catalogue nor a balanced curriculum was possible at this stage. The students were to pay their fees to the society, which in turn planned to recompense the professors for their time. The whole thing was a very private sort of arrangement, conducted with the utmost circumspection. A great many people knew of it, but few cared to discuss it. The teaching of women, though now regarded as worthwhile and perhaps even necessary, was still considered somewhat beneath the dignity of a Harvard professor, not perhaps as demeaning as keeping a shop, but certainly nothing that enhanced a scholarly reputation.

At first, the only men who agreed to it were those who badly needed to supplement their Harvard salaries. President Charles Eliot, however, was well aware that many of his junior instructors were somewhat underpaid, and he had no objection to outside activities, provided that these were undertaken on the professor's own time and well outside of the sacred precincts of the Yard. During Eliot's presidency a young man applying for a teaching post at Harvard was usually told in a roundabout way of the additional opportunities offered by the society. In several cases, it seems to have been a most effective inducement, a sort of prototype fringe benefit. Even a quite senior professor might occasionally take a turn at speaking to the ladies, finding it spiritually as well as financially rewarding. One merely had to repeat one's regular lectures. No concessions were either expected or made.

The idea for the society was first suggested to Elizabeth Cary Agassiz, the widow of the renowned biologist Louis Agassiz. The proposal came from a Mr. Arthur Gilman, who wished to educate his daughter Grace. Many years earlier, before her husband's work was so well recognized, Mrs. Agassiz had run a select and successful school for young ladies in her own home, reluctantly closing it only after family responsibilities made it impossible to continue. Mr. Gilman remembered that little school with nostalgic affection. It had been precisely the sort of place he would have liked for Grace. 'Opposed to coeducation, we did not care to send our daughter to High School," he said, "and we objected also to sending her daily to Boston in the horse cars."

He assembled a small group of like-minded parents at his home, and they agreed that Mrs. Agassiz should be consulted. Her previous educational experience, her impeccable Boston family connections and her close Harvard relationships would be invaluable to any plan they devised. Although Elizabeth Agassiz was then nearly sixty years old and thoroughly occupied in writing a biography of her late husband, she promised to serve on the committee and contribute in any way she could. An understated memorandum was quickly prepared, "worded -with care," in Mr. Gilman's phrase. He wished to avoid "two popular misconceptions" that could be disastrous. The first was "that the plan in any way favors or tends to coeducation" and the second, "that Harvard College is in any way responsible for it."

Mrs. Agassiz was soon up to her aristocratic chin in paperwork, collaborating with Mr. Gilman on a list of Harvard professors—friends of her late husband's—who might be persuaded to teach a few young women in their spare time and lend prestige to the endeavor. Professor William E. Byerly of the Mathematics Department would take a class for an emolument of $3 an hour per student. Professor J. P. Cook, the chemist, insisted on a laboratory before he would consent to appear. Professors Benjamin Peirce and F. H. Hedge made no such stipulations, but the eminent William James would not accept less than $4 an hour and made it clear that his high fee "would probably exclude any solitary pupil" from his classes in psychology and modern philosophy. He was, however, willing to make some concessions. A group of three pupils could have him for $6, and he was willing to speak to classes of four, five or six for a mere $1.50 an hour from each girl. For any class larger than six, the fee dropped to a flat $10 an hour—William James himself at ordinary discount prices.

The Agassiz name had proved even more magical than Mr. Gilman dared hope. He soon realized that he had outlined something far more elevated than the high school he had originally envisioned. His young daughter Grace was clearly not ready for such a program, and she was regretfully sent off to Bradford Academy instead. It was decided that the Cambridge female students would "pursue a regular college course of four years." Each young woman would receive a certificate upon successful completion of each course, and eventually these would be "merged into one, which will be signed by all the instructors." The presumptuous word "degree" was never mentioned at this stage.

All the preliminary planning was accomplished in a mere month. By March 2, 1879, three applications for admission to the Society for the Collegiate Instruction of Women had already turned up in Mrs. Agassiz's mailbox, although the institution existed only on paper. In June, Mrs. Agassiz escaped to her summer home at Nahant, where she continued her interrupted work on the biography and wondered from time to time where the prospective students would live or attend classes, should any of them actually appear. General entrance examinations were announced for September, and the response was both gratifying and disconcerting.

Twenty-seven applicants, many of them already teachers, were accepted, though only three signed up for a full complement of offered classes. Elizabeth Agassiz had to find both classroom and boarding accommodations for them, a job that would have been difficult in June but was almost impossible in September. She seems to have discovered somewhat tardily that she was considered head of the society and responsible for almost everything connected with it. A few Cambridge neighbors were persuaded to accept students as paying guests, and a Mrs. Carret on Appian Way agreed to rent four rooms of her private house as lecture halls. Mrs. Carret, however, didn't wish to have it known that she had turned her parlor into a school and insisted that the fact be concealed. To oblige her, the now rather desperate Mrs. Agassiz bought yards of muslin and personally hung curtains at the Carret windows. These were kept drawn so that curious passersby would be unaware of the small groups of young women studying inside. A few of the professors were brave and generous enough to teach the girls in their own homes, which helped considerably.

Even an invisible college, however, requires a library, and this demanded some particularly ingenious arrangements. In December the committee voted to rent an empty room at the corner of Appian Way and Garden Street, and to hire a thirteen-year-old boy "to carry books from the Library and return them as called for by the young ladies." The "Library" in question was the Cambridge Public Library because President Eliot's support of the venture did not extend to admitting women to the Harvard bookstacks. (The following spring Mrs. Agassiz asked President Eliot if her girls might have borrowing privileges at the university facility, and while he seems to have been amenable enough, provided the women promised not to sit down and read, the Harvard Corporation rejected the idea outright.)

For its first three years the society muddled along in this twilight zone, but in 1882 the advisers of what was eventually to be Radcliffe College voted to incorporate and officially elected Mrs. Agassiz president. The working title of the organization had been The Society for the Collegiate Instruction of Women by Professors of Harvard University, but the last crucial five words were left out of the new charter. Mrs. Agassiz considered them particularly vital to the success of the venture since the Harvard faculty was really all the institution had to offer. Finally, she succeeded in having the phrase reincluded, but in a modified form which promised somewhat less. The compromise was "with the assistance of the Instructors of Harvard University." Mrs. Agassiz had to settle for that, which she hoped would be enough to put her project into a competitive position with other women's colleges, all of which had classroom buildings, dormitories, laboratories and libraries, as well as a permanent faculty. Wellesley and Vassar were frankly luxurious, and by 1882 Mount Holyoke and Smith had grown and prospered considerably.

An explicit Harvard connection had to be established, but Mrs. Agassiz ran into trouble the moment she tried to regularize the society's position. The back street arrangement suited Harvard perfectly. Alexander Agassiz opposed anything more explicit, as did the rest of Mrs. Agassiz's family and most of her friends. Her diary for 1893 notes that she had a "Little talk with Alex about the Annex this morning. He is discouraging and I think he would rather discourage the [Harvard] Corporation, should he see any of them." What her stepson Alex and the others stubbornly resisted was the implication or suggestion that Harvard sponsor or underwrite the women's college. The project might be a good idea all by itself, but they didn't regard it as a fit endeavor for so glorious an institution as Harvard. If the attempt were to fail or even to prove less than illustrious, Harvard itself could be compromised. The university refused to offer any aid or comfort except the purely voluntary services of well-intentioned or impecunious professors, and it preferred not to advertise even that concession.

Elizabeth Agassiz was obliged to raise the necessary operating funds by any means she could devise. In 1883, therefore, considering herself rather mature to go racketing around New England with a green velvet bag as Mary Lyon had done, Mrs. Agassiz organized a series of "Parlor Meetings" in Boston, to which she invited her most eminent relatives and friends. Her methods were delicacy itself. By then there were about forty pupils, and those who were taking the full course needed at least $200 for tuition—$50 more than Harvard itself charged. Moreover, the girls had to pay for room and board. "Our students are scattered by twos and threes in Cambridge families," Mrs. Agassiz assured her audience. "They quietly pursue their occupations as unnoticed as the daughters of any Cambridge residents." That was a vital point, because there was still widespread opposition to a houseful of young women in the vicinity of Harvard. The scattered scholars posed less of a threat. "The school stirs no prejudices, excites no opposition, involves no change of policy for the University," Mrs. Agassiz continued. "Our students themselves manifest no desire for coeducation. The element of competition with men does not enter into their aims."

Having tranquilized her listeners with all these negatives, Elizabeth Agassiz moved softly into the single positive. What she did want was $100,000, so that her scholars could come to Harvard "with full hands," asking for recognition and a promise that Harvard professors would continue to teach them. The money would constitute a sort of performance bond, though it sounded more like a dowry than an endowment. Mrs. Agassiz wanted to *give* Harvard the $100,000 because, as she said, "anything less would make us, financially speaking, an unsafe acquisition for the University." Brahmin that she was, she put the welfare of Harvard first, instinctively. "Even if we should succeed in raising the whole of this sum," she said, "it would not put the education of women on a par with that of men, at Harvard," though "it might give the college the means of continuing on a somewhat broader base, the work already begun. We cannot but hope that if the College accepts us, we too shall have . . . our bequests and legacies like some departments of the University."

These parlor talks may have been calming, but they weren't as lucrative as had been hoped. By 1884 only $93,000 had been raised, and Harvard coldly refused that paltry sum, denying any official recognition of the Annex at its corporation meeting. No one, at that point, had any idea of Harvard's price or even if Harvard *had* a price. It was strongly suspected by many cynics that it did, but the Society for the Collegiate Instruction of

Women was in no position to make a better offer. It was hinted that the popular designation of the women's course as the Annex was embarrassing to Harvard, implying a relationship that did not actually exist. The tag stuck nevertheless. It was both convenient and optimistic, and to abandon it would have been to admit that there was no hope of a liaison.

In the fall of 1885 Mrs. Agassiz bravely decided that some of the rejected dowry should be used to buy a house. The concession to Harvard sensibilities had resulted in nothing more than discomfort and inconvenience for the women students, and there were now so many of them that lecture space and lodgings were impossible to find. A spacious old mansion had become available, and the price for sixteen rooms of turreted splendor was a reasonable $20,000. Loyal "Friends" subscribed half the sum, and the rest was taken from the treasury, leaving about $80,000 soundly invested. After six years of official nonexistence, the invisible college had emerged. It was hoped that from that moment on it would be harder to ignore.

Four years later the institution was still struggling under its unwieldy maiden name, but it had acquired a nearby lot and built a physics and chemistry laboratory. Now, presumably, it would be able to attract and keep a chemistry professor. The ownership of all that real estate, however, seemed to go to the students' heads. The young women had seemed content with their ambiguous status and their anomalous "certificates," but now they suddenly demanded "academic degrees." Women at other colleges were receiving them, and the ladies of the Annex were becoming restive. They had been taught, however covertly, by Harvard professors, and there was a growing feeling that the world should know and that President Eliot himself should countersign the diplomas.

Mrs. Agassiz now presided over assets totaling $150,000, and she agreed to pay another call on Harvard, offering "all our present property" in return for diplomas, but "not asking for any rights or privileges" above and beyond that. Although President Eliot seemed to like the proposal, the corporation remained adamant. The suit was rejected for the second time. Edward W. Hooper, treasurer of Harvard, wrote the icy letter of refusal. "I am quite willing to see Yale or Columbia take any risks they like, but I feel bound to protect Harvard College

68

from what seems to me a risky experiment." The most ardent supporters of the Annex idea were humiliated and predicted an early end to the whole experiment. What Harvard rejected, Cambridge did without. It had always been that way, and it didn't seem likely that one elderly lady, no matter how impeccable her background, would ever succeed in changing matters.

The final "no" was common knowledge all over Boston, and Mrs. Agassiz saw no further reason to minimize the problem. She discussed the matter fully and freely with her friend Mrs. John C. Gray, who was married to the Royall professor at Harvard Law School. Professor Gray was sympathetic, though he had not been involved in the controversy until that moment. He promised to see what he could do. There might be some obscure legal point that could be useful. Nice legal points were his particular specialty, and he regarded the difficulty as an intellectual challenge. There clearly had to be an alliance of some sort between the institutions, but why a betrothal? Why not a guardianship?

Professor Gray had recently been researching the more exquisite nuances of English law, and he had unearthed the stipulation that all colleges must have "visitors"—qualified outsiders who function as academic watchdogs making sure that proper standards are upheld. The "visitors" are selected by the college needing them, and there seemed to be no precedent for refusal. English law applied in America, and therefore, Professor Gray reasoned, the Society for the *Collegiate Instruction of Women* need only appoint Harvard as its "visitor," and Harvard would be legally and morally obliged to serve. There would be no need, under such an arrangement, for any money to change hands. Professor Gray suggested that the visitor-visitee relationship be made subject to cancellation "by either party on four years' notice." He thought that this escape clause would make the responsibility more palatable to intransigent members of the Harvard Corporation, who otherwise might have considered the plan coercive. As a visitee of Harvard the society would naturally receive an appropriate degree—not, perhaps, *the* degree, but something at least equivalent. To deny it would indicate that the women had not received proper instruction, and that would reflect very badly on the great visitor. Mrs. Agassiz was triumphant—and immensely grateful to Professor

John Gray. The originality of the plan seems to have emboldened her. "The form of our diploma should be carefully studied," she said. "It should not be differentiated from the A.B. of Harvard as a 'ladies' degree."

A "memorandum of agreement" between the president and fellows of Harvard College and the Society for the Collegiate Instruction of Women was immediately drafted. The name of the party of the second part, however, proved so cumbersome and awkward that it was decided to use the designation X instead. "The Annex" was too undignified and informal, and the party of the first part had always resented it. No one wanted to delay the proceedings until a more permanent name could be found. X would do. The provisions were simple and to the point. The role of visitor was made as clear as possible, and so was the fact that "diplomas of X would be countersigned by the President of Harvard and would bear its seal." It wasn't an intimate relationship by any means, but it was a high-button shoe in the door. Intimacy might come later. A few unreasonable men on the board may have felt that they had been betrayed by one of their own, but Harvard didn't wrangle with Harvard in public, and the agreement was signed.

The opposition temporarily retired and consoled itself with the thought that the Massachusetts legislature could still refuse to charter the venture. It almost did, on the ground that the college was too poorly endowed to maintain the necessary standards of excellence. Mrs. Agassiz, now almost seventy-five years old, but tactful and eloquent as ever, persuaded them otherwise. "If our endowment is small," she said to the assembly, "the active and cordial cooperation of the professors and teachers of Harvard is better than money for us." The legislators, many of whom were Harvard men themselves, could hardly disagree, and X was chartered. In 1894 it was rechartered as Radcliffe College, commemorating Ann Radcliffe, the first woman to donate money to Harvard. That act of generosity had occurred in the year 1642 and the name had several advantages. It was euphonious, short and suggested no connection whatever with Harvard to any living person.

VII
The Founders: Bride

NEWS of the educational underground flourishing at Cambridge spread quickly, and a "we too" movement developed almost at once. Scores of academically deprived young women living in various university towns reasoned that if Harvard itself could be inveigled into a liaison, other men's colleges might also be amenable. There were optimists everywhere, and a pervasive feeling that the 1890s would be a decade of leap years. As long as the ladies were willing to settle for ambiguous status—no name on the mailbox, no public appearances and no common property—they were confident that something could be arranged.

Columbia University, in fact, had first been propositioned in 1876, by a socially prominent women's club known as Sorosis. The group (it was one hundred years too soon to call them sisters) presented a polite petition for the admission of women to the university, and they were turned down flat. Although Frederick A. P. Barnard, then president of Columbia, was an ardent and outspoken supporter of higher education for women, few New Yorkers of either sex seemed to share his enthusiasm. Barnard's ideas were resisted by the clergymen, business people and society leaders who composed the board of Columbia trustees, and some of his most vocal detractors were women themselves. At the time, advanced education was widely believed to drain the blush from a girl's cheeks, the light from her eyes and the tenderness from her heart. The bluestocking had already become a cartoonists' delight, even though there were hardly any to be seen on the sidewalks of New York. Frederick Barnard proselytized at every opportunity, but the list of conversions was short. In his memoirs he reports a typical encounter. "One of the most highly cultivated ladies in New York society" heard his theories at a dinner party and commented, "I would preserve the bloom on the peach as long as possible." "So would

71

I," Barnard answered, "I would favor no measure which would leave the slightest trace upon the delicacy of the bloom; but I would have the peach valued for something more than its bloom merely." The anecdote ends right there. The "cultivated lady" departed, still certain that learning and beauty were mutually incompatible.

By 1879, however, in spite of fairly general indifference, a formal Committee on the Collegiate Education of Women had been formed in New York, and Columbia University was approached for the second time. The newly constituted organization asked only that "the statutes of Columbia be construed as not to prohibit women from certain courses under certain conditions." By then the petitioners had learned that negative phraseology and deliberate vagueness seemed to work best in these matters, but the Columbia trustees disposed of this proposal as summarily as they had rejected the first one. Reconstruing statutes could be particularly chancy for Columbia because the original charter of that university had been rather haphazardly worded. It promised "education to the youth of the city," and if the noun "youth" were allowed to mean young people of both sexes, the university might well be stormed by females from as far away as Brooklyn and even Long Island. The Columbia Medical School had already been confronted by a woman applicant, (a recent graduate of the University of Michigan) who pointed out that Webster's dictionary defined "youth" simply as "young people." It had been a sticky business, but the medical school had taken refuge in the sixth and seventh definitions, which held that "youth" referred especially to "a young man or someone not yet attained to full manhood." That kept the lady out, but it had been a near thing, and no one wanted to take any further risks.

At the same time that these proposals were being drafted and rejected, a very small number of young women were actually attending lectures at Columbia in spite of the rules. There were a few ways that this could be managed, all illicit and precarious. In rare cases, invitations could be wrangled from the professors themselves. If the "guest" minded her manners, chose a seat in the very back rows of the auditorium and didn't crackle papers or ogle the gentlemen, she might reappear for several weeks before attracting any notice. Some professors were nearsighted, others were absentminded, and a tiny minority were truly liberal. Professor Ogden Rood of the Physics Department, for instance, was known to be particularly tolerant of unauthorized visitors, and several young women succeeded in hearing his entire course of lectures. Other instructors would also admit ladies, assuming them to be the sisters, cousins or fiancées of properly registered young men. Probably no more than twenty women ever infiltrated Columbia by these various ruses, but the loopholes did exist for those who were daring, brazen or curious enough to slip through them.

Information acquired by this system must have been rather like owning a smuggled work of art—one could display it only at the risk of cutting off the source of supply. Bootleg scholarship may have been better than nothing, but not much. In any case this pleasant interlude lasted for only a very short time, because the petitions focused attention on the cowering ladies in the back rows, and they immediately became an issue of contention. When it was discovered that one of the ex officio students was actually the daughter of a Columbia trustee, the brief détente came to an abrupt and final end. All women were explicitly barred from classrooms by a new bylaw, and the more lenient professors were asked to check for mixed company before they even began to speak. The women of New York, barely on square one by the 1880s, were totally sidelined. A desperate few considered the trip up the Hudson to Poughkeepsie, but that was completely out of the question for a day student.

In April, 1882, enough interest had apparently been generated in women's education for the Union League Club to hold an open meeting on the subject. The event was elegant and well attended, and 1,400 leading citizens were sufficiently moved by the oratory to sign a third petition addressed to the trustees of Columbia. That one seemed a bit harder to dismiss than the earlier versions. For one thing, the 1,400 included some very important and influential people, and for another, Cambridge University in England had recently established a women's college. While New York might consider itself *hors de combat* as far as Boston was concerned, it did enjoy a spot of competition with the English. If women's education had become fashionable, New York dared not ignore it—though it still, of course, could oppose it.

The request that emerged from the Union League meeting was even more exquisitely worded than the first two had been. It asked that the "benefit of education" at Columbia be granted to "such properly qualified" women as might desire it. Since there was no college preparatory school for girls in New York City at that time, the numbers of potential scholars would be kept to a minimum. That phrase was a safeguard, and it apparently gave the Columbia trustees a welcome sense of security. The next sentence, however, was fraught with danger. It mentioned the admission of women to "lectures and examinations," and that did not slip by so easily. After giving the entire proposal their most careful attention, the trustees decided that admission to lectures simply could not be granted. They were willing, however, to allow women into examinations, reasoning that without the benefit of the lectures, few, if any, would be able to pass the examinations, and the status quo would be preserved. Columbia would be known as a forward-looking place, right in the vanguard of educational reform, but it would also remain precisely the same and all-male. Instead of the Harvard plan, which provided for classes but no degrees, Columbia would offer degrees but no classes.

The petition was granted with its limitations made perfectly clear. A "Collegiate Course for Women" would be established, and every student in it was to be "entirely free as to where and how to pursue her studies, whether in some school, private or public, or at home, or under the auspices or direction of any association interested in her welfare and advancement, and providing her with the means of education." Columbia agreed to act as the examining body and notary for anyone who found a college or the equivalent. The young women were to understand that "entirely free" did not mean that they could enter Columbia's classrooms or avail themselves of any of its facilities except a desk and chair for the final examinations.

This enormous concession made, Columbia sat back to watch the response. Of the thirty young women who attempted to take advantage of the plan, only one ever extracted a diploma from the university during the four years that the option was available. Her name was Mary Parsons Hankey, and the degree she was given was called Bachelor of Literature. Miss Hankey died a few months after winning it, happily unaware that a BL diploma meant nothing at all. The other twenty-nine candidates seem to have been unable to locate a second Columbia that would prepare them to pass the tests given by the first one, and they were obliged to drop out of the program. The sad case of Miss Hankey was exploited to show that women could not physically survive the rigors of higher education, and the disappointing records of her classmates were used as proof that girls lacked both interest and motivation. Columbia considered the results of the experiment conclusive and called it a failure.

Before the university could completely abandon the project, however, a rather remarkable student contrived to take and pass the entrance examinations. She knew, of course, that she was not really *entering* anything, but rather embarking on a long and solitary grind, but she wasn't deterred. Her name was Annie Nathan, and she was somewhat less intimidated by the idea of independent study than most girls who considered the Collegiate Course. Annie Nathan had never attended a regularly constituted school at all, not even a small private one. Her mother had taught her to read, and her father had generously provided her with books and an occasional hourly teacher, "none too adept," in Miss Nathan's own phrase. Beyond that she had always been on her own. It was an irregular arrangement, but then, the Nathans were an irregular family. Part of the small group of Sephardic Jewish settlers who had reached New York in the 1620s, they seem to have had more than their share of hardship and scandal during the intervening two and a half centuries. As described by Stephen Birmingham in *The Grandees,* the Nathan history is genuinely Gothic. While they weren't entirely impoverished by 1880, the family fortunes hadn't been replenished for a hundred years or so, and the glitter of the name was considerably diminished. There was an unsolved murder in the background, considerable alcoholism, a number of unsanctified attachments and love affairs and more than a rumor of drug addiction.

Various Nathans wrote memoirs of these events, and though there isn't much agreement among them, there's a great deal of source material. Annie Nathan, in *Barnard Beginnings,* offers a carefully edited version of her childhood, explaining it all calmly. In that book, published in 1935, she says:

> I hasten to add that my lack of schooling was in no sense a question of lack of funds or opportunity, but simply owing to

the fact that being the youngest child of four, my dear mother had kept me under her tutelage longer than the others. . . . Later on, after my mother's death, I became the apple of my father's eye, and he refused to let me go to school when the weather was bad. We couldn't then afford a carriage, so I simply decided that I would no longer go to school to be kept home whenever the skies frowned. I was insatiably ambitious, and frequently, returning from some visit which I had made with my father, ordered my teacher to instruct me in this or that, so I would cease feeling ignorant and embarrassed.

(For a more dramatic account of those years, one must read Annie Nathan's *other* and more outspoken book, *It's Been Fun*, 1951.)

In any case, Annie did manage to qualify for Columbia's Collegiate Course, "preparing entirely by myself, without assistance." After passing the preliminary examinations, Annie told her incredulous father how she had been spending her time between family visits, household duties and nightly whist games. It must have been a most affecting scene. According to the account in *Barnard Beginnings*, Mr. Nathan drew his daughter "gently and lovingly to him" and sadly announced, "You will never be married. Men hate intelligent wives." Annie admits that her "heart sank" at this prophecy, but she did the assigned reading and appeared for the midyear and final examinations anyway. She was only eighteen, delicate and classically pretty, and she seems to have persuaded herself that she just might be an exception to her father's gloomy rule. (Her older sister, Maud, was already a leading suffragist, and Annie determined to stay well away from that tumultuous and controversial movement. As a result, she and Maud became implacable enemies and never spoke to each other if they could help it. Each Nathan girl opposed the other's crusade, and the rift lasted for their lifetimes. The estranged sisters, in fact, were the talk of the town for half a century.)

As a first-year student Annie juggled her reading lists and her beaux successfully, never allowing them to overlap, and turned up for the June examinations confident, exhilarated and almost engaged. She never suspected that the test would be based on the classes she had missed, instead of the books she had so thoroughly studied. Shocked, she reports that she answered fully the questions that she understood, then "coolly wrote in the examination paper that certain of the questions evidently referred to the professor's lectures, which I had not had the privilege of hearing." Miss Nathan not only passed, but was married within a few months, safe on all counts.

After her wedding Annie Nathan, now Mrs. Alfred Meyer, decided that she could probably educate herself just as well without the agony of the examinations. Columbia had relented to the point of allowing women to use its library, though they were still excluded from the lecture halls. Annie made full use of this new dispensation and spent all her free time in the reading rooms. Her husband seems to have been sympathetic and understanding, and her loving father was vastly relieved.

The Collegiate Course had been a complete farce, and Mrs. Meyer was receiving far more help and guidance from the new Columbia librarian than she had ever got from her so-called professors. Melvil Dewey was not only the famous inventor of the library decimal system, but an innovator in other fields as well. Most important to Annie Meyer, however, was his knowledge and articulate advocacy of women's education. He listened to her account of her frustrating year as a Columbia student and agreed that the plan had been absurd. His remedy was heroic. Melvil Dewey suggested that Annie herself start a real college. Dewey saw no particular reason for women's colleges to be founded by elderly millionaires. In his opinion, a twenty-year-old bride would be a much more logical choice. Mrs. Meyer agreed entirely, but she foresaw certain problems. Her new husband was a physician and by no means wealthy. The Nathan family, though venerable, had withdrawn almost entirely from New York social life and had allowed most of their once powerful connections to lapse. Annie was not even the graduate of a school, let alone a college. Her sister, Maud Nathan, was making headlines right and left, and the publicity wasn't all favorable. "The fact that the job was bristling with difficulties—some of them seemingly insurmountable—made it all the more thrilling to undertake, all the more worth while," wrote Mrs. Meyer.

She got down to work at once. The first step would probably be to assemble distinguished backers, and Annie began by paying a call upon a Mrs. Wendell, the mother of an eminent Harvard professor and a sympathizer in her own right. Mrs. Wendell listened patiently and, after Annie left, broke into tears at the thought of the whole preposterous idea and the inevitable heartbreak ahead. Luckily for the future of the project, Mrs. Wendell was able to restrain herself until Annie was safely gone and didn't even tell her of her reaction until years later.

After sounding out a few more people, none of whom seemed much more confident than Mrs. Wendell, Annie devised a systematic two-year five-part plan for herself. First she intended to learn everything possible about existing women's colleges in America. "I was so naïve and misinformed as to be greatly surprised when Mr. Arthur Gilman, Secretary of the Harvard Annex, wrote me that so far as he knew no college in the country was self-supporting." She would collect all the facts and figures on the subject and then "get in touch personally with every man and woman in the neighborhood of New York who might possibly support the movement to establish a college for women." Perhaps being antisuffrage (and anti-Maud) might help her win friends. It was an attitude that other educational pioneers had adopted before her, though none of them happened to have a suffragist in the immediate family. When she had her supporters, Annie intended to "strengthen public opinion in favor of the higher education of women . . . by means of interviews and letters in the papers, as well as editorials inspired or written by myself." Once the prejudice against college education for women had melted away, Annie realized that she would still have "to win over both individually and as a body, the Trustees of Columbia" to the idea of an affiliated women's institution. Only then could she proceed with Phase 5, which was simply "to build up a body of men and women who would command the confidence of the public and would undertake to direct the college." Annie Meyer allowed no more than six months for each item on her list.

In order to expedite these tasks, which covered a great deal of geographical as well as ideological ground, Annie bought herself a bicycle. She was one of the first women in New York to do so, and hers was not intended for recreation in Central Park. Perched on it, Annie Meyer looked considerably younger than twenty and much more fragile than her hundred pounds. No one would ever have taken her for the prospective founder of a college, and that turned into a distinct asset. Few people, glancing out their casements at the tiny figure standing on their stoops, refused to open their doors to a lost little girl.

Once inside the brownstones Annie Meyer politely declined milk and cookies and came to the point. By then it was too late, and the astonished householders found themselves listening to her carefully prepared proposals. These usually included a total disavowal of suffrage, and that may have made her acceptable in places where Maud was *non grata*. One by one, she got her signatures, and they were an impressive and well-balanced lot. Coeducation was still anathema to most people, and that word was never uttered. Mrs. Meyer was careful to explain that her college was to be *affiliated*, related to Columbia as a child to its parent. There was a great difference, she added, between an *affiliate* and an annex or an addition. An affiliate didn't impose. It would know its place. She hinted that it would be neither seen nor heard. As described by its charming prospective founder—Mr. Nathan's dutiful daughter, Dr. Meyer's glowing bride and the notorious Maud's estranged sister—the college hardly sounded threatening at all. Not everyone Annie visited promised money, but moral support was easier to get than she had dared hope.

Phases 1, 2 and 3 went smoothly and quickly. Phase 4 was the most difficult. By the time she reached it the Columbia trustees knew all about Annie and were on their guard. Her small size and her bicycle were no longer a certain guarantee of entrée. The board included several intractable foes of women's education, among them Dr. Morgan Dix, the head of Trinity Church and one of the most powerful men in New York. By 1888 Mrs. Meyer was a mature and sophisticated twenty-two, but even so, she kept postponing that particular interview. Dr. Dix had been described to her as "a Rip Van Winkle who had slept, not twenty, but two hundred years." His broadsides from the pulpit on the subject of universal higher education made King James' tirade on the *Monstrous Regiment of Women* sound absolutely tender. "Woman," said Dr. Dix, "becomes offensive and detestable when the clamor for rights appears to be taking the form of competition with men on a field which God has reserved for men only."

Annie dreaded the confrontation with Dr. Dix most of all. If she had been one of his parishioners, the prospect might have been less awful, but she wasn't even a Christian. "For the first and only time," Annie Meyer wrote, "I implored my husband to accompany me on my errand of persuasion." Dr. Meyer escorted his wife to the rectory door and left her. "My knees were wobbling," she said, "and I could scarcely bear to think what my voice would sound like if I could control it sufficiently to be heard at all."

Despite his bearish *ex cathedra* reputation, Dr. Dix at home was an affable charmer, and the name Nathan sounded familiar to him. Was Annie related to his dear old friend, Harmon Nathan? Of course. All Nathans were related. Harmon, fortunately, was one of the respectable ones, untouched by the recent scandals that had brushed so many other relatives. Dr. Dix explained gently to his quaking interviewer that he was not really opposed to women's education as such, but only "against wild women." "I disapprove," he said in his most mellow pulpit voice, "of unwomanly tactics, of creatures who are not men and certainly not women." No one could place little Annie Meyer in that hideous category, and Dr. Dix assured her that he would agree to a "separately financed college for women, manned by the instructors of Columbia and properly safeguarded by dignified and responsible sponsors." He even mentioned a hidden clause in the Columbia charter that would provide for such an eventuality. Annie's knees "again began to wobble; but this time not from anxiety, but from the suddenness and completeness with which all anxiety was removed." She had left the terrifying Dr. Dix for last, and he had been unbelievably easy. "I knew," she wrote, "that the battle was won."

There were, however, a few details still to be worked out before the first class would meet. Annie Meyer needed trustees, a charter, buildings, a faculty and funds, but none of it seemed so hard to get as Dr. Dix's blessing. By the end of 1889 the budget was set: $1,800 for rent, $1,000 for furnishings, $3,500 for professors' fees and $1,200 for the lady principal—$7,500 would do it, Mrs. Meyer thought, though she would have liked a bit more for a janitor, heating, lighting, postage and incidentals. After exploring various low-rent districts and rejecting them, Annie and Alfred Meyer personally signed a lease for a house at 343 Madison Avenue. It was rather far uptown, but Gramercy Park was priced out of reach, and there was nothing closer available. The yearly rent was $3,250, almost twice what the Meyers were paying for their own brownstone. "Had things gone wrong," Annie wrote, "we should have had to make inroads into our capital." On October 7, 1889, Barnard College opened, named for the retired Columbia president who had believed that there should be more to a peach than its bloom.

There were only seven regularly enrolled freshmen that year, though two dozen other students appeared for special science classes. Mrs. Meyer was glad to have them. They gave the house at 343 Madison Avenue a certain serious air that it might have otherwise lacked. Sister Maud, of course, was predictably furious. Annie had got her college ahead of schedule, but votes for women were still thirty years away. That, of course, did the tortured Nathan relationships no good at all. In the end, however, things seem to have balanced out. Maud Nathan is still firmly ensconced in recent editions of *Who Was Who,* trailing lists of organizations down the column, but Annie's names, married and maiden, have been dropped entirely. Most people have gradually come to believe that Barnard was founded by Frederick A. P., the Columbia president who conceded that knowledge didn't necessarily ruin a young woman's complexion.

VIII
The Founders: Physician

IN 1877, when Dr. Joseph Taylor informed a few intimates that he was leaving his fortune for the foundation of a new women's college, the news was received with a mixture of surprise and chagrin. It wasn't easy to imagine the calm and judicious Dr. Taylor joining a trio that included a deluded brewer, a capricious spinster and a fanatical ex-attorney who fancied himself the Lord's Anointed. Though Mary Lyon had been a woman of unimpeachable character, she had died in 1847, and ever since, the cause of female education had been attracting some questionable types. Dr. Taylor seemed to have very little in common with any of them. He was a lifelong bachelor, a devout and prominent member of the Society of Friends and a trustee of Haverford College. Moreover, he lived just across the river from a fine selection of deserving colleges, several of which admitted women in accordance with enlightened Quaker principles. His friends and colleagues on the Haverford board of governors were unable to see why Dr. Taylor should bypass these worthy and established concerns in favor of an empty hilltop in Bryn Mawr, Pennsylvania, and they were even more bewildered when he emerged from his peaceful retirement to embark on one of the most punishing commuter jaunts ever devised. In order to supervise the progress of his college, Dr. Taylor, at the age of sixty-nine, would ride his horse from his country estate to the town of Burlington. After stabling it in a friend's barn, he would take a train to Camden, where he had to change to a ferry for the trip across the Delaware. Once on the Pennsylvania side of the river, Dr. Taylor raced for the trolley car to the Main Line station, where he might, with luck and perfect timing, catch the train for Bryn Mawr. After a full day of fieldwork at the college site, he would leave for home; by train, trolley, boat, train and horse in reverse order. He kept up this brutal pace from the day construction began in August, 1879, until his death five months later of a heart attack.

The college was the second and last impulsive act of Joseph Taylor's ordered life. As a boy of seventeen he had studied medicine, and he finished his training before his twentieth birthday. He settled in Germantown and confidently nailed up a nameplate. Though he had purchased the practice of a retired doctor, his extreme youth and boyish appearance seems to have frightened even legacy patients away, and he spent a disproportionate amount of time gazing out of his windows and rearranging his equipment. The Philadelphia area was well supplied with more mature physicians, and Joseph Taylor, restless and bored after a few months of sitting in his empty office, joined a ship bound for Calcutta as its medical officer. That gave him an instant, if somewhat limited, practice. Since there was no competition on board, Dr. Taylor had a complete monopoly of the sick and injured. In lieu of a salary, the ship's physician was allowed a cargo space in the hold, and Taylor returned home with $1,000 worth of oriental novelties. He disposed of these at considerable profit and quickly decided that commerce could be more exciting and lucrative than medicine. An older brother had established a tannery in Cincinnati, and Joseph went west to join him.

Within weeks, he found himself in another new world—grinding tanbark and touring the border states to buy hides. His medical background was no particular asset in this work, but overqualified as he was, he made no complaints and, after some years, became a full partner in the tannery. By then, however, he had thoroughly tired of that career and developed severe eye trouble. The oculist he consulted suggested a long sea voyage, and Joseph Taylor happily set sail for England, where his vision improved at once. After eight months abroad he dutifully returned to the tannery but found the business and Cincinnati even more tedious than before. England had made him pensive, and Abraham Taylor, the senior partner, strongly urged his brother to resign and devote himself wholly to things of the mind and spirit.

He needed no persuasion and moved back to the East, buying a farm near the historic site of the Burlington Friends' meetinghouse. The town was an intellectual enclave, and Joseph Taylor took full advantage of everything it had to offer. He invested his savings cautiously, avoiding flashy speculations like the horseless carriage and the telephone, but doing well

83

nevertheless. Once he was away from the hide and hair of Cincinnati, his eyes caused him no further difficulty, and he read widely, concentrating particularly on educational theory.

Though Dr. Taylor worked diligently for Haverford College, its "male only" policy disturbed his sense of justice and did not seem to coincide with the Quaker notion that women's minds were as valuable an asset to the community as men's. In principle, Quaker women could be recognized as ministers, but there was little opportunity for the formal training that would fit them for leadership. The vaunted liberal attitudes tended to be more theoretical than actual, and Joseph Taylor was disturbed at what he considered the waste of female intellect. As a retired gentleman he had ample opportunity to observe the footling activities of the women in the neighborhood, and the pettiness of it all saddened him. The few colleges that enrolled women usually confined them to a narrow selection of so-called collegiate courses, which seemed designed not only to segregate them but to keep them at a lower level of achievement. America needed a corps of women prepared to teach the primary grades, but overqualified graduates could present serious problems. They might soon become impatient with toddlers and demand the right to teach grown men at places like Harvard and Yale. That was absolutely unthinkable until the middle of *this* century, but at the end of the last one there were a great many people who worried about the efficacy of female teachers with boys of eleven or twelve. By the 1880s a majority of Americans were willing to grant women enough education to cope with K through 6, but only the most visionary believed in so much as a jot more. There were still administrators who thought that coeducational public schools were a temporary economy for the newer and poorer states and that prosperity might yet make such penny-pinching unnecessary. "Mixed schools, like camp meetings," announced the president of the Polytechnic College of Pennsylvania at a mid-nineteenth-century convention of educators, "had grown out of the early necessities of the country and when circumstances permitted, would naturally disappear from amongst us." His report, approved and cheered by an overwhelming vote, concluded: "An all-wise Creator has ordained that the spheres of man and woman should be different, so their education must be pursued separately, otherwise neither can be brought to the highest point of perfection." Dr.

Taylor was alarmed at these sentiments and foresaw a day when women could lose even the tiny foothold already gained.

In addition to these windy discursions, which were required reading for all college trustees, Dr. Taylor had his Philadelphia *Evening Bulletin,* which supplied him with daily dispatches from the female educational front. By 1869, when a few women had gained grudging admission to the clinical lectures at Pennsylvania Hospital, the paper reported the event as a rout. "When the ladies entered the amphitheater they were greeted by yells, hisses, 'caterwauling,' mock applause, offensive remarks upon personal appearance, etc. . . . During the last hour, missiles of paper, tinfoil, tobacco-quids, etc. were thrown upon the ladies, while some of these men defiled the dresses of the ladies near them with tobacco juice."

To the courtly Dr. Joseph Taylor in his tranquil retreat, such treatment seemed worse than no educational opportunity at all, and he shuddered to think of a cultivated young woman's being forced to submit to it. Coeducation was clearly a mixed blessing in every possible sense, and Dr. Taylor envisioned at least two unfortunate effects arising from it. Either women would be so intimidated that they would never take advantage of the slowly widening opportunities offered to them, or their traumatic experiences would so harden and toughen them that all grace and gentility would be destroyed.

As a man who had always taken great (if nonspecific) pleasure in the conversation of the subdued and elegant women in his small social circle, Joseph Taylor could not bear to think of future generations being obliged to sacrifice propriety for learning. There had to be more places where women could improve their minds without the risk of physical indignity. Dr. Taylor brooded about jets of tobacco juice splattering the skirts of lady students and imagined someone like his sister Hannah being subjected to "offensive remarks" upon her appearance while struggling to take notes between rude remarks. It seemed to him that women—those mysterious and delicate creatures he had always admired at a safe distance—deserved much better.

One of his closest friends, a Dr. James Thomas of Baltimore, had a remarkably intellectual daughter, Martha Carey Thomas, whom Joseph Taylor had known virtually from infancy. Such girls presented a great moral problem to nineteenth-century Quaker families. Parents could either thwart their ambitions, which was the usual course, or take the enormous risk of sending them off to some remote New England town to be taught by others of less friendly persuasions. Young Miss Thomas, for instance, had seen Vassar and decided that it was little more than a finishing school. Wellesley was scheduled to open in 1875, but few Quakers would consider exposing a daughter to the notorious and evangelistic Mr. Durant, who might "save" her for a missionary career among the Hottentots. Mount Holyoke might have been a possibility for someone else, but Martha Carey Thomas would not consider any place that still called itself a seminary. In 1872, after she had finally persuaded her father to let her go away to school, the choices were still pitifully limited.

After a series of disappointing tours of various establishments, the Thomases settled upon the Howland Institute, a new girls' academy near Ithaca, New York. It was too distant from their home, but the catalogue was impressive, and the work seemed advanced. Both Martha Carey Thomas and a close friend and cousin, Bessie King, matriculated there, and their families hoped that they would look after each other and keep the faith. The decision and the anguish that preceded it were common knowledge among the Quaker settlements, and Dr. Joseph Taylor was one of the most interested observers of the whole affair. Parents of brilliant and precocious daughters sought advice and help wherever they could find it.

Martha Carey Thomas herself might have had an ulterior motive in insisting on that particular school in Ithaca. Cornell University had been opened in 1868 as a place where "any person can find instruction in any subject." "Any person," Martha Carey Thomas immediately realized, meant women, and she was even more pleased to learn that the founder, Ezra Cornell, was a Quaker. Howland Institute was the best vantage point imaginable from which to observe Cornell, and Martha Carey Thomas hardly let the new university across the lake out of her sight. By 1874, the year she finished Howland, she was delighted to discover a women's residence hall rising on the Cornell campus. She had almost willed it into existence.

Upon her return to Baltimore after graduation Martha Carey began her next campaign at once. Her father, Joseph Taylor's old friend and confidant, needed further counsel and support. His child was being stubborn and unreasonable. She had apparently regarded Howland as a mere stepping-stone to Cornell and was determined to continue her studies there. What was worse, Mrs. Thomas sided with her daughter. Dr. Taylor mediated. Martha Carey Thomas eventually won, and her father sadly and reluctantly allowed her to take the entrance examinations for Cornell. He withheld his consent until three weeks before they were scheduled, perhaps in the forlorn hope that Martha might not have enough time to prepare for them.

It was painfully clear to Dr. Taylor, who had seen this family crisis from its very beginning, that a proper Quaker college for young women would solve a great many similar problems. Though it was certainly true that Martha Carey Thomas was an exceptional girl, she was by no means unique. Joseph Taylor thought how many more there must be just like her, gifted and energetic young women whose talents would never be fully developed. He followed Martha Carey Thomas' academic career with avuncular interest and was pleased to hear, in 1877, that she had received her Cornell degree. The rumor that she wished to drop her first name and wanted to be known as plain Carey Thomas was somewhat distressing, however, indicating to the already worried Quakers that coeducation was defeminizing as well as demeaning. (At home and to her friends, she had always been known as Minnie, which sounded much too casual and undignified for a young woman of her remarkable attainments.) When it was discovered that Carey Thomas, not yet satisfied, was applying to Johns Hopkins for postgraduate study, all their worst fears were realized. Her father, Dr. Thomas, was a trustee of the new Baltimore university, and he was profoundly embarrassed by the entire affair. Miss Thomas and her academic adventures were the talk of Quaker communities in Baltimore, Philadelphia and southern New Jersey, and she became a test case, the focus of considerable troubled attention.

Carey Thomas was admitted to Johns Hopkins "on certain conditions," which were apparently not made precisely clear to her. Jubilant, she simply assumed that the phrase referred to qualifying examinations and turned up in September eager to get them over and begin work on her second degree. She was quickly disabused of this notion. The "certain conditions" were "without class, tutorial or seminar attendance." (Johns Hopkins seems to have been the first university to try this subterfuge, which was later successfully used to keep women away from Columbia.) The plan was designed to dissuade the most indomitable female, and in most cases it did. Carey Thomas was by no means domitable, but on at least three separate occasions that year she described her existence on the fringes of Johns Hopkins as "a living death." The prospect of studying there for two years as an unperson was enough to shatter even the strong-willed Miss Thomas. She quarreled bitterly with her mother, wrote, "I do believe I shall shoot myself," in her diary, lost most of her faith in God, ended her only tentative romance and abandoned herself to bouts of uncontrollable weeping. The prodigy had become an inadvertent, classic and conspicuous example of the perils of higher education for women under the prevailing conditions.

In her father's opinion, Carey was wholly irrational. She continued to demand, amid floods of tears, that she be allowed to finish her degree in Germany. There, she had heard, women were sometimes allowed in the classrooms. Despite her misery at Hopkins, she was determined to win a doctorate. "There is nothing for it," her mother said, "thee must cry thyself to Germany." Now that the weeping had a definite goal, Carey intensified her efforts, and Dr. Thomas, who had been impervious to argument, finally showed signs of dissolving, particularly when Mrs. Thomas added her sobs to those of her daughter. At the first tentative indications of success with Dr. Thomas, Carey advised her closest friend, Mamie Gwinn, to go to work on *her* father. This young woman, desperate to accompany Carey to Germany and almost as determined to become a PhD, added a few touches of her own. Mamie produced fainting fits as well as tears, and after a few terrible weeks both exhausted young women were finally told they could study together in Germany, and their passage was arranged. Peace returned to the Friends' meeting, but at a great price. By then, the autumn of 1879, there was fairly general agreement among the Quaker settlements that a women's college in the vicinity would fill a genuine and urgent need. Had it only existed five years earlier, it would have been the perfect place for Carey Thomas.

IX
Under Way in South Hadley

THE seventh edition of Cass and Birnbaum's *Comparative Guide to American Colleges* has 748 pages of listings in fine print, and the authors do not claim to have unearthed or included every last institution of higher learning in the country. A modest allowance for omission and caprice, however, still leaves approximately 1,200 places in the United States accredited to grant degrees. Although a tiny minority is at least technically limited to men only, a determined woman can often inveigle her way into those, sustained by the 1972 Federal College Aid Act. The Equal Rights Amendment will be the ultimate weapon, but it isn't yet in force. Even the service academies have yielded to siege, and the midshipperson will be a reality by 1976. The rest of the holdouts—religious schools or private undergraduate colleges founded for a single sex—have long since admitted members of the other sex to various courses and to master's and doctoral programs. There's actually such an embarrassment of opportunity that militant feminists tend to duck the whole subject of education. In the wrong hands it can be a dangerously counterrevolutionary weapon.

In November, 1837, an intellectually ambitious girl had a choice of Mount Holyoke or nothing. (Oberlin excepted.) Although there had been a few other and almost simultaneous attempts to establish advanced ladies' academies, most were to prove pathetically transient, often vanishing before they could graduate a single class. The eighty young women who entered Mount Holyoke the first November had virtually no basis of comparison, no alternative, and no chance of transferring elsewhere until 1865, when Vassar would be ready to receive them. By that time any disillusioned entrant would be at least forty-five years old and probably resigned to whatever her fate had been.

To be the only place of a kind may not guarantee student

morale, but it probably helps. Its uniqueness was an enormous asset for Mount Holyoke for at least twenty-five years, almost impossible to overestimate. The seminary survived and flourished, assisted by its wise and visionary principal, its small but vital endowment and the incontrovertible, unromantic fact that it was a monopoly—benevolent, altruistic, philanthropic, but a monopoly. That made all the difference, because the vista that confronted the first arrivals was rather bleak and intimidating. After long and exhausting journeys by various combinations of stagecoach, ferry and, rarely, railroad, the girls found themselves at a tall red-brick building which stood isolated upon an expanse of sand. Though the façade was liberally supplied with doors, the steps leading up to them had not yet been set in place, and the structure seemed totally inaccessible, like a ship grounded upon a reef. There were no blinds or curtains at the windows, the stoves to heat the rooms were still scattered about the public parlors, supplies of furniture had been delayed by bad weather, and much of the bedding promised to Miss Lyon by various ladies' aid societies hadn't materialized. Although South Hadley lies in the midst of a naturally wooded landscape, overzealous builders had cleared the originally attractive site of every shrub and tree. The barely finished structure was at that awkward stage when it is almost impossible to tell the brand-new from the utterly abandoned. Anyone with a fanciful notion of a women's college might have been sadly disappointed, but since there were no existing models, there seems to have been few serious cases of disillusionment.

Once they had been deposited in view of the future doorstep, however, the young ladies could hardly turn back. South Hadley, in 1837, seems to have been a three-day trip from practically everywhere, and even Boston students had to leave home at four in the morning in order to get to the seminary by evening. Those who first glimpsed the campus at night were the luckiest. By moonlight the rawness and desolation were slightly less apparent, and the building, glowing with oil lamps, could have seemed imposing and almost cosy. In the gray chill of a November afternoon it was merely desolate on its barren acres, and the earliest arrivals must have had agonizing struggles with their misgivings. They were led across the sand to the only usable door, a basement entry at the back. Once inside, they found themselves in the dim dining hall, half of which had been turned over to a group of haggard seamstresses. These women were busily sewing quilts, a familiar sight to a nineteenth-century girl, but hardly reassuring to the cold, tired and hungry traveler. A few improvised tables stood depleted in the gloom, spread with refreshments which had been Spartan from the start. Much of the kitchen equipment, like the furniture, stoves and bedding, had gone astray, and the whole seminary community subsisted on bread, butter, cold water and mashed potatoes for several days after the official opening. Even this limited menu strained the available resources, and Mary Lyon was obliged to begin her breakfast preparations at eleven at night in order to have anything ready for the girls by the next morning.

The retrospective accounts of the beginning of Mount Holyoke, published on subsequent anniversaries, make much of the high spiritual tone of the event, but the actual facts seem somewhat more rugged than the various authorized versions would have them. The young women of the 1830s were assiduous diarists and candid letter writers, and several of their eyewitness reports have been preserved. There was apparently very little time for either prayers or sermons during those first weeks. A Vermont student, one of a family of four daughters who enrolled with the original group, informed her father that she first met Deacon Stafford on his hands and knees in the main hall. He had shed his canonical jacket and collar and was cheerfully, though inexpertly, nailing straw matting to the floor. His eminent clerical colleague and co-trustee, Deacon Porter, could usually be found tidying up the rubble-strewn grounds. The sand around the building had been Deacon Porter's practical inspiration. It helped cover the mud and debris left by the builders and made the hike to the back cellar door somewhat more decorous. Even so, the young ladies had to lift their skirts to unprecedented heights, but without the sand, matters would have been much worse.

Both worthy deacons were among the original trustees of Mount Holyoke, and both were eventually to have residence halls named for them. Deacon Andrew Porter, however, acquired an additional and unique immortality. His name is perpetuated in a traditional college dessert known to generations of Mount Holyoke alumnae as Deacon Porter's Hat, which it resembles in form (cylindrical), color (off-black), durability (excellent), and consistence (feltlike). Deacon Porter's Hat was an inevitable and recurring item on the college menu for the first century and a quarter. Now it is served only on commemorative occasions. Hard sauce enhances it, but not noticeably.

The administration and factulty all seem to have made a special effort to stress the adventurous aspects of the situation, appealing to the girls' natural pride and latent courage. It was a psychologically sound approach, and really the only one possible. "We were weary," the Vermont correspondent continued, "but none of the repining, homesick girls of modern boarding schools were there, for we were coping with realities, not fancies, and under the inspiration of a magnetic leader." "Young Ladies," Mary Lyon said, "you will recall these little experiences in the real hardships of the Far West." There is no record of the response of students who had no intention of ministering to the Navaho or Sioux but the idealists were exhilarated. Their particular adventure had begun ahead of schedule, and Springfield, Massachusetts, seemed to mark the start of the frontier.

The "little experiences" might not seem particularly trying to a hearty twentieth-century backpacker, but they were thrilling enough in the protected context of the time. Some students were dispersed to various South Hadley houses for the first nights, and others slept on mattresses that had been spread on the seminary floor. Because the woodshed still had not been roofed over, the young ladies were obliged to carry their firewood up from the basement. Water for washing and drinking was also hauled to the separate floors. Life became somewhat more genteel as soon as the woodbins were finished and the cisterns that served each story of the building had been filled, but the rigors of the early weeks far exceeded the intellectual pioneering that most girls had envisioned.

The whole project, in fact, was more fun than anyone had dared hope. Undergraduates from Amherst came over and helped move furniture around, and the social restraints imposed later hadn't yet been devised. Of course, once the desks and beds were in place and everyone was assured of three meals a day and a permanent place to sleep, the emphasis quickly shifted, and the girls were solemnly and frequently re-

Annie Nathan Meyer, the
irresistible founder.

The original Barnard
brownstone at 343 Madison
Avenue; Mrs. Kelly lived
downstairs and the front rooms
were rented out.

Barnard

New York had certain advantages.
Barnard students, 1910.

Hoops·are Neo-Platonic, circa 1925.

Inside the Canteen Over Here, World War I.

Bryn Mawr

Bryn Mawr Archives

"One aim and concentrated purpose."
M. Carey Thomas of Bryn Mawr.

Pembroke Hall, 1972,
Pennsylvania Gothic.

Bryn Mawr Archives

"Put thy sweet hand in mine and trust in me."
Faculty, Woodrow Wilson and the first class at Bryn
Mawr—1886.

Bryn Mawr Eclectic.
A student's room in Denbiga Hall, 1899.

Mt. Holyoke

Mary Lyon, 1797–1849.

The verandas were purely ornamental.
The original Seminary Building.

A very upper-class phenomenon, prom at
Mount Holyoke, 1938.

Flaming, gilded and otherwise sadly altered youth, about 1930.

Victory gardeners, World War II.

Zoology in the Jazz Age, 1925.

Active sports, 1866: drills with Indian clubs.

First-class citizen in the Mount Holyoke machine shop.

minded that they were studying in an institution "built by the Hand of the Lord" and dedicated to His service. The chaos of the opening weeks, however, had already enabled many of the students to meet young men from the surrounding area. That was an unexpected bonus for the pioneers and one that seems to have mitigated many of the discomforts. Later classes missed both the hardships and the compensations. "I remember when John Dwight was setting up furniture one evening he saw Nancy Everett for the first, but not the last time," the same conscientious diarist wrote. "How happy we were in making the best of our inconveniences, and how we appreciated every article of furniture as it came."

In anticipation of the inevitable difficulties, Mary Lyon had insisted on a minimal maturity for entering students. Unlike most contemporary boarding schools, which eagerly accepted applicants as young as twelve, she would consider no one under sixteen. Most members of the first classes were actually considerably older, many of them in their early twenties. Several had already been teaching in village schools, semiqualified as they were, and most of the others either shared that same ambition or assured Miss Lyon that they did. Not many of the entrants could have embarked on so outlandish a project either for lack of anything else to do or from idle curiosity alone. In later years Mount Holyoke would make great use of the idea that educating a girl meant educating a whole family, but that aphorism hadn't yet won much acceptance. Teaching was the only justification for continued study. There was, after all, room for only eighty, and twice that number had applied. From the very beginning Miss Lyon was able to select the best risks: those who were conscious that they were participating in a great experiment and were convinced that they had to prove worthy of it. It was an unsophisticated admissions system, but it worked. The religious atmosphere, the comparative isolation and the enforced domestic jobs functioned as deterrents to more frivolous types, and there was less attrition than anyone expected.

The household chores, however, received considerable publicity and were to be one of the most controversial aspects of the whole venture. There was a widespread belief—and perhaps some malicious hope—that students would object to the work or that it would interfere with their academic performance, but the most general view was that the girls would simply neglect the tasks and live in squalor. The journals of the time dwelled at tedious length on these depressing possibilities, predicting an early end to this most peculiar corollary of Miss Lyon's self-styled "Peculiar Institution." Even the supporters of the plan were sure that the work program would be discarded as soon as the seminary could afford to hire servants. The founder herself freely admitted that the domestic department was "too complicated and requires too much care to be continued were it not for its great advantages. If dollars and cents alone were concerned we would drop it at once," she said, "but this feature also serves as a sieve, holding back the indolent, the fastidious and the feeble—of whom we never could make much—and giving us the finest of the wheat—the energetic, the benevolent, and those whose early training has been favorable to usefulness."

And she got them. The low fees put higher education well within the reach of the many, and that was certainly one reason why the plan aroused so much hostile curiosity. If it succeeded, almost every American girl might eventually expect to attend college, and that was too cataclysmic a thought to bear contemplation. The spheres of men and women, so neatly separated, so regular in their immutable courses, would collide and smash. Papas, brothers and husbands would be left to fend for themselves while matrons, sisters and brides parsed Latin sentences and juggled algebraic equations. Women would soon come to believe that their days of peeling potatoes and serving meals were over as soon as they received their certificates from Mount Holyoke Female Seminary and that once these documents were safely in hand, they could proceed to ever more glorious pursuits. (Most men took a completely contrary view, believing that housework should follow education.) The opponents of the seminary seized the brooms and fought back, ridiculing and subverting the domestic plan whenever and however they could.

The household chores, which Mary Lyon insisted were merely incidental to her larger design, quickly became the single most conspicuous and publicized factor about her school; over-emphasized, derided and misunderstood. Her patient descriptions only seemed to reinforce the misconception of the Holyoke student as unpaid skivvy. A disproportionate amount of her time was spent in explaining that it meant a mere hour a day for each girl, that it was a welcome and wholesome diversion from study and a chance for relaxed sociability. Most of the girls agreed, writing home to their families and friends how pleasant it was to bake bread, shell peas and polish silver for the greater good. Their mild Victorian tempers became aroused only at the imputation that Holyoke was *teaching* them the household arts, when in fact the jobs were so small a part of the total experience. Early letters are full of assurances that the community was nine-tenths scholarly and only one-tenth domestic. But the doubts smoldered on for an entire century. (When Mount Holyoke students were required to resume sweeping and dusting during World War II, after a hiatus of fifty years or so, acquaintances at other colleges where austerity programs had been imposed for the first time simply assumed that Holyoke had been doing it all along. One alumna, a member of the class of 1943, who volunteered to pick asparagus in a victory garden, was astonished to discover that it was widely believed that agriculture had always been a required part of the curriculum and not even an elective.) The aura has been almost impossible to shake. "Now that manual labor is so chic," said a member of the present administration, "we actually get applicants who ask us if we're still a working commune. They're crushed when I tell them that the last butter churn vanished before the Civil War."

With all of the nineteenth-century maundering about Woman's Sphere, it might seem as if the idea of required domestic duties would be soothing, but that wasn't the case. The opponents of higher education for women were not at all appeased by the vision of the Mount Holyoke girl with a broom in one hand and Euclid in the other. The resistance depended so heavily on the notion that advanced education made a bluestocking and spoiled a bride that any evidence to the contrary had to be suppressed.

According to this rather tortured reasoning, Mount Holyoke represented a greater threat to the established order than a more traditional academy would have done. The wan female scholar, her health destroyed by study and her household skills unlearned or forgotten, was a favorite and useful stereotype.

The merry work circles of South Hadley, keeping tuition down as they kept intellectual standards up, deprived the conservatives of their most potent argument. Critics came to the seminary and all but choked on the decent meals they were served in demure and orderly surroundings. Some of the skeptics gracefully reversed themselves and became ardent advocates of the system, but intransigents remained a problem for years. Observers who grudgingly acknowledged that the rooms were neat and the food was palatable frequently disparaged the academic standards of the new institution.

Throughout its first three decades Mount Holyoke remained on the defensive, denying that it was a domestic science school and battling for the academic respect it deserved. Miss Lyon, after much soul-searching, waited with forbearance for the recognition due her. The students were somewhat less patient. One has only to glance at a copy of Smellie's *Intellectual Philosophy* to understand why the most modest girl would have wanted credit for mastering it. Eventually, a few concessions were quietly made, and a minimal maintenance staff was hired. Housemaid's knee then very gradually ceased to be an effective argument against sending a daughter to Holyoke.

In addition to the detractors who persisted in belittling the curriculum and standards, Mary Lyon and her scholars had to contend with a smaller but equally contentious minority who saw the insidious taint of Popery in the plan. There was a particularly bitter irony in these charges, because the finishing schools actually run by the Catholic Church seemed immune from such criticism. Nineteenth-century Americans knew—or thought they knew—what to expect from Rome and took suitable precautions, but Mary Lyon's special seminary had no real precedent. There was general anxiety that it might be a convent *in disguise*—the most dangerous sort of all. The low fees, the simple accommodations, the no-nonsense curriculum and those unladylike communal jobs aroused more doubts than they allayed. There were a few rebellious spirits even among the mature and carefully chosen scholars and enough references to "St. Mary's," "Mother Superior," "The Convent of St. Lyon" and "Cell 65" to alarm an assortment of fiancés and parents. Catholic convents were designed to absorb their alumnae, when necessary, but Protestant nunneries (existing only in the minds of the fearful) made no such provision. The very idea, however, was enough to cause chills in many New England households, where maiden aunts and widowed relatives were a constant responsibility and perpetual burden. Removing one's marriageable daughters so far from view could turn out to be false economy, with dire long-range consequences. The fashionable girls' schools in Boston, New York or Philadelphia did occasionally produce a handsome return on Papa's investment, whereas a sensible Mount Holyoke education might only fit a girl to instruct naked heathens in the alphabet and shorter catechism. A post as schoolmarm in the Northwest Territory at the going rate of $5 a month was considered no great plum either. A wise parent carefully weighed the risks before sending his girl up to South Hadley, where the social opportunities, if any, would be narrowed to the impecunious young ministers in attendance at Amherst. Miss Lyon, it was rumored, was such a stickler for propriety that she forbade the girls to sit on the verandas, where they might give passersby the wrong impression of the institution. All "gentlemen callers" had to be blood relatives of Mount Holyoke students and able to document kinship on the spot. Amherst "cousins" without the proper credentials on their persons were unceremoniously dispatched, and ladies found guilty of misrepresentation were reprimanded and even expelled. The 1850s were particularly wild years, with dismissals "for violations of the rules of propriety and good order, in connection with receiving calls from gentlemen" coming by trios and quartets. Before that, the sheer novelty of the institution had apparently guaranteed discretion, if not always perfect celibacy.

The overt religious atmosphere of the seminary continued to produce other strange problems. The young women were of an impressionable age and inclined to be dazzled by returned missionaries who spoke to them of opportunities for service among the unenlightened. Mary Lyon welcomed many of the clergymen to the school to lecture and inspire the girls, but there was soon a disturbing and somewhat unexpected tendency toward emulation. The seminary audience could get literally carried away by religious fervor at these revival meetings. Visiting missionaries made the Sandwich Islands, Persia, India and the Philippines sound so much more exciting and rewarding than

97

Illinois, Ohio or even California that rather large numbers declared their eagerness to serve in these very remote outposts. Word of the phenomenon spread, and it was widely assumed that Miss Lyon was deliberately training the fairest flowers of New England for export only. She herself felt that "the project of young single ladies going on a foreign mission was apt to appear ludicrous," but the notion persisted, bolstered by the dramatic and much publicized departure of a few.

Graduates who actually went forth from Mount Holyoke as foreign missionaries were always a minority, but they naturally attracted a great deal more notice than the alumnae who married New Haven attorneys or Boston manufacturers. Of those who did leave for dangerously exotic shores, most departed as the brides of clergymen, but the celebrated cases were the exceptions who freely chose to go as maiden ladies. They, of course, were the examples that thrilled their fellow students and caused all the alarmed editorials in the Springfield *Union* and the Boston *Advocate*.

There was great popular interest in foreign missions during the 1830s and '40s, and every village church had its adopted heathens. The congregations were glad to support the benighted with gifts of Bibles, diapers, cash and an occasional assistant pastor, but that was usually considered sufficient. Daughters were encouraged to join the sewing circles and stitch up Mother Hubbards for the newly converted Polynesians, keeping their enthusiasm for foreign service within reasonable bounds. Though the letters that brought news of spiritual progress among the savages were stimulating, most women listened to these missives in church and returned content to their safe firesides, vowing to remodel their worn petticoats and hold another strawberry festival. The missionaries themselves were in constant peril from mysterious tropical diseases, tribal wars, intemperate climates and the grueling labor itself. Tours of duty lasted for years, and the mortality rate was appallingly high. "Most ladies," repeated Mary Lyon in 1843, "can do more for the missionary cause at home than abroad. Wives, mothers and daughters have much to do to elevate the standard of liberality in those they love. You may even lead a brother to give himself to the missionary work."

But the erroneous impression that Holyoke functioned as a

sort of missionary talent agency was almost impossible to dis-
lodge, and Miss Lyon was swamped with requests for volunteers. She dutifully told her students and faculty about the
openings, but with some understandable reluctance. Since the
seminary was the only training ground for its own staff, the loss
of even one gifted teacher could mean a crisis. The response to
the missionary appeals continued to astonish Mary Lyon, and
she was particularly affected when a Reverend Mr. Perkins
proved so persuasive that he spirited away her own valued personal assistant, Fidelia Fiske. Perkins was clearly a spellbinder
in the great tradition. Though he came to South Hadley hoping
to interest two graduates in going to Urumiah, Persia, to work
in a new girls' school, *forty* members of the college community
immediately responded to his appeal. Naturally, he selected the
most diligent and experienced of the applicants, and
Urumiah's gain was South Hadley's loss.

Mary Lyon's consolation speech to Miss Fiske's mother con-
veys something of her mixed feelings about the whole missionary enterprise and the Reverend Mr. Perkins' all too remarkable success among her protégés. "I also give up a daughter,"
she said. "I have thought she might comfort you in your declin-
ing years and at the same time labor for our dear seminary with
me. . . . If we are to give her up, we shall, in so doing, understand as never before the gift of the Son of God." When Miss
Lyon returned to Mount Holyoke, a student reported that "her
face shone like an angel's, it seemed to me, she was so joyful in
the sacrifice." Another pupil, however, described the actual departure of Miss Fiske in less rapturous terms. "Miss Fiske wept
not herself, but smiled and said, 'When all life's work is done we
shall meet again.' Tears and sobs were our only reply." Miss
Lyon appears to have been the most deeply touched of all. "It is
easiest, safest and sweetest to trust [God]," she said, and then
embarked upon several weeks of solitary and "uninterrupted
thought and prayer for her beloved charge."

The farewells became more difficult with the passing years,
and a definite note of perturbation becomes obvious. By 1845
several more newly trained teachers had embarked on these
tours, and increasing numbers of students were clamoring to
join them, Mary Lyon's niece among them. "I have nothing to
say," wrote Mary Lyon that year, "but to ask that the will of the

Lord be done, whether we are with or without means to carry out our plans." The hymn judged most appropriate for these emotional occasions was "God Moves in a Mysterious Way."

Though Mary Lyon confided to one of her closest friends that "I have passed through many scenes of tender interest . . . manifestly increasing my grey hairs," she never actively discouraged those young women who seemed determined to go abroad. Despite her private thoughts and fears about the matter, she is remembered as their greatest inspiration. In time, Mount Holyoke alumnae seem to have found other outlets for their energies more in keeping with their founder's original intention. By 1860 or so the American West offered just as many challenges for teachers, and considerably better chances for marriage. After the Civil War, Holyoke graduates could be found in all the new territories, living out the plots of countless future horse operas, the original models for the mythic young schoolteacher who tamed the frontier. After the war a number of Holyoke alumnae became involved in the education of newly freed slaves. Miss Sarah Dickey, '64, established the Mount Harmon School for Colored Girls in Mississippi, and her project remained a Mount Holyoke adoptee for thirty years. Students supported it with money, books and superfluous clothing. That was, of course, a less touchy era.

Even after the missionary and housework issues faded, at least one compelling argument against the seminary remained. A student could assure her family that she didn't object to the domestic chores or swear that she wouldn't abandon her home for Urumiah or even Idaho, but there was no way that she could convince a worried parent that she wouldn't fall ill. Epidemics of diphtheria, typhoid, scarlet fever, typhus and other contagious diseases were a very real threat in that era, and any enclosed community was particularly vulnerable. In the summer of 1840, just as Mount Holyoke was gaining some tentative approval, nine students died of an unidentified fever. Dozens of girls who had planned to enter in the fall were frightened away, and although the seminary managed to fill the empty places from its waiting list, an old, reliable and still valid objection was revived.

The health factor was never dormant for long during those first decades. Typhoid raged in Massachusetts in 1853 and again in 1854. No matter what precautions were taken, the seminary had to face the possibility of a death or two even in a good year and cope with the general panic that inevitably followed. Effective vaccines are relatively recent, and the nineteenth-century public regarded boarding schools with the same trepidation that later generations would feel toward swimming pools and movie houses. The summertime polio scares of the twentieth century can only begin to suggest the acute anxiety in which nineteenth-century parents lived all year round. Virtually nothing was known about infections at that time except the single fact that crowding increased the dangers. A single fatality could—and did—set the cause of higher education back for years. A minority of boys might be obliged to risk their lives for a degree, but middle-class girls had no effective arguments by which to justify the dangers. One does not court death to satisfy a whim. These fears were an enormous obstacle to the growth of women's colleges and devilishly hard to refute. As a result, hygiene became an understandable obsession with the pioneers in women's education, shaping every aspect of seminary life— rules and regulations, curricula and the amount and kind of religious observance.

The morbid stress on salvation, the constant sermons and the passionate prayer meetings were natural in the context of the time. Religion was really the only way the colleges could come to terms with the fact that 10 percent of the students might die in any given year. Were it not for antibiotics and immunization, every college and university in America would probably still have required worship. An orthodox belief in an afterlife made a dreadful kind of sense in 1837, and for some years following. It only dwindled when ordinary life expectancy reached seventy or so. Until then it wasn't hard to fill a college chapel fifteen times a week.

If Mount Holyoke seemed to work overtime at saving souls, the seminary also made a strenuous effort to save bodies. By 1854 there was a full-time physician on the faculty, and a woman at that. Her name was Dr. Sophronia Fletcher, and her duties included lecturing in physiology as well as practicing medicine. A female doctor was a noble idea, but the first one didn't last very long. A letter from a Miss Usher describing her methods survives and may explain why. "One of the girls had a slight sickness, and she gave her a mustard plaster, one sitzbath, two packs, two electric shocks, and what else I don't know. The girls don't give way as much as before to a slight illness, for if there was a toe-ache, Dr. Fletcher stands ready to be marshalled forward." Rather abruptly, Dr. Fletcher was replaced by a male with a less eclectic approach to his profession. He may have inspired more confidence, but he also had more dreadful problems.

Three girls died of scarlet fever during Dr. Kithredge's first year, and there was another frightful round of typhoid. The seminary was fumigated, painted and whitewashed, and Dr. Kithredge immediately established a health committee which was to explore and recommend new avenues to physical fitness. During his tenure there were several dramatic advances. He advocated, among other things, "daily contact of the body with sunbeams, direct as well as reflected, pure air in the study room and especially in the sleeping room, and a good wholesome diet." He also instituted a medical checkup of prospective students in order to discourage the overly frail from entering. After a decent and tactful interval had passed, he urged the appointment of another female physician to instruct the girls in delicate matters of female physiology. This woman, Dr. Mary Homer, apparently turned out splendidly. She made gymnastic exercises mandatory and saw to it that seminary food included vegetables, fruit and especially graham flour, then assumed to be a panacea for almost everything. Dr. Homer lectured her classes with the avant-garde aid of a female "manikin," a coup that no man could have accomplished.

The campaign for an all-season gymnasium was intensified during the Homeric era and ultimately succeeded. By the late 1850s attending Mount Holyoke had become no riskier than staying home. The seminary then proudly published its vital statistics, announcing that the mortality rate among its students had actually fallen below the national average. Those in charge of raising further funds for the gym lost no time in making their needs known. A graduating senior made one of the most dramatic pleas of all. "There were some critics," she said, "who believed young ladies were murdered here every year. Let them no longer lift their holy hands in righteous indignation, but put them forth to prevent even the beginning of such a calamity." The governor of Massachusetts opened the subscription on the spot, and within three hours $1,500 had been pledged. (Mary Lyon, who had died in 1849, would have been deeply gratified. She had always advocated physical exercise, once stating that neglecting it was a "sin against the seventh commandment." Since that is the one which proscribes adultery, it is assumed that she made one of her only Scriptural errors on that occasion.)

That, however, was in 1861, and there were suddenly more urgent concerns than the health and safety of girls. The dangers of a seminary—no matter how great—suddenly seemed negligible in comparison to the dangers of a Civil War battlefield. Moreover, there was a desperate need for nurses, a kind of service for which the Mount Holyoke alumnae were remarkably well prepared. The "peculiar" aspects of the seminary—so controversial in 1837, seemed providential by 1861. Women teachers had been regarded as an economy, but overnight they became an absolute necessity since there were no young men at all to staff the schools. Girls who could double as janitors were greatly in demand. The opponents of higher education for women soon found themselves bereft of all their major arguments and obliged to suspend even the minor ones for the duration. The advocates, on the other hand, who had the wisdom to stay well out of the burgeoning movements for political and economic equality, found that their discretion was another point in their favor. (Eventually the exigencies of war were to thaw some of the most obdurate opposition to suffrage, but that took longer.) The immediate side effect of the American Civil War was that it improved the educational status of women by depriving them of husbands, fiancés, fathers and brothers. The barely thinkable notion that a woman might have to make her own way in the world was forcibly thrust on America. When feminist history is finally rewritten, the real heroes of the movement may well turn out to be the Civil War dead. Without that upheaval and those appalling casualties there would have been few openings in the economy and no real impetus toward either education or the political autonomy that came after. By 1945 we might have had a column or two in Cass and Birnbaum, but not much more.

X
Emphasizing Pterodactyls

VASSAR Female College opened in September, 1865, not quite six months after Lee had surrendered to Grant at Appomattox. The Main (and only) Hall was filled to capacity with 353 prospective students, a rousing response to an enterprise that the founder first called "humble," then "benevolent," "noble," "great" and finally "magnificent," but one that the rest of the country continued to regard simply as dubious. The first Vassar class included the young widow of a Union assistant adjutant general, and her presence lent a certain validity to the whole idea. She was a particularly poignant object lesson, someone for whom a college background might be a solution, if not quite a consolation.

By 1865 the demand for teachers everywhere so far exceeded the supply that objections to training women for the job were almost entirely stilled. In lieu of money, the work offered security, respectability and a chance to serve humanity. It wasn't hard to persuade impressionable girls that teaching was part of God's grand design for them. Moreover, the Emancipation Proclamation had abruptly thrown a million freedmen upon the economy, and the prospect of the illiterate ex-slaves left to fend for themselves was utterly appalling. The job of helping them was one that demanded selflessness, patience, commitment and altruism, exactly the traits that the new women's colleges promised to inculcate. A girl educated at Mount Holyoke or Vassar would be far better suited to such work than the impoverished and resentful ladies of the Confederacy, whose accomplishments were not generally of a very practical nature. By the mid 1870s more than a dozen alumnae of one set of "Peculiar Institutions" were deeply involved with former slaves—refugees from the other and most "Peculiar Institution" of all. Though most of the women who went South to teach ex-slaves did so under the auspices of vari-

104

ous church and mission societies, Sara Dickey, Mount Holyoke '69, devoted her entire life to the school she founded in Mississippi. The Northern seminaries thrived in this atmosphere, and Mr. Vassar's "magnificent enterprise" got excellent reviews in thoughtful journals like *The Outlook, Harper's* and especially *Godey's Ladies' Book*. The critics were amazingly kind, not only praising the new ventures, but often glossing over their shortcomings in the gentlest possible way. Only one writer mentioned the vainglorious sign MATTHEW VASSAR, PROP. that hung at the main gate. If some of the compliments seem somewhat backhanded, it may be because literary modes have changed considerably in the last century. "How much ignorance is required in a woman to induce and sustain proper female delicacy is a question that has never been answered," heavily commented the New York *Post* in a typically favorable editorial.

Practical Americans reasoned that the cost of sending a young woman to Mount Holyoke at $60 a year or even to Vassar at $350 could be regarded as an investment in the future of the country. One gentleman from Brooklyn actually enrolled all seven of his daughters at Vassar as soon as it opened its doors. A classmate of theirs wrote home to *her* father that the all-inclusive bill for that family was $2,500 to $3,000 a year. If her intention was to justify her own relatively small expenses, she must have succeeded. Out of any seven nineteenth-century daughters, the odds were that at least two would remain spinsters, and the "Brooklyn gentleman" may have thought he was buying a kind of group insurance.

The first collection of Vassar students was so widely assorted that the ambitious college plans had to be drastically revised at once. The ages of the entering class ranged from fourteen to twenty-four (the Brooklyn family must have run the gamut all by itself), and it was immediately and embarrassingly apparent that hardly anyone was qualified for the level of work that had been planned. Though advanced courses graced the catalogue, the girls lacked the prerequisite backgrounds to take them, and many had to settle for the introductory classes. Even the most highly motivated young woman was understandably reluctant to spend seven or eight years of her life at Vassar, and the brutal truth was that usually students were obliged to leave without ever taking the college degree. "Only one-quarter of the girls

105

are thoroughly grounded in anything," said President Raymond of those early years, adding sadly that "their previous education had been a wretched sham." He immediately established the remedial department, and Vassar was obliged to function largely as a preparatory school for itself until 1888. For most of this period the degree candidates were a very small minority of the total student body, and there were years when the school could grant only one or two diplomas.

Vassar began with twenty-one overtaxed women teachers and nine underworked male professors. The men gave most of the "college" courses. There were offerings in English language and literature, ancient and modern history, math, physics, natural history, philosophy and astronomy. The last department was a point of special pride for the college because the instructor was the remarkable Maria Mitchell, who was something of a meteorite herself, the first woman to be elected to the American Academy of Arts and Sciences. In 1847 Miss Mitchell had discovered a comet and had been awarded a gold medal by the Danish king. She was one of the original faculty members and already well known for her pioneering work with sunspots, nebulae and satellites. Attracting her to Vaasar was a triumph, and her presence there buttressed the still tenuous notion that women could be serious scholars if given the chance.

The whole of Vassar College was under one roof—classrooms, dormitories, laboratories, library, dining halls and infirmary. The only separate building was the riding academy, and that was not completed until 1866. A 400-person household must have been unwieldy and somewhat claustrophobic, but there were certain advantages. The personal behavior of the young ladies could be closely supervised every moment of the day and night, and that was considered most important. Had they been scattered in cottages, their comings and goings could not have been so readily observed. The Great Hall idea had ardent advocates, despite the unavoidable noise and confusion that resulted.

Each residential subdivision was the responsibility of a corridor teacher, whose duties included monitoring every aspect of student life, up to and including the number of baths a girl took each week. (Two were absolutely required, and more might be managed by someone particularly enthusiastic about the modern Vassar arrangements.) There was hot and cold running wa-

ter, a great novelty at the time, and few girls had to be reminded of their obligations. "I took a splendid bath today," reported
one student to her family in 1865, "I think you will have to get a
bathing place fixed by the time I come home or I don't believe I
can hardly stand it, for I enjoy it so much taking them here."

The college archives contain an extensive collection of early
correspondence, and there seems to have been remarkably few
complaints. That, however, may be because incoming and out-
going mail was carefully proctored, and the objectors may wisely have kept their thoughts to themselves. Another duty of the
corridor teachers was to deliver the post, and they were instructed to "notice so far as they may be able the extent and apparent character" of the letters and to report to the lady principal "such cases as seem to need attention." How these decisions
were made remains a mystery. The postmarks may have
offered a clue, with letters from New Haven, Princeton or Cambridge automatically going into a special stack for closer investigation. One doesn't like to think of the corridor teachers re-
sorting to steaming or otherwise tampering with the federal
mail, but they obviously did have effective methods. A typical
example of "attention" turned up in April, 1866. A young lady
was found to have been "carrying on and seeking a clandestine
correspondence with a young man in the city, to whom she was
a stranger, and in representing him to the officials of the college
as her cousin and receiving visits from him as such." The cul-
prit, whose name is never mentioned in the records, was banished from Vassar. Miss Hannah Lyman, the Lady Principal,
did not make exceptions.

The old pamphlets filed in the Vassar collection of memora-
bilia clearly defined Miss Lyman's duties. She was to judge the
propriety of calls on the young ladies, to correct faults of conversation and to guard "against coarse or insipid frivolities of
rustic and fashionable talk." The Lady Principal had a wooden
platform in her quarters specially designed to test the decency
of skirt lengths. Students were asked to step up on it before
leaving on holidays in order that Miss Lyman could make sure
that no part of a shoe could be seen. "Young ladies are not supposed to have feet," Miss Lyman proclaimed, and during her
administration, they didn't. Instead, they had rather tattered
hems, but that was considered the price of good breeding.

The rules were inflexible. Shopping lists had to be submitted to Miss Lyman and approved by her before a student could purchase so much as a notebook in the town of Poughkeepsie. Once having secured permission to do errands in town, the student had to engage a chaperone for the jaunt. The regulations about traveling alone did not distinguish between short trips and long ones. When the college opened, each bedroom had a list of rules affixed to the door, like the rates in a hotel. There were only about a dozen regulations that were explicit enough to post, but the unwritten code was complex and troublesome. It was easy enough to discipline oneself to turn off the gas at ten in the evening instead of blowing it out, but the subtleties were often impossible to grasp until they had been violated. Girls learned them by being called to Miss Lyman's office and chastised. After the reproof, the quaking student was encouraged to kneel in prayer with the Lady Principal, and together they would ask the Lord for forgiveness. After that, the rules were not easily forgotten or circumvented. Prayer was for first offenders. A second lapse was cause for expulsion.

During Miss Lyman's absolute reign, each Vassar girl was required to prepare a précis of the Sunday sermon and submit it to her corridor teacher, as proof that she had been spiritually as well as physically present at the services. The synopses were carefully checked for undue similarities of phrasing, and those that seemed to show evidence of collaboration were turned over to the Lady Principal for appropriate action. There are a few indications from surviving manuscript letters that the girls found this requirement tedious, but only because they were subjected to so many sermons in the course of the week that it was almost impossible to separate one from another.

During Vassar's first two decades there were required chapel exercises twice a day, as well as the usual periods of silent meditation each morning and evening. Sundays were, of course, special. The 7 A.M. chapel was replaced by a Bible class, and there was no time limit on the sermon that followed. In 1866 one student clocked Dr. Raymond at a record of seventy-three and a half minutes, considering that something to write home about even in an era when tolerance for pulpit rhetoric was remarkable. On Sunday and Thursday evenings President Raymond led all-campus prayer meetings, which were always longer and more demanding than those conducted by lesser personages on every other night. An ordinary and routine Vassar week, therefore, involved at least thirty-five distinct and programmed religious experiences (forty if you count required Bible class), and even the most devout student could run into difficulties as she attempted to sort them out by Sunday night.

Students actually seemed to spend more time on their knees than in their classroom chairs, and there were years when piety rose to disconcerting heights. Vassar seemed to reach such a peak in 1872, when prayer meetings were so thronged that the college considered knocking down a wall in order to create more space for them. The enthusiasm seems to have abated slightly while the alterations were under discussion, however, and Old Main remained structurally intact. After hoopskirts went out of fashion, there was more than enough space to kneel. One of Vassar's most cherished traditions during these decades was the annual Day of Prayer when all classes were replaced by a veritable fiesta of devotional meetings. In 1876, when President Raymond postponed the day, disappointed students protested so strenuously that the calendar was changed back. At about the same time there was a spontaneous undergraduate movement to change the weekly holiday from Saturday to Monday. The most devout girls had begun to worry that a Saturday without classes tempted the less pious to study on Sunday. Editors of the *Vassar Miscellany* opposed the switch on the grounds that academic obligations *before* the Sabbath would allow no time to reflect and prepare for the day itself.

By 1877, however, a few students had openly begun to criticize certain sermons, especially those that seemed condescending. The parson who aroused the greatest opposition had made the dreadful mistake of comparing his Vassar congregation to a field of lilies, adding that "the sole aim of the lily was to minister to the aesthetic nature of the manly oak." He so outraged his listeners that there was talk of not asking him back unless he promised to apologize. But such outbursts were still rare, and the majority seem to have remained respectfully docile. The Bible was taught "geologically," by "dear Professor Tenney," who carefully sidestepped the sizzling issue of evolution. Years later a member of the class of 1874 wrote in the *Vassar Quarterly*: "Agassiz was still alive and combatting Darwinism, and in those days if one believed in evolution, one mentioned it in subdued tones." Few mentioned it at all. Even the professor of natural history managed to lecture without discussing "the debatable question" of how life arrived on earth. Cornelia Raymond, the daughter of Vassar's first president and the head of the Society of Religious Inquiry during her undergraduate years, reports in her *Memoir of a Child at Vassar* that despite the suggestive name, the society's most ambitious project during the 1870s was "making Christmas mottoes to be fastened on the walls of the hospitals for charity patients on Blackwell's Island." The heretics were obviously still a tiny and unobtrusive minority.

At Mount Holyoke, evolution was actually confronted as early as 1872, but apparently behind closed doors and by invitation only. Miss Lydia Shattuck asked several of her best natural history students to meet in her private apartment, and after they were all assembled and seated, she gently presented Mr. Charles Darwin's revolutionary new theory. Accounts of the event hint that Miss Shattuck was in accord with Darwin and that she dealt sympathetically with his thesis. At Vassar, however, it was decided to avoid the whole issue, and there was considerable pressure on the Mount Holyoke science department to follow that example. Mere seminaries should not rush in where colleges feared to tread. Both these institutions had promised "an education peculiarly fitted to women," and evolution was the perfect test case. It was exactly the sort of distressing intelligence from which ladies should be protected. The matter eventually was resolved very simply. Teachers presented the hypothesis very quietly during the week, emphasizing pterodactyls and glossing over primates, and the ministers preached vociferously against it on Sundays. To everyone's relief, religious faith showed no signs of diminution. On the contrary, many Holyoke students found Darwin's theories so outlandish that they became more orthodox than they had been before they ever heard of him.

Though the Mount Holyoke students of the 1860s and '70s were not proctored by corridor teachers, they were still expected to report themselves for any infraction of the rules governing personal behavior. This system had been in operation from the very beginning, and members of the administration favored its continuance as a method of strengthening the "moral power" which was such a special characteristic of the Mount

Holyoke student. "I think young ladies would much prefer being placed upon their honor as in the self-reporting system to being under the espionage of corridor teachers as at Vassar," wrote Mrs. Mary Chapin Pease, a member of a committee studying the rules.

Still, the mood at Mount Holyoke had grown increasingly restive in the years after the Civil War, and there were frequent indications that the weekly self-reporting sessions might have outlived their usefulness. Many students and faculty members found them humiliating and atavistic. The burden on the girls was enormous since they were expected not only to confess publicly to their own violations, but to announce those of others. Saints and sinners agreed that the system had to go. It penalized everyone, turning the obedient into prigs and fracturing long-standing friendships. The opposition referred to the assemblies as "the pillory" and loathed them. Alumnae mothers who remembered the embarrassments of previous decades often chose to send their daughters elsewhere—or nowhere—rather than subject them to the stern and outworn discipline of confession. There was a growing feeling that Mount Holyoke's antique rules smacked of Popery without even the saving grace of privacy. It was a charge to which Holyoke had always been particularly sensitive, and any mention of it was enough to rouse the seminary to instant action.

By 1875 it was obvious that Mount Holyoke was no longer an educational monopoly, and there were well-founded fears that it could very easily become an anachronism. Nominally, it was still a seminary, and that alone was enough to make current students defensive and prospective students disdainful. The faltering image wasn't helped by an open letter written in 1875 to the president-elect of Smith College by the Reverend Edward C. Towne of North Easton, Massachusetts. The Reverend Mr. Towne's widely reported letter attacked Mount Holyoke's "badly Puritan" routine, with its unhealthy emphasis on "fear, zeal, anxiety, solemnity, doctrinal strictness and church formalism." The outspoken clergyman called the whole affair "a prodigious mistake" and expressed his wish that President L. Clark Seelye would find another and better way to manage the new college in Northampton.

This letter and the inquiries it inspired eventually led to the

111

resignation of the principal of Mount Holyoke. Ostensibly and classically, Miss Julia E. Ward left for reasons of health, but not before she had made it clear that she suffered as much from "a lack of mutual trust and confidence" as from her physical ailments. Toward the end of her reign the honor system had shown severe signs of wear, and even the most conservative members of the faculty were ready to acknowledge that students were simply ignoring it. In 1877, for the first time in Mount Holyoke's history, there had been no student interest in a religious revival. Instead, undergraduate energies seemed channeled into defiance of Miss Ward, and some unthinkable incidents had occurred. There were not only subversive card parties behind locked doors, but at least one very open game in a hotel in Springfield. They were playing "not like novices," according to the astonished report of a "friend" of the seminary who had seen them. The cardplayers were instantly dismissed, and no exception was made for the daughter of a missionary in China.

It was the end of an unmourned era. There was a general investigation, and the entire student body was asked what they knew of these affairs. Several girls chose to leave Mount Holyoke at this crisis, not convinced that a knowledge of cardplaying was a crime in itself. "I knew it was not my duty to go tell," wrote a young lady named Hattie Savage that year. "And I don't want to be told that because I don't love everything about this institution and love the rules I am hindering a revival. Neither do I feel at all sure cardplaying has hindered a revival. Oh well. There are more rumors now. They say there is a good deal of smoking cigarettes in school." The rebellious Miss Savage was safely out of Mount Holyoke before the peak of revolution was reached a year or so later. She missed the secret wine suppers of the late 1870s, which is a pity, since she sounds like the sort of young woman who was just a bit in advance of her time.

XI
Hands and Hearts

IF the fourteen young women who made up the first class at Smith College seem to have escaped some of the footling regulations that characterized life at Vassar and Mount Holyoke, it was probably because they were so small a group that no extraordinary measures seemed necessary. Smith, at its opening in 1875, was hardly larger than an ordinary Victorian family, extended only by a permanent faculty of three. Upon the students' arrival President Seelye informed the girls that "the unwritten code of good society was to be observed by them as by well-bred women elsewhere," adding merely that they would be expected to attend church every Sunday and "not violate nor offend the proprieties of Sunday observance in a New England town." Miss Sarah Humphrey, who taught history, would oversee the social life of the college. As a historian she could be depended on to know the nuances of traditional Sunday observances. The plan sounded more offhand and casual than it actually was because the "New England town" in question was a mere ten miles from South Hadley and shared all the same austere Sabbath customs. As a result, Northampton Sundays were not particularly festive holidays despite the Reverend Mr. Seelye's apparent liberality.

The "unwritten code" at Smith was as rigid as anything invented by the Medes, the Persians or the lady principals of Mount Holyoke and Vassar. Smith students soon learned that they were not supposed to walk "merely for pleasure," that Sunday callers were "not expected" and, according to the recollections of a member of the class of 1880, that the greatest breach of propriety of all would be a visit from an Amherst friend, solicited or not. There were not even any loopholes through which an Amherst "cousin" could slip, pleading urgent family business. Sunday strolls were permissible only if they terminated at church, and the more ingenious scholars immedi-

113

ately opted for the most remote houses of worship they could find. Smith college was too tiny to have a chapel of its own, and that fact seemed to offer the only opportunity for social encounters. The overly venturesome, however, had all of a long, cold New England winter to ponder their choice and decide whether a three-mile hike through the snow was worth the possible glimpse of an Amherst student bent over his psalter. There were several denominational changes after the winter recess, and by the time the spring term began most of the Smith students could be found in the front row of the Northampton Congregational Church, where the whole town could readily observe them.

All fourteen entering students were lodged in Dewey House, the first of the several modest cottages that served as Smith dormitories. Miss Sophia Smith's ideal of one-story houses had been slightly modified, but the spirit of her wishes had been kept. The living arrangements were designed to elude attention, not attract it, and they succeeded. No reporters descended on Northampton. There was nothing to make a trip from Boston worthwhile: no exotic plants, Greek statues or crenelated turrets. The scholars themselves, fumbling their way to bed by the light of candles stuck in potato halves, must occasionally have had some doubts of their own existence. Shivering in the semidarkness, they could only remind each other that Smith was the only *true* women's college, unadulterated by so much as a single preparatory student. That distinction warmed and encouraged them for several years.

Although illumination by potato candleholder was only temporary, it was obvious even before the college opened that the $300,000 bequeathed by Sophia Smith would not provide for quite as glorious an establishment as the one envisioned. The benefactress had been reluctant and cagey to the end, entailing her fortune so that no more than half could actually be used for buildings and grounds. The financial slump of 1872–73 seriously aggravated the problems. A brand-new women's college seemed the least worthy cause imaginable, and Smith found few outside backers. Although it opened on schedule, the college was obliged to use the town library and to borrow almost all its teachers from Amherst, Mount Holyoke, Massachusetts Agricultural College and Williston Academy. Miss Smith's will had provided that the second half of her bequest be invested by the trustees and the income alone spent for all of the college's operating expenses. That would have been reasonably difficult during a surge of national prosperity, but in the mid 1870s it was all but impossible to find a dependable stock or bond. Moreover, when Miss Smith had finally capitulated to the idea of having the college in the town of Northampton instead of in her beloved Hatfield, she had made a further stipulation: Northampton would not get the college unless its citizens were to "raise and pay over the sum of twenty-five thousand dollars to the Trustees of the college." Miss Smith's will gave the population of Northampton two years in which to demonstrate interest and good faith by producing the money. The word "blackmail" was thought by some skeptics to be applicable to this arrangement. Worse, if the pledge was not made good at the end of that period, Smith College would revert to Hatfield, at no charge whatever to that town. These rather mean-spirited provisions did not exactly galvanize the people of Northampton into spontaneous outbursts of generosity. There were, in fact, a great many who were more than willing to let Hatfield have the honor and privilege of playing host to the new institution. Northampton already had its monument in the form of Mr. Clarke's Deaf and Dumb Academy, and that was considered distinction enough. Eventually, the ransom was raised, but enthusiasm was by no means unanimous.

Even the friends of higher education for women were somewhat ambivalent. The idea of coeducation was gaining ground, and Boston University proposed to admit both sexes very shortly. Cornell had begun to do so upon its opening in 1868, and that made a grand total of two universities open to women in the Northeast alone. In 1871 Amherst was debating the possibility of allowing girls to study there, and no one seriously thought the subject would still be under discussion more than a century later. Coeducation seemed to be the wave of the future, and even if it turned out to be a mere ripple, Mount Holyoke was just across the mountain, plans for Wellesley had been announced, and the Vassar students were still struggling to qualify for the college courses. Smith College seemed redundant even to the optimists. The town fathers tried to put extortion out of their minds as they asked themselves dispassionately who would go to Smith when, where and if it were ever to be established. The inevitable answer was no one. As it turned out, they came perilously close to being right.

Smith had been planned as "fully equivalent" to a men's college, not merely similar to one. The requirements for admission were to be substantially the same as at Harvard, Yale, Brown, Amherst and other New England colleges "inasmuch as the high schools and most of the academies wisely furnish the preparatory instruction to both sexes." That sounded so impressive and splendid that almost a year elapsed before the public realized that "fully equivalent" meant that aspiring students for Smith would have to be examined in Greek and Latin grammar, Sallust's *Catiline,* Cicero's *Seven Orations,* the first six books of the *Aeneid,* Xenophon's *Anabasis,* the *Iliad;* algebra to quadratic equations and geometry, as well as in arithmetic, geography, English and history. The Trustees' first prospectus, moreover, had rather grossly overestimated the wisdom of the preparatory schools and academies. They were not, it appeared, really offering this extensive smorgasbord of electives "to both sexes." Girls who wished to qualify for Smith were usually obliged to find private tutors in math and ancient languages, while those few who attempted to take the required subjects in the high schools that had them were refused admittance to those particular classes. . Even their parents were subject to abuse, ridicule and threats. Dr. Seelye reported that at least one of his fourteen scholars came to Smith despite the fact that her father had been anonymously warned that he "would have to buy her coffin before her diploma."

The stringency of the requirements quickly revived the not-so-dormant arguments about female health and study, and a renewed debate raged in the pages of the Springfield *Republican* for months, once again undermining the whole frail cause of higher education for women. "Female nervous systems" wrote one persistent correspondent, "are wrecked by a process of stimulation for examinations, exhibitions, and prizes, and by a regime which ignores the great natural laws which make them, between the ages of 15 and 45, essentially a separate and higher order of beings than men, destined for a purpose wholly feminine. . . ." The fact that a woman physician signed this essay seemed to lend it an extra measure of credence, and the skeptics received it enthusiastically. The furor eventually subsided, but not before scores of potential students had been discouraged or frightened away.

The trustees courageously tabled these various considerations and went ahead with their plans, asking the Reverend L. Clark Seelye to serve as president of the new college. He firmly declined. Dr. Seelye's niece had just become one of the few girls actually to graduate from Vassar, and he had returned from that ceremony convinced that there was neither enough money left by the peculiar conditions of Miss Smith's will for a true college nor even any pressing need for another. Construction costs had risen, the economy was depressed, and it now appeared that the town of Northampton would have to find another $50,000 in order to win the bid. The $25,000 already collected was not adequate for even a single classroom building. Professor William Tyler of Amherst was chosen to make a last appeal to the townspeople, and he did a remarkable job of it. He didn't mention his colleague Seelye by name, but he admitted that the trustees had met with "imperfect success" in their search for a qualified president. "Such men," said Tyler, "are in great demand. They already hold important positions with a sure and ample support and an established reputation. . . . They ask what pecuniary basis we have to build upon; and when they are told . . . they say it is not enough to make a college in our day. . . ." Warming to his subject and his audience, Tyler continued with even more persuasive arguments: "Give us a Northampton Hall built by Northampton hands and Northampton hearts and the ablest and the best men of the land will be glad to cast in their lot with the College . . . and the faculty will bring the students, and the faculty and the students' money will flow in to enlarge and expand, to secure growth and progress for years to come. . . ."

After Tyler's eloquent speech, two brave men pledged $1,000 each, on condition that their fellow citizens would subscribe the rest. There the matter rested. The trustees eventually decided to ignore their financial problems and to concentrate on persuading Dr. Seelye to reconsider, in the hope that a president would inspire confidence. This time the plea was phrased somewhat differently. "If you should take the presidency . . ." wrote the eminent Professor Edwards A. Park of Andover Theological Seminary, "you would be a means of preventing well-established colleges from introducing women into their existing course of study and would thus save the community from a great amount of evil." That was a circuitous argument, but hard to rebut. Seelye could preserve Amherst from coeducation by becoming president of Smith. If he loved Amherst, he'd do it. What could be nobler? On this basis, Dr. Seelye finally agreed and devoted the rest of his long life to Smith College, secure and reasonably happy in the knowledge that he was simultaneously doing Amherst the greatest service possible.

The new president needed consolation because by the end of the first year, 1876, there were a mere dozen students at Smith College. Sixteen more girls were admitted for the second year, virtually exhausting the national supply of female mathematicians with a knowledge of Sallust. Naturally, no great prosperity accrued to the town from the presence of twenty-eight impecunious young women, and considerable pressure was applied to Smith to lower its unrealistic standards. No women's college had yet survived without a preparatory department, and the trustees were urged to institute one at Smith without delay. After anguished deliberation, a compromise was reached. Smith would not dilute itself with a preparatory school, but it *would* admit "special students," a euphemism for girls who could not fulfill the troublesome requirements in math and classics. Enrollment boomed immediately. Art and music were added to the curriculum, and Smith began to seem less eccentric. The provision for "special students" made a tremendous difference, and thirty-nine young women turned up for the third year's class, to the vast relief of the Northamptonites who had invested their money in the project.

By 1879 the Academic Hall finally built by Northampton hands and hearts was overflowing. Two hundred students filled its recitation rooms during the day, and the large social parlors no longer seemed so ostentatious. The college girls were beginning to make a small but perceptible difference to the local economy, and the reluctant contributors to the cause congratulated themselves upon their foresight. More cottages were planned, a gymnasium incorporating a bowling alley and a stage was built, and the college felt secure enough to offer some of the visiting faculty members permanent appointments and regular salaries.

The only disquieting note was that this flowering was clearly attributable to the "special students," who were proliferating at an alarming rate. Though many were commendably serious about education, others seemed to regard Smith as a sort of academic variety store, picking and choosing among the course offerings as if they were selecting ribbons for their bonnets. Some stayed just long enough to charge a few French phrases or a smattering of geography to their indulgent papas before returning home with the special aura that belonged by rights only to mistresses of Greek and quadratic equations. "Every year," wrote Dr. Seelye in his memoirs, "there was a large proportion of students who were perhaps more inclined to amusement than to study." Some, he added kindly, "were gradually changed by their environment so that they became good scholars," but others were unaltered, and "their original predilection tended to increase the College festivities and sports, and greater vigilance was necessary to maintain the College standards."

Smith, which had been intended as the most rigorous of the women's institutions, was inadvertently becoming the most deplorably relaxed. It had grown so rapidly that students were boarding all over town, often with landladies who were either unfamiliar with the "code of good society" or regrettably lax about enforcing it. There was evidence that some Sunday walks to church included detours around Paradise Pond, where other and graver breaches of propriety could easily occur. The ten o'clock bedtime rule was being openly flouted, and there were reports of midnight oyster festivals behind blanketed windows. It was immediately and painfully obvious to Dr. Seelye that the young ladies who had been exempted from Greek considered themselves exempt from other stipulations as well. The Victorian family, once full of common purpose and noble aspiration, was splitting into cliques, and the first true fully equivalent women's college seemed to be going astray. After much deliberation and anguish, it was reluctantly decided to limit the number of special students in the hope that frivolity would diminish accordingly. The unwritten social code was spelled out on printed leaflets, and lenient landladies were warned that they would be stricken from the approved list if the rules were not rigidly enforced. The curriculum was often revised so that the course for nonclassical scholars would be every bit as demanding as originally intended. "Fully equivalent" became merely "equivalent," but the line was firmly held at preppies. There were none.

XII
No Sex in Mind

NEW ventures usually begin where older ventures leave off, but Wellesley was a deliberate exception. Henry Durant started fresh, as if his college were the very first institution of its kind. He deplored what he considered the moral laxity of the Gilded Age and did his best to turn the calendar back to a more congenial time. Inside his enchanted garden it was 1840 or so, and sometimes 1625. Wellesley was his personal Eden as long as he lived, and he remained its patriarch until his death in 1881. He was not just a reformer, but a reformer himself reformed, and such men tend to be inflexible. As a trustee of Mount Holyoke Durant had been able to observe both its faults and its virtues very closely, differing with many more progressive observers about which were which. (Since the demand for philanthropists with an interest in women's education far exceeded the supply, men like Durant were parceled out very carefully, and many things were overlooked.) Durant had also kept an eye on Vassar and was well aware of the plans for a women's college in Northampton. Students at Smith, he learned, were to be allowed to choose their own churches, and the rumor upset him. That was precisely the sort of trend that he hoped to reverse by his policy of mandatory evangelism. Durant was immensely relieved when he found that only fourteen souls were imperiled at Northampton, though he still feared for the worldlings at Vassar. There, in spite of the commendable religious atmosphere, young ladies were practicing the schottische and the hesitation waltz in their calisthenium before departing for holiday parties in New York.

Dancing, opera and theater were to be flatly forbidden to Wellesley students, and the prohibition applied to vacation time as well. The Wellesley spirit was so deeply imbued that some students observed their regular half hour of silent meditation even while traveling home on the Boston and Maine. Durant's plan for cultural inspiration was to invite approved poets like John Greenleaf Whittier, Matthew Arnold and Henry Wadsworth Longfellow to read their works at the college. That effectively minimized any risks that might have come from unnecessary exposure to the outside world. Only Longfellow was reluctant to come, but Durant finally convinced him. After an enthusiastic crew of inexperienced oarswomen had rowed the poet around Lake Waban, the standard honor for all distinguished visitors, Longfellow vowed to return only if he would be excused from this ritual.

Though most of Durant's policies were quite original, he thoroughly approved of the Mount Holyoke idea of domestic chores and was determined to revive that plan at Wellesley. Applicants were instructed to leave their fine clothes at home and bring only their plainest and most functional dresses with them, turnouts that wouldn't be damaged by an hour of daily sweeping and dusting. "A calico girl is worth two velvet girls" was one of Durant's favorite maxims, and he meant it. There was more than a hint of worldly renunciation in the Wellesley prospectus, which also mentioned that food would be both simple and wholesome. "Pies, lies and doughnuts will never have a place at Wellesley College" was another Durant edict. The first students found this to be something of an understatement. Supper, though served on the elegant Wedgwood plates, usually consisted of bread, butter and molasses, washed down by milk or water and very occasionally followed by an apple. No one was allowed to supplement this diet with boxes of food from home, though once in a while a special exception was apparently made. When Charlotte Conant received a gift of two pears from her father, she obediently presented them to the proper authority for confiscation. To her surprise and delight, the pears were carefully divided into eighths, and each girl at the table was allocated a single snip. Charlotte's thank-you letter to her parents explained that this was "the only way we can have anything sent to us, and even that is frowned upon."

Durant's belief, often and tiresomely stated, was that the primary purpose of education was to strengthen religious feeling, and everything at Wellesley was arranged to that end. Instead of the pageants and plays staged by students elsewhere, Wellesley girls were encouraged to entertain themselves with debate.

A favorite topic of Mr. Durant's was: "Resolved: That the influence of Christianity has been a more important factor than the activity of the human intellect in producing modern civilization." He never wearied of hearing his girls argue this subject, and while he didn't actually join in the contests, it was obvious to the participants that he strongly favored the affirmative. Those who took the opposing point of view were careful not to make their cases too strong since an overly vehement speech was certain to bring about a post-contest chat with the founder about salvation.

Henry Durant was much too shrewd a businessman to risk limiting enrollment to Greek scholars and advanced algebraists. His investment was immense, and the venture had to pay its way. Wellesley, like Vassar and Smith, proposed to grant college degrees, but it did not discourage preparatory students. Three hundred and fourteen young women were admitted on September 8, 1875, and another 200 had been regretfully told that they could not be accommodated. The cost of a year at Wellesley was initially set at a mere $250, reasonable even in those days. Reports of Wellesley's incomparable luxury had circulated widely, and most of New England had read descriptions of the carpeted floors, mirrored bureaus and generous closets—amenities not to be found at any other college. The fairyland on Lake Waban was a legend before it opened and almost everyone's first choice, so desirable that eagerness to attend it apparently led many applicants to overestimate their qualifications. After a confusing few weeks of placement tests, it was obvious that only 30 of the 314 entrants were even partially prepared for college work.

For its first six years, Wellesley was really the largest and most glorious secondary school ever. Since Mr. Durant had somehow neglected to apply to the Commonwealth of Massachusetts for the right to grant college degrees, that may have been just as well. Permission to confer the BA was received only a few weeks before the first commencement in 1879. The oversight seemed to have gone unnoticed until the original class was well into its second year, and the procedure was a lengthy and difficult one. Durant, in fact, was obliged to resume the practice of law in order to plead his own case. Religion might come first, but he realized that no one would pay tuition for four years only to receive his blessing. The legislature, remembering some of the founder's previous and dubious clients, proved obdurate, but Durant prevailed. This time he had God firmly on his side.

According to the journal of Florence Morse Kingsley, who attended the college in 1876, there were girls at Wellesley in the first few years who hadn't yet "learned how to tie their shoestrings or braid their hair properly when they come." Though Mr. Durant wanted Wellesley to be the "calico girl's college," the "velvet girls" descended on his project by the trainload, expecting service that matched their surroundings. Once there, they had to be looked after, often to the annoyance of the more mature and serious students. After giving the place a month's trial, Mary Elizabeth Stillwell wrote:

> Wellesley is not a college. The buildings are beautiful, perfect, almost; the rooms and their appointments delightful; most of the professors are all that could be desired, some of them are very fine indeed in their several departments, but all these delightful things are not the things that make a college. . . . I came here to take a *college course,* and not to dabble. . . . More than half my time is taken up in writing essays, practicing elocution, trotting to chapel, and reading poetry with the teacher of English literature, and it seems to make no difference to Miss Howard or Mr. Durant whether the Latin, Greek and Mathematics are well learned or not."

Miss Stillwell obviously would have been happier in Northampton, where the classics were appreciated, but she did make the best of Wellesley and eventually became president of her class. Along with many other students, she seems to have found the pervasive spirit of evangelism irksome and antiquated. She did not, however, join in the frequent send-ups of Mr. Durant that soon became the chief amusement of her contemporaries, who practiced skits in the privacy of their meditation parlors and laughed at the founder behind his back. Miss Stillwell merely commented that Durant "was losing all his influence and doing just the opposite of what he intended. Every spark of religious interest is killed," she wrote, and while that might have been an exaggeration, the level of fervor dipped considerably below Durant's expectations. By the time the seventh Sunday observance was over even the most devout were a bit weary of it all and ready to listen to a parody of the bedtime sermon.

Other Wellesley rules seemed borrowed intact from a nursery. The girls were chastised for slamming doors and whistling, for talking above a whisper after lights-out, for "idle and flippant" words about the faculty and for concealing edibles in their rooms. They were warned against writing letters to "general correspondents on Sunday," though a note to one's pastor might pass the postal inspection. The more imaginative soon learned to address all their mail to hypothetical "reverends," a dodge which never seemed to arouse the least suspicion. Students were cautioned by their physiology teacher against tight clothing and advised to avoid wearing skirts that hung from the hips. Those who owned unsuitably snug outfits were asked to send them home for alterations. "So, Mamma," wrote Charlotte Conant, who seems to have been a model scholar, "I am going to put buttons on my underwaist and button all my clothes on to that."

A lavishly illustrated article written by Edward Abbott in *Harper's New Monthly Magazine* for August, 1876, inexplicably shows several willowy and elaborately gowned Wellesley girls in intimate conversations with dapper young men. None of their skirts appear to be loosely buttoned to underwaists. Some of the students are actually drawn leaning casually against the trees or seated on the grass, postures that would certainly have been discouraged by Miss Ada Howard, the Lady Principal in charge of deportment. The pictures are elegant and beguiling, and the text makes scarcely any mention of the petty rules and regulations that governed every aspect of college life. The requirements for admission, especially in comparison to those at Smith, seem moderate, and the author adds that students with "irregular or imperfect" preparation are not sent home but "placed in training for the freshman class." He suggests that Wellesley applicants be prepared for tests in reading, writing, spelling, geography, U.S. history and Latin grammar. Candidates for the college course would need a bit of algebra and geometry as well. French and German were recommended, but not mandatory. Mr. Abbott was a trustee of Wellesley, and after the appearance of this veritable advertisement, applications poured in, guaranteeing a full palace for at least a decade.

Although the 1870s and '80s were not the most innovative decades in the history of the colleges, the accomplishments were tangible enough. More than a thousand schoolteachers were turned out; at least a dozen doctors, scores of nurses, librarians and editors; a creditable number of pioneers in social work; and some amazingly prolific poets, journalists and novelists. Each of the colleges had an impressive collection of missionaries it could call on to prove its usefulness in the sight of God. Wellesley soon led that field with twenty, outstripping Mount Holyoke in no time at all. The choice of respectable professions was narrow, and the first generations of alumnae were diverted from fields that might have made them celebrated or notorious. A career on the stage was unthinkable, and while many college women were "artistic," few seem to have been artists. Of the literary ladies, those who came closest to genteel fame were the poets. With luck and the right music they often found a special immortality in the hymnbooks, like Katharine Lee Bates, the Wellesley author of "America the Beautiful." Those who achieved the greatest eminence, as a group and individually, were the educators. They had a numerical advantage, of course, but teaching did seem to attract the best and the brightest.

Charlotte Conant, the cooperative freshman who sewed buttons on her basques to oblige the physiology instructor, had one of the more distinguished careers, founding Walnut Hill Academy by the time she was thirty-two. After graduating from Wellesley, she was offered a post at Northfield Seminary, where she spent a rather uncomfortable year teaching classes that included women far older than she, as well as very small children. All faculty members at Northfield were expected to be authorities on the Bible, as well as mistresses of their secular disciplines, and Charlotte Conant was assigned a course in the Pentateuch. Despite her misgivings, her Wellesley background apparently enabled her to manage it so well that she was offered the job of assistant principal for the next year.

By then, however, her tolerance for evangelism was exhausted, and after a year at home, she joined the staff of Miss Clark's small coed day school at Rutland, Vermont. Socially and intellectually, that was a marked improvement over Northfield, though the school was constantly in financial difficulties. Charlotte Conant's Wellesley experience had convinced her that the women's colleges could never reach their full potential if they were forced to dilute their curricula with high school courses, and she spent the next six years planning a preparatory school tailored especially for Wellesley, though her Walnut Hill girls were free to choose Smith, Vassar or the Harvard Annex. The academy opened in 1893, managed by Miss Conant and her former college roommate, Florence Bigelow, who served as co-mistress. Their educational methods were enlightened and refreshingly liberal, and the school flourished. Miss Conant's typical career was followed with justifiable satisfaction by the advocates of women's college education and she was regarded as an almost perfect example of what a girl could—and should—do with her new advantages.

During the 1870s and '80s that did not seem to include crusading for legal rights. There was very little overt—or even covert—agitation for suffrage on the campuses, a fact which is not really as paradoxical as it seems. Few women could afford the luxury of advocating *two* causes, and the right to education was still too fragile to jeopardize. Wellesley was particularly docile in this respect, and its undergraduates continued to vote automatically and overwhelmingly against their own enfranchisement until 1910, *after* the states of Washington, Utah, Idaho, Colorado and Wyoming had actually granted the ballot to women. Wellesley didn't change its mind until 1912, and even then, feeling was by no means unanimous. There were anti-suffrage groups on campus even when the Nineteenth Amendment was finally passed.

Vassar, which was to enjoy a precocious and slightly exaggerated reputation for political radicalism in later years, was still not the most comfortable place for a suffragist in the mid-1870s. Harriot Stanton, the daughter of Elizabeth Cady Stanton and herself the eventual founder of the Women's Political Union, remembered her undergraduate days in Poughkeepsie as a "Slough of Despond," in an "institution composed entirely of a disenfranchised class, which was definitely discouraged by the authorities from taking any interest whatsoever in its own political freedom." Harriot did succeed in galvanizing her classmates into a Democratic Club, "the first time politics had crossed the sacred threshold of this higher institution of learning," and when news of her efforts reached Samuel Tilden, he sent her an autographed daguerreotype. After that triumph, however, the club disbanded, and Miss Stanton was left to compare the "somnolence" of Vassar with the vitality of Cornell, where she had wanted to go in the first place. Unfortunately, her education was not underwritten by her firebrand mother, Elizabeth Cady Stanton, but by a very conservative aunt, who agreed to pay Harriot's tuition only on condition that she attend Vassar. One suffragist per family was considered enough. A few days after her graduation Harriot Stanton enrolled at the Boston School of Oratory, where she quickly filled the gaps left by the previous four years.

She was, however, a rare exception, if not unique. The women's colleges existed on the precarious benevolence of men and prudently avoided any activity that would alienate their supporters. There was still scattered resistance to the idea of sending girls to college, and misdirected zeal could revive it overnight. Even after it was clear that girls were physically, mentally and spiritually undamaged by the work, the case was by no means won. New threats appeared before the old ones quite expired.

In 1895 the entire women's college movement was shaken by the announcement that fully half the graduates had remained spinsters. No amount of interpretation or juggling of these statistics could blunt their impact, though those concerned with women's education tried valiantly. "Figures will always lie," pleaded Frances Abbott in the November 1895 issue of the *Forum*. "It is impossible to write the history of a living institution, especially one so young as a woman's college." After making this disclaimer, however, the author attempted to do exactly that, using Vassar as the model. Between 1867 and 1894 Vassar had graduated a total of 1,082 women, of whom only 409 had married, a disappointing total of less than 38 percent. Miss Abbott (two-name women writers were almost always spinsters in an age when matrons used their given, maiden and married names for occasions as formal as appearances in print) bravely tried to arrive at "a truer proportion" by examining the figures year by year, but no matter how many points she stretched, she never succeeded in marrying off more than two-thirds of a class. The class of 1867 did best, with three out of its four members safely wedded by the age of fifty-eight, but even that record fell short of the nineteenth-century ideal. Moreover, neither Wellesley nor Smith seemed to be producing a fair share of brides. At that time fully 80 percent of American women between the ages of twenty-five and thirty-four were married. Those figures were for the population at large. For college graduates, however, whose problem was partly that they were *not* at large, the discrepancy was startling.

The spinster explosion was taken very seriously by the American public, and the colleges were naturally held responsible for it. There was general agreement that every married couple in America was obliged to produce a minimum of three children in order for the Republic to survive. The ignorant poor were doing more than their share, but the more privileged classes seemed to be abdicating their responsibilities. Even college *men* dawdled on the way to the altar, and when they arrived, it was rarely in the company of a college woman. Graduates of the women's schools, when they found husbands, were having an average of only 1.7 children, setting a disgraceful example, which would soon lead the country to extinction.

One misguided attempt to justify the colleges implied that educated women were no great loss to the race since they were "more or less lacking in normal sex instincts" and that the colleges probably served a useful purpose by segregating such women from the rest of society. The writer, speaking *ex cathedra* from the pages of the respected *American Journal of Heredity,* added as a consoling afterthought that "it is doubtful if they are a superior class except intellectually." This curious point of view soon acquired enough adherents to be called a school of thought, and for the next fifteen years or so the *Journal of Heredity* functioned as a forum for all those opposed to college education for women. The attacks steadily increased in intensity, and a whole new generation of detractors appeared. One of the most prolific writers for that publication was a Dr. Robert Sprague, who could be depended on for at least three contributions a year. His titles, inflammatory in themselves, barely hint at the passion in his text. In *Education and Race Suicide,* one of his most influential essays, he asked, "Is the woman's college as now conducted a force which acts against the survival of the race which patronizes it?" only to answer himself with a resounding and predictable yes. He then proclaimed that "the civilization that uses its women for stenographers, clerks and schoolteachers instead of mothers has but one racial fate."

On every hand, *soi-disant* experts were differentiating between "the normal all-round red-blooded woman" and the wan, one-dimensional college student. There were solemn suggestions that the colleges reorganize themselves in order to serve the "domestic and motherly instincts" of the red-blooded class, leaving the anemic academic types to fend for themselves. The sciences, classics and even literature would immediately be replaced by domestic arts, and the time previously spent in learning "dead" subjects employed in healthful, though unspecified exercises designed to invigorate the reproductive system. The spokeswomen for the beleaguered colleges sidestepped this question and concentrated on arguing that education should be genderless, since the human mind had no known primary or secondary sexual characteristics. Often during this gloomy period, the educators were invited to take heart from the notion that "celibacy of the cultured classes . . . is not peculiarly to be deplored" since educated women make poor mothers, "not giving themselves up to children with complete abandonment." Many geneticists of that era favored the theory that "intellectual ability was not a dominant Mendelian characteristic that all breeds true to parental type," a premise which led easily to the belief that educating women was a waste of time and money.

All this constituted a massive setback for the existing colleges and operated as an impediment to the establishment of new ones. The arguments may seem ludicrous now, but they caused enormous misunderstanding and confusion and were surprisingly difficult to combat. There was not much datum available, and methods of collecting and interpreting it varied widely. The spinster count continued to rise inexorably, and the colleges could defend themselves only by weakly insisting that once their graduates married, they rarely divorced and that the children of these unions, though few, were remarkably strong and healthy. They added that their unmarried alumnae entered professions like teaching, public health and social work, where they nurtured hundreds of young people instead of only a single family. Rather plaintively, the educators maintained

129

that there should be an alternative for those who might, after all, not be so well suited to motherhood. The eminent Vassar astronomer Maria Mitchell took every opportunity to repeat that "Vassar girls marry late, but they marry well." M. Carey Thomas, the brand-new president of Bryn Mawr, tried to convince a totally incredulous public that it was possible to *combine* marriage and a career. She put it awkwardly, however, by stating: "Our failures only marry," and incurred even more hostility. The whole country quickly misquoted the phrase as "only our failures marry," and Bryn Mawr, the youngest of the colleges, received a disproportionate share of the prevailing criticism. By 1900 it was beginning to seem as if the women's colleges might have done too thorough a job of motivating and protecting their students—that they might, in fact, have outdone themselves.

XIII
Strong Characters

UNDERSTANDING why the colleges remained somewhat aloof from the larger crusade for women's rights involves making certain allowances, but once that is done, it's easier to forgive them for not producing platoons of passionate suffragists. Although the Seven can now claim the most vociferous and controversial of all the new feminists, there are some interesting reasons why it didn't happen until the second time around. For one thing, the religious orthodoxy that prevailed on the campuses must have been a powerfully inhibiting force. The Bible makes the second-class status of women almost an article of faith and is the ultimate justification for its perpetuation. Since the average college career of the 1870s and '80s involved some 3,000 exposures to Scripture, there couldn't have been many skeptics left by graduation day. If conventionally observant young women of that era found it extraordinarily difficult to give themselves wholeheartedly to the Struggle for the Ballot, true believers often regarded its principles as outright heresy. The frequent college polls on the suffrage question show how ambivalent undergraduates could be toward votes for women and how long the misgivings lasted. College girls had already taken a great risk with their social desirability and often seemed inclined to cover their bets. A scholar might find a husband, but a scholar-crusader would give any man pause. Religion may also partly explain why the early educators and the advocates of women's rights often seemed to be wary and suspicious of each other.

Though the causes seem complementary in retrospect, at the time they were devilishly hard to reconcile. Except in the bizarre and extreme case of the Nathan sisters, there was rarely any real enmity, but scholars and voters did not often appear on the same platforms or march in the same parades until 1910 or so. Since there weren't nearly enough advocates and benefactors to go around, the competition for support was keen enough to strain an already frayed connection. The suffragists tended to favor attention-getting stunts like blocking trolley tracks and chaining themselves to legislators' gates. A few occasionally even resorted to stone throwing—an English technique that had proved effective in London. The educators regarded this kind of early street theater as undignified and tasteless and felt obliged to disassociate themselves from any connection with it. Though many of the college teachers, like Maria Mitchell, were throughly in favor of equality, they did draw the line at making public spectacles of themselves. The trustees and the presidents of the colleges, most of whom were still fundamentalist clergymen, would not have approved.

Of all those who led the women's colleges at the close of the nineteenth century, only M. Carey Thomas, dean and president of Bryn Mawr, could be called a feminist in the larger sense, and she continually proclaimed that her "one aim and concentrated purpose shall be and is to show that girls can learn, can reason, can compete with men in the grand fields of literature and science and conjecture"—a tall order right there, and one that didn't leave much surplus time and energy for other aspects of the struggle. Miss Thomas, moreover, was a member of the Society of Friends, a fact which allowed her a bit more leeway in the interpretation of the Gospel. Once Bryn Mawr was reasonably well established and its first priority accomplished, M. Carey Thomas did take a more active role in the suffrage crusade, but she admitted even then: "The ballot is the symbol of a stupendous social revolution and we are frightened before it." That was in 1910. Two years later, after Miss Thomas had patiently explained to her Bryn Mawr assemblies exactly why Theodore Roosevelt and his prosuffrage Progressive Party should be preferred to Woodrow Wilson, her students still opted for Wilson by 2 to 1.

Wilson had taught briefly at Bryn Mawr in 1888, but that was before most of the undergraduates of 1912 had even been born, and their motives could not have been sentimental affection for a former professor. In any case, Wilson had left Bryn Mawr in a fit of pique, making it unpleasantly clear that he disliked teaching women and considered the job, the salary and the limited library facilities of the new college a great disappointment. His relationship to Miss Thomas had been frosty at best. She considered him arrogant, and he found her aggressive. They were careful to avoid each other as much as possible on that small campus, and a terse reference to Wilson in Carey Thomas' papers serves very nicely to illustrate their uneasy relationship. Discreetly, she avoided making any personal comment, but simply followed the name Woodrow Wilson with a line from Tennyson—"Put thy sweet hand in mine and trust in me." The quote was not one of her favorites, and she chose it because it was a perfect summation of Wilson's feelings about women in general and Carey Thomas in particular. Her students seem to have been more forgiving. Wilson was, after all, eventually to become America's peace candidate, and that might account for undergraduate loyalty to him.

Miss Thomas herself never came to terms with her own femininity, which she regarded as a most unfortunate barrier to feminism. Her ambivalence was very nearly her undoing, and its effects were to be disastrous. There is a classic anecdote that shows the depth of her confusion, and it is included, inconspicuously, in the appendix of Edith Finch's biography of her. Speaking to an English audience at the height of her career, Miss Thomas attempted to prove her theory that women could combine marriage with a profession and that the policies of Bryn Mawr were designed to encourage exactly that advanced idea. "A short time ago," she said by way of illustration, "a married woman member of the faculty of Bryn Mawr came to me and said, 'I am going to have a baby, Miss Thomas. Must I give up my position on the faculty?' And I replied, 'Not at all. Have it in the summer.' " Miss Thomas waited a moment to let the full impact of this statement reach the last rows, then added, "She had to have leave of absence because she did not have the baby in the summer. I forget why."

Other stories, however, are less amusing and have more solemn and disturbing ramifications.

Carey Thomas' relationships with male professors were never really warm, and variations of the Wilson story caused frequent rifts at Bryn Mawr. Miss Thomas would have preferred an all-female faculty, but by 1900 not many women had achieved the dazzling academic credentials she demanded. Moreover, a few token men served an ulterior purpose. Their names could be mentioned to quiet, if never really to squelch, the disturbing and persistent rumors that Bryn Mawr was something more than an ideologically feminist institution. According to Bertrand Russell, who became related to Carey Thomas by marrying her cousin Alys Pearsall Smith, the president of Bryn Mawr had "a profound contempt for the male sex," and Woodrow Wilson was but one in a long line of faculty casualties.

In the first volume of his lengthy autobiography, published in the 1950s (a tactful quarter century after Miss Thomas' death), Lord Russell devotes several frank pages to the curious Thomas ménage at Bryn Mawr, where he and his wife were uneasy houseguests while they lectured at the college. The Russells had happened to be there in 1896, during a particularly intense phase of Miss Thomas' convoluted emotional life. At Bryn Mawr, Carey Thomas shared the Deanery with Mamie Gwinn, the girlhood friend with whom she had traveled and studied in Europe. "At the time that we stayed with them," Lord Russell wrote, "their friendship had become a little ragged. Miss Gwinn used to go home to her family for three days in every fortnight, and at the exact moment of her departure each fortnight, another lady, named Miss Garrett, used to arrive, to depart again at the exact moment of Miss Gwinn's return." This traffic seemed remarkable even to the sophisticated Russells, and its implications were obvious to them. (Eventually, Mary Garrett was to replace Mamie Gwinn as co-resident of the Deanery, but that did not occur until 1904, after Mamie Gwinn had decamped forever.)

At the time of the Russells' visit, in the late 1890s, Miss Gwinn had fallen in love with a complex and Svengali-like young man named Alfred Hodder, who was then teaching philosophy at the college. Hodder had been a Harvard friend of Gertrude and Leo Stein, both of whom became privy to the succeeding intrigue. If the Hodder-Gwinn-Thomas relationship seemed extraordinary to the Russells and Steins, its effects on a small Quaker college town were mind-boggling. On the surface of things, Alfred Hodder and Mamie Gwinn were the most improbable candidates for mutual passion imaginable. At the time that he met Miss Gwinn, Hodder was solidly married and a father—a not unsolvable condition even then, but one that did tend to be more inhibiting than it has since become. Of all the female faculty members and students at Bryn Mawr, Mamie Gwinn seemed to have the least potential for an extramarital romp. Edith Finch, whose 1947 biography of Carey Thomas is both restrained and tasteful, describes Mamie Gwinn as "a curiously enigmatic figure . . . both repellent and fascinating; dark-haired, dark eyed, white skinned, tall, elegant; physically indolent, languid in movement, studied in gesture; selfish, sometimes malicious; and mentally brilliantly, subtly active"— all in all, a volatile and rather dangerous mixture. When Alfred Hodder arrived on campus, Mamie Gwinn was in her late thirties. Years before, she had explicitly renounced men and marriage forever.

According to the accounts of all who knew her or studied the art of exposition in her classes, Mamie Gwinn had such a distaste for ordinary human contact that she conducted her course in writing without ever meeting her students. There were no reports, no reading lists and no verbal discussion of the work covered. Girls who elected composition with Miss Gwinn were told to drop their prospective essay topics into a black tin box. Miss Gwinn would retrieve the suggestions, approve or reject them and then await the completed paper, which was to be delivered by the same impersonal route. Eventually the corrected essays were returned to the box with Miss Gwinn's "often scathing" comments in the margins. That was all. Theoretically, there were three hours during the week during which students might confer with her, but word quickly spread that one attempted this only at considerable peril. In the entire Bryn Mawr literature there is only one recorded and verified instance of a student's breaching Miss Gwinn's security. It appears in the Finch biography and offers a rare glimpse of this elusive personality. The intrepid undergraduate who insisted upon seeing Miss Gwinn was shown into a dark room of the Deanery, where she found her teacher apparently dozing on a couch. "How do you write an essay?" the girl is said to have asked, and after staring at the intruder in silence, "her eyes seeming to burn in her white face," Miss Gwinn "arose, moved to the desk, and taking up a sheet of foolscap, folded it down the middle. 'You write your essay here on the right hand side of the sheet, leaving the left side blank for my comments.' " Miss Gwinn was not bothered soon again.

Her associations with her colleagues on the faculty seem to

have been no more intimate. At dinners in the Deanery, while Carey Thomas entertained outside guests and members of various college departments, Miss Gwinn would sit sullenly and silently staring at her plate, all too obviously waiting with impatience for the interlopers to depart. "She made her calculated impression, always, of knowing all the answers had she chosen to give them, and of thinking the struggling conversationalists a little dull," reports Edith Finch. Nevertheless, this forbidding woman was the inexplicable choice of Alfred Hodder and more amazing still, he so enthralled *her* that she contrived to meet him clandestinely and with increasing frequency for six years before she left the Deanery and eloped with him. During this awkward period Mamie Gwinn continued to live with Carey Thomas as before and did her best to keep her escalating romance with Hodder a secret. Inevitably, however, the rumors reached Miss Thomas, and the nightly quarrels of which Bertrand Russell wrote began. The affair, he says, "roused Carey to fury, and every night, as we were going to bed, we used to hear her angry voice scolding Miss Gwinn for hours together." In 1904 Mamie Gwinn made her ultimate decision, and neither she nor Hodder ever returned to Bryn Mawr in Carey Thomas' lifetime. They went abroad, and Hodder died after they had been married only a year, "worn out from riotous living," according to Bertrand Russell, who adds by way of an epitaph, that Hodder had "a very brilliant mind and in the absence of women could talk very interestingly."

This story, as well as Miss Carey Thomas' succeeding relationships with other women, is handled with exquisite circumspection by Edith Finch in *Carey Thomas of Bryn Mawr,* but no amount of euphemism can obscure the fact that Miss Thomas was, in the preferred nineteenth-century phrase, "a Sapphist" and that college policies were dominated by a core of her intimates. In recounting the Gwinn episode, Miss Finch writes:

> . . . as the nineties wore on their attachment began to crumble. Carey Thomas's life was complicated by the bewilderment and heartache and the blows to a sensitive pride that the breaking up of personal relationships always brings. . . . Toward the end of the century, Mamie Gwinn, always an exigent partner, was becoming a disaffected one. . . . She who had hither-

to arrogantly eschewed acquaintance with any man succumbed to his [Hodder's] fascination. Mamie Gwinn, moreover, had not the courage openly to avow to Carey Thomas her new love or her complete reversal of opinion as to the ideal life of a woman.

The Finch biography confirms indirectly what Bertrand Russell was to state so boldly:

In the last years of Mamie Gwinn's life at the Deanery Mary Garrett's visits had become more frequent and extended, and not long after Mamie Gwinn's departure, she came there to live. Though Carey Thomas's imagination, perhaps, was never caught, as Mamie Gwinn had caught it, by the upright, unromantic Mary Garrett, she was genuinely touched by her justice and generosity, and more and more warmly bound by her self-effacing loyalty and cooperation.

Mary Garrett never defected, and after her death, in 1915, Carey Thomas was completely inconsolable, falling into so profound a despondency that she was unable to fulfill her obligations as president of the college. Mary Garrett had named Miss Thomas sole heir to a considerable family fortune, and this gesture only exacerbated matters. Miss Garrett's disinherited and disgruntled relatives did nothing to scotch the proliferating tales of undue influence and unnatural association, and these slurs aggravated Miss Thomas' suffering. The president of Bryn Mawr became a virtual recluse, and her incapacity inflamed the ugly speculation still further. The loss of a professional colleague, no matter how valued and indispensable, did not seem to warrant such extremes of mourning, and Carey Thomas' behavior forced even those who had never acknowledged the nature of the bond to reexamine it. Miss Finch reports that "an acquaintance, meeting [Miss Thomas] by chance in Philadelphia and stirred to sudden impatience by her melancholy aspect, remonstrated frankly that 'it was not worthy of her to sink into herself, to neglect her duties, and to go about depressing others with her grief.' " Thereafter, Miss Thomas made a tremendous effort to "carry on existence as before . . . to find her anodyne in . . . work for the college and the suffrage cause," but although she tried valiantly, she had left it too late.

By then Miss Thomas' rapport with the trustees, the faculty and the alumnae association of the college had deteriorated so drastically that a concerted movement was under way to remove her from office. It was led by the wife of a former Bryn Mawr professor, a woman who had also served as president of the alumnae association. This dual background had provided her with a formidable arsenal of information, some of it accurate and all of it titillating. Vague and unsubstantiated charges of financial chicanery and general incompatibility were trumped up against Miss Thomas, but the precipitating issue was the abrupt and perhaps unjustified dismissal in 1916 of three dissident male faculty members. One of the men had a powerful supporter in a senior professor who took the story to the city editor of an influential daily paper, the Philadelphia *Public Ledger*. A detailed account of tensions at Bryn Mawr was duly written and published, accusing Carey Thomas of "despotism and unjust dealings" with her faculty and stating that the faculty itself insisted that such despotism "be obviated by the introduction of some form of faculty government." There had been earlier instances of trouble and friction at the college and several previous occasions when disquieting rumors seemed to threaten the continued existence of the school, but nothing like the full-scale revolution that finally erupted in 1916.

The *Public Ledger* devoted its lead columns to the controversy for six weeks, soliciting and printing voluminous letters and allegations from any and all interested parties. None of the published material was favorable to Miss Thomas, though a staff member at the *Ledger* office did admit later that some of the mail had actually been supportive of her. The tone of the editorials and commentaries soon degenerated into a vituperative personal attack on the character of the president, and although the faculty eventually gained the greater autonomy it desired, the college was nearly destroyed in the process. Decentralization of power had been the ostensible issue and a perfectly valid one, but it was, of course, merely a respectable and convenient front for the situation that had caused the furor in the first place. By the time the Philadelphia *Public Ledger* had exposed correspondence from dismissed instructors, resentful alumnae and shocked trustees, there were few secrets left, and the reputation of the college was badly battered. Miss Thomas emerged from the impeachment ordeal victorious but not wholly vindicated: still president of Bryn Mawr but harrowed and vulnerable.

In later years she became somewhat more discreet in the conduct of her personal life and slightly less autocratic in her dealings with the professors, but the restoration never achieved the perfection of the inviolate original. The gossip about Miss Thomas was diffused, but it never really died.

A childhood injury had left her permanently lame, and her pain increased with age. She grew increasingly dependent on Cannabis, using it as an analgesic in the form of silver covered pills. She carried a large supply with her wherever she traveled and took it frequently and often publicly. Though the drug was not then illegal, her use of it did not go unnoticed. One way and another the president of Bryn Mawr managed to excite comment and controversy throughout her remarkable career.

After her retirement, in 1934, Miss Thomas abandoned the faint pretenses she had adopted while in office. Toward the end of her life she lived and traveled with Edith Lowber, a Bryn Mawr protégée twenty-one years her junior. Carey Thomas was to outlive Edith Lowber, too, a loss that seemed to drain the last of her waning resiliency. At the age of sixty-five she began to write both a history of the college and her autobiography, but neither project was ever finished. The history was arduous, and the autobiography proved impossible. After many false starts she destroyed most of her personal papers. Hers was simply not a story that could be honestly told in her lifetime, and she was, above all, a supremely honest woman. The Finch biography, assembled in the late 1940s from the shreds and scraps that Miss Thomas had left and fleshed out by interviews with those who had known her, is conscientious, but so wary as to be opaque.

Some very explicit references to the difficult and anguished emotional lives of the Thomas clique do crop up elsewhere, and one of the most lucid accounts of the story was done by Gertrude Stein, in an early prose style she soon rejected. As a medical student at Johns Hopkins after her graduation from Radcliffe, Gertrude Stein lived in Baltimore and was inevitably drawn into Carey Thomas' circle of special friends. Miss Stein became so intrigued by the tales of their intellectual and amorous entanglements that she wrote a *roman à clef* about Carey Thomas, Mamie Gwinn and Alfred Hodder, changing their names, but leaving no doubt about the identity of the college in question.

The book was called *Fernhurst,* a name taken from the town in Sussex, England, where Carey Thomas spent summer holidays. Gertrude Stein and her brother, Leo, had visited the English village of Fernhurst in 1902, as guests of Bernard Berenson and his wife, Mary. Mary Berenson, like Alys Russell, was also a cousin of Carey Thomas, and the triangular love affair was the talk of that household during the Stein's stay. Knowing Alfred Hodder and already obsessed with the subject of lesbian attachments, Gertrude Stein found the material irresistible. *Fernhurst* was completed in 1904 but not published until the 1950s, when a collection of forgotten Stein manuscripts was brought out by Liveright under the title *Fernhurst, Q.E.D. and Other Early Writings by Gertrude Stein.* (*Q.E.D.* was the very first work, and also deals with a homosexual love affair, but that one was Miss Stein's own.)

Fernhurst was obviously based on the stories circulating about Bryn Mawr, and the allusions are unmistakable. "The dean of Fernhurst is hard-headed, practical, unmoral in the sense that all values give place to expediency and she has a pure enthusiasm for the emancipation of women and a sensitive and mystic feeling for beauty and letters," Gertrude Stein wrote. It was a naïve book, but utterly straightforward. Hodder's name in the novel is changed to "Philip Redfern," and the editor of the Liveright edition, Leon Katz, suggests strongly that though the circumstances are Alfred Hodder's, the character himself is made to resemble Woodrow Wilson. It's a reasonable supposition, though the story is complicated enough without it. All of Carey Thomas' conflicts with male professors had certain points in common. Gertrude Stein's thinly fictionalized version follows fact closely until the very end. In *Fernhurst,* "Janet Bruce," the Mamie Gwinn character, does *not* elope with Hodder-Redfern. Instead, she returns chastened and forgiven to the Deanery, and "Fernhurst was itself again and the two very

140

interesting personalities in the place were the dean Miss Thornton with her friend Miss Bruce in their very same place." That was a happier ending and clearly the one that Miss Stein desired.

After completing the book, Gertrude Stein tucked it away, but whether she was dissatisfied with it as a work of art or reluctant to circulate it for other reasons has never been explained. The episode continued to fascinate her, and she could not bear to waste it. Five years later she changed all the names again and incorporated the same strange tale into her long novel *The Making of Americans.* By then Gertrude Stein had achieved her mature literary style, and she told the Fernhurst tale twice over—once as originally written and a second time in her new and repetitious manner. It was, she said, "a lovely story."

Though the most conspicuous, Carey Thomas was not the only member of her family to attract literary attention. Her sister, Helen Thomas, also inadvertently found her way into a Stein novel. In *Q.E.D.,* her first book, Gertrude Stein uses the name Helen Thomas to represent the object of her *own* affections. In this book, as in *Fernhurst,* the homosexual theme is awkwardly but openly handled. (*Q.E.D.,* when it finally surfaced in the 1950s appeared with the names of all the original main characters revised. Its author had heedlessly borrowed those of her actual Baltimore friends and acquaintances, and since some of the people concerned were still alive at that time, the alterations seemed necessary for both legal and humane reasons.) The *real* Helen Thomas, Carey's younger sister, had married Dr. Simon Flexner in 1903, the year *Q.E.D.* was first written. Before that wedding, Helen Thomas had been the inseparable friend of Lucy Donnelly, who was a professor at Bryn Mawr and a woman who would always figure importantly in Carey Thomas' life. When Helen Thomas married Dr. Flexner, Lucy Donnelly wrote in her despair to Bertrand Russell, who had met all the women involved during his stint as a lecturer at Bryn Mawr. Bertrand Russell's tender letters of consolation and advice to Lucy Donnelly, referring explicitly to Helen Thomas, appear in the first volume of Russell's autobiography, along with his memories of Carey Thomas' famous affair. Of all the Americans he met during his travels in the United States, Russell was to remain fascinated by the curious Thomas clan for half a century, and no wonder. They were a thoroughly remarkable lot.

Passionate relationships between women, particularly those with advanced political ideas and great intellectual ambitions, were usual in that era and seem to have been accepted as a matter of course. It was a tolerance based on naïveté rather than on full understanding, but it protected a great many people and permitted them considerable freedom. Since women were generally viewed as a sexually deficient species, virtually neuter until "awakened" by a man, the most intense female associations could elude suspicion almost indefinitely. Men were thought to have base instincts and animal passions, but good women were presumed "above all that," at least until obliged by circumstances to perform their conjugal duties. Repugnance for the sexual act was expected to increase with the fineness of the female clay, and college women, as the most rarefied of the species, were regarded as almost immune to desire. Bryn Mawr, founded expressly for the advanced education of "young women of the higher classes," was perhaps even more special than other colleges which modestly addressed themselves to turning out parsons' wives and frontier schoolteachers. In all cases, however, girls left to themselves were thought to be devoid of libido, and their devotion to one another, no matter how extravagant, was seen as an example of purity and idealism.

This versatile theory could be used as an argument *for* separate education or *against* it. Those who believed in the segregation of the sexes insisted that learning succeeded best with no rude distractions; those who opposed it were able to fall back upon the "race suicide" theory, pointing to the low marriage statistics for college women and prophesying that the future mothers of America would eventually be drawn entirely from "the lower orders of society." The rumors about Bryn Mawr kept these notions alive long after they might have withered of malnutrition. In fact, many of the nineteenth- and early twentieth-century women involved as students or suffragists in what now seem patently lesbian relationships eventually did marry, and led very conventional lives thereafter. This was certainly true of several in Carey Thomas' immediate circle, the group that Gertrude Stein found so congenial during her Baltimore years. The situation was not unique in those days of women's struggle for the vote, for a place in the arts and sciences and for the redress of social injustice, but in most cases the affairs seem to have gone unrecorded, unpublicized and perhaps unrecognized. The Sapphist phenomenon may be a natural concomitant of the women's movement, and the fact that the crusaders of the 1970s are now completely free to discuss the subject has not made it any easier to manage or control. The opponents of change in the status of women have always had this particular weapon and have rarely hesitated to use it. Moreover, allegations of lesbianism have lost very little of their historical power to alienate the public and fragment support for fundamentally decent and honorable causes. The activists take the risks; the rest scurry for cover and enjoy the benefits. It's not a pretty picture, and it never was.

XIV
Rarely Debs and Never Proles

DURING the first three decades of the college's existence Bryn Mawr students, like their contemporaries elsewhere, apparently agreed that advocacy of suffrage would do little to advance either their careers or their chances of marriage. Opportunities in both areas continued to be sadly limited, and the spinster explosion hadn't abated.

The majority of women were still becoming teachers, and of all professions teaching is the most hostile to nonconformists or agitators. That fact alone explains much of the undergraduate indifference to suffrage, though it doesn't take up all the slack. Part of the difficulty seems to have been that the women's rights movement found its greatest strength among two segments of society that were not yet attending college: the upper class and the working class. College students at the turn of the century were rarely debs and never proles, but solidly bourgeoise, girls from what Mary Lyon had called the "middle walks of life." They were the daughters of parsons and doctors, missionaries, merchants and reasonably prosperous farmers. It was a homogeneous group, unleavened by many volatile elements. Women like Mrs. Astor, Mrs. Vanderbilt and Mrs. Belmont had the leisure and unassailable social position that permitted them to engage in suffrage activities with impunity; trade union crusaders like Rose Schneiderman, who had spent her youth in a Lower East Side sweatshop, had nothing to lose and everything to gain. To the few thousand girls in college in the early 1900s, however, the cause offered a few delights or rewards that seemed worth the risk. Only the most visionary could possibly have succeeded in identifying either with the likes of Mrs. Astor or such exotics as Rose Schneiderman of the Cap Makers Union, Clara Silver of the Buttonhole workers or Mary Duffy of the Overall Makers. That war was being fought on another front.

There were, however, a few students, like the fabulous Inez Milholland of Vassar, who were sufficiently committed to make a career of the struggle. Miss Milholland's involvement, like Harriot Stanton's, began at home. The movement tended to be dynastic, and suffrage leadership usually ran in families. Unless one had a sister or mother on the barricades, it was difficult to keep the faith at college. The Milhollands, though not as single-minded in their devotion to the cause as the Stantons, were supportive and supplied Inez with bulletins and progress reports throughout her college career. When they informed her that Harriot Stanton, then Mrs. Blatch, was touring New York with a small group of suffragists, Inez Milholland invited them to come to Vassar. The president in 1908 was the venerable James Monroe Taylor, the last of the Baptist clergymen to head the college and no great friend of the activists. He refused permission for any such gathering, though he must have known that both Mrs. Blatch and the economist Helen Hoy were Vassar alumnae.

Inez Milholland defied him and risked expulsion by holding the meeting anyway, selecting a nearby cemetery as both neutral and hallowed ground. It was an imaginative solution since Dr. Taylor would hardly have cared to cause a commotion among the headstones. Forty daring students attended and heard Harriot Blatch, Charlotte Perkins Gilman and Rose Schneiderman explain why college women should give more of themselves to the battle. Mrs. Blatch had brought a large yellow banner which said, COME LET US REASON TOGETHER, and she kept it aloft throughout the meeting, a gesture intended to reassure any passersby that the gathering was not intended to be surreptitious. Fortunately, there were no mourners that day, although there were apparently a few reporters assigned to follow the campaign trail wherever it led. The following morning the New York *America* headlined the event in large type, SUFFRAGISTS INVADE VASSAR. HOW RUDE! and campus interest picked up considerably. The next year several dozen Vassar girls and a few Barnard students (Annie Nathan Meyer was appalled) volunteered to serve as ushers when Mrs. Pankhurst, the leader of the English suffrage group, spoke to standing room only at Carnegie Hall.

Inez Milholland, '09, rode on to even greater fame and glory, and her name was never out of the papers for long. She set the all-time record for elegance under fire by leading parades seated on a large white horse, dressed in a white broadcloth suit, white boots, a pale-blue cloak and a dramatically plumed hat, and at the time of her premature death in 1916, she was considered Vassar's great martyr to the cause. Neither Harriot Stanton Blatch nor Maud Wood Park of Radcliffe, both of whom eventually contributed a great deal more, ever captured the public imagination the same extent. Perhaps because of the charismatic Inez, Vassar acquired the most impressive activist reputation, and by 1911 more than 57 percent of the seniors had declared themselves in favor of suffrage. By default, Poughkeepsie had become the best place to be radicalized, though the efforts of the newly formed College Equal Suffrage League did excite considerable interest at the other campuses. Mount Holyoke promptly formed a chapter, and when the league tried to hold a debate on the issue, there was suddenly no one left to speak for the opposition. (A Wellesley team, led by Alice Vant George, '87, secretary of the Massachusetts *Anti-*Suffragette Association, would have been a logical answer, but the organizers didn't ask.) In May, 1912, twenty-five Mount Holyoke students and five faculty members marched in the Boston suffrage parade, and the college paper reported that Mount Holyoke was the only college to be officially and distinctly represented in the procession. "Officially and distinctly," however, were the operative words. Holyoke merely had its own banner, but that was an encouraging sign that a delayed détente between the educators and the suffrage movement had finally taken place. By the time of the Philadelphia parade in 1915, all the women's colleges were represented, and Wellesley's contingent was one of the largest.

As marchers in the suffrage parades the students could briefly imagine themselves emancipated twentieth-century women, but once they folded their flags and returned to the campuses, they reentered a time warp. There had been extensive and gratifying changes in the curricula since the early days of required Latin orations and mandatory church history, but socially the rules and regulations remained almost medieval. By 1900 or so the lady principals were no longer monitoring letters and checking hem lengths, but a surprising number of quaint restrictions were still in force.

146

Descriptions of college life written during the last years of the
nineteenth century were still all too valid ten years later. A long
and detailed article in the May, 1898, issue of *Scribner's Magazine* by Abbe Carter Goodloe, then a Wellesley undergraduate,
offers some rare insights into the paradoxes of the time and the
traditions that developed around them. Though mixed dancing was not allowed at Wellesley, the girls were permitted to
dress as men at formal all-girl parties, and Miss Goodloe's comments seem untouched by either irony or dismay. "The cotil-
lions in the gymnasium, where half the young girls impersonate
their own brothers, are celebrated for their entire success and
brilliancy," she wrote, adding in perfect innocence that "there
has never been a time in the history of the college where students have not shown both special aptitude and great inclination to amuse themselves, and never more so than at present."
These curious charades apparently had to suffice until the epochal senior prom of 1913, several long years after all the other
colleges had capitulated to petitions for ballroom dances with
men. Luckily, the custom of masquerading in white tie and tails
never spread beyond Wellesley. Though all-girl dances were
also held elsewhere during the nineties, the other colleges
seemed to frown upon the added fillip of male costumes.

Scribner's Magazine, perhaps in response to bewildered inquiries, promptly followed the Wellesley article with one by a
Smith student, Alice Fallows. That appeared in July, 1898, and
covered nearly as much ground as the first one. After proudly
listing the available courses and the wide range of sports and
club activities, which by then included golf, bicycling, long
walks and "dreamy rows on Paradise Pond," skating, snowshoe-
ing, tennis and basketball, Miss Fallows eventually told the public what it wanted most to know. "Smith dances," she said, present "a spectacle peculiar to the college. From the gallery it
looks like a butterfly ball. Not a single black-clad man mars the
effect, but the floor is filled with girls in delicately tinted evening dresses, weaving the figures of the mazy waltz or following
an unaccustomed partner through the intricacies of the two-
step." This short but informative series caused no perceptive
rise in applications to the women's colleges.

At Vassar, where approved young men were admitted to the
annual promenades during this era, a string orchestra played
while the girls and their escorts walked in time down the Hall of

Casts and back to a common room for lemonade and cookies. Mount Holyoke took extra precautions of providing students and their guests with cards listing appropriate topics of conversation for the strained intervals between parades, and shy couples, stuck for opening gambits, could choose from a printed list that included "Truth," "Friendship," "Progress," "Space" and other topics of general interest. For inexplicable reasons, "sports," "weather" and "studies" were not recommended. Either they were thought suggestive, or it was assumed that anyone needing help would have already exhausted them.

Mixed parties helped weaken the influence of the secret societies that had flourished at the colleges for several decades without attracting much official notice. At first, these clubs had existed mainly to flout the more exasperating rules, when a dozen or so of the more irrepressible spirits would gather to picnic on illicit delicacies, gulp a few tentative sips of wine and perhaps puff cautiously at a Turkish cigarette. These little frolics were tolerated by hidebound administrators who considered them the lesser of two evils—encounters with young men being the greater. They actually served a useful purpose, taking some of the edge off the oppressively holy atmosphere that still prevailed on the campuses.

By 1900 or so, however, the secret societies had acquired most of the less agreeable attributes of sororityhood, and the officials could no longer discount them. Girls not selected for membership were made to feel miserably excluded, and the panoply of initiations, rituals, meetings, Greek letters and dues caused deepening rifts among the student community, creating a climate totally contrary to the Great Ideals that all seven colleges shared. Some of these clubs were ostensibly literary or artistic, but essentially the groups were social, and the elect tended to be the debs of the class rather than the intellectuals. The clubs that actually lived up to their higher purposes were even more insidious. They monopolized the publications, the pageants, the plays and other extracurricular activities, and not always with the best aesthetic results. Student life at Smith was virtually run by an infrastructure of these organizations, and Mount Holyoke, despite its reputation for high principles and plain living, had five powerful secret societies in 1902, each with about thirty members.

Even the most optimistic administrators were eventually forced to acknowledge that the secret organizations were no longer limiting their activities to the post-curfew munching of sardines and biscuits and that something would have to be done to prevent total dissolution of college spirit and morale. There was not yet a Seven College Conference to consider such matters, but President Mary Woolley of Mount Holyoke abolished the clubs there by fiat in 1910. Secret societies, however, continued to flourish at Smith until 1940, when two of the larger groups—Orangemen and A.O.H.—grudgingly and finally agreed to phase themselves out. Even then, however, there was a sizable group of members who mourned their clubs as casualties of the Second World War. "Are secret societies necessary?" asked one sentimental and wistful member in a 1940 article in the Smith paper. "Probably not. Neither are hair ribbons, but those of us who wear them would feel put upon if the college forbade us to appear in them. In this vale of tears, it seems unnecessary to carry the reform spirit so far that one begins abolishing anything so innocuous." But the defenders steadily lost ground, and the veiled photos of members that had given the Smith yearbooks a curious and titillating distinction vanished along with the other overt demonstrations of girlish exclusivity. The secret society phase of college history tends to be glossed over by historians as an embarrassment that few care to recall, and those who were privy to the mysteries have guarded them carefully.

XV
Over Here

THE outbreak of the world war helped liberate students from some of the more oppressive anachronisms, but significant vestiges of the old order did linger. At Wellesley, war brides were allowed to finish their courses, but they were not permitted to live in dormitories after the wedding ceremony. Their soldier husbands might be 3,000 miles away with the AEF, but it was still thought inadvisable to mix matrons with maidens in the same residence halls. That quirky rule was followed at the other colleges as well, by an informal but general agreement. After attending their lectures and handing in their assignments, the brides went meekly into the exile of off-campus furnished rooms. This compromise was decided upon in order to preserve the innocence of virgin classmates. As soon as the war was over, the married women were politely asked to apply elsewhere. They had presented an unusual and delicate problem, and it was tacitly agreed that they could best be accommodated at other sorts of institutions. (To be fair, it should be added that the men's colleges also preferred bachelor undergraduates, though the same reason could hardly have applied.) This rule was to remain more or less in force until the Second World War, though after that, it was almost impossible to legislate a return to celibacy, and the colleges and universities reluctantly abandoned the attempt.

When the United States formally entered the first war, students and faculty at the Seven Sister schools unanimously pledged themselves "to prepare . . . physically, mentally and so far as possible, specifically for usefulness." At Mount Holyoke and Wellesley, the physical preparation at first consisted of afternoon military drills, supervised by gym teachers, who suddenly found themselves transformed into platoon leaders. The regiments quickly became so proficient at parade that they were soon attracting an audience of townspeople for every muster. They were an impressive and reassuring sight, but not quite as "useful" as they had hoped to be, and a more practical outlet for patriotic energies soon took the place of the drill teams.

At Mount Holyoke, 600 girls set a splendid example by volunteering to work on a six-acre farm every week for the duration of the war. At the first turnout the little pasture was so jammed with eager farmerettes that the crew was cut to 400 and the amount of land doubled to twelve acres. The planters still tended to collide as they hoed and weeded their rows, but the farm returned a profit of $64.70. Delighted by this success, the college turned twenty-eight acres over to the girls. The disappointed were invited back, and with twenty-two hands per acre, Mount Holyoke produced 2,000 bushels of potatoes, enough to keep itself in carbohydrates all winter long. After that, students branched out into canning fruits and vegetables, doing so well that the farm had to be continued after the Armistice in order to use up all the seeds, fertilizer and extra mason jars. At Wellesley, enthusiasm for war farming reached such heights that intramural tomato and potato picking contests all but replaced every other diversion. Their twenty-acre field was so well managed that the college was chosen as a training camp for the Women's Land Army of America. Vassar's agricultural record was just as brilliant. There the girls not only grew vegetables, but helped with the college livestock. Academic life acquired a whole new dimension during this period. The milking lessons, given by a professional dairyman, were described in a surviving notebook as "just like learning to play the piano."

Unwilling to be outplanted by country cousins only because they couldn't dig up Riverside Drive, Barnard acquired acreage in Westchester County and permitted students to commute to it from New York. The city girls became so proficient that farmers in the vicinity, most of whom had stopped by to jeer, stayed on to offer the crews $1.20 a day as hired hands. Whole teams signed up, though after paying for their room and board, they had very little left but their suntans and the knowledge that every callus made the world a little safer for democracy.

Barnard also made another and perhaps more prophetic contribution. From their vantage point above the Hudson, students were in an ideal position to observe the troopships docked in the river and the clumps of lonely servicemen wandering beneath the campus, so near and yet so far. After considerable persuasion, the administration agreed to remodel an elderly boathouse for use as a canteen, and Barnard girls had a rather lovely war, entertaining the officers and reveling in a freedom that hadn't yet arrived on the Sister campuses.

Popular as these various projects were, they represented a relatively minor part of the total war effort, and the other achievements were more impressive, if somewhat less amusing. Students and alumnae volunteered as nurses and ambulance drivers, and hundreds of them went to Europe with the Red Cross, the Salvation Army and other relief organizations. The colleges promptly instituted courses in "vocational" subjects like typing, dietetics, telegraphy, first aid and bookkeeping, so that women might fill essential jobs left vacant by soldiers. By Armistice Day each of the women's colleges had its veterans, many of whom had served with considerable distinction. Faculty members, alumnae and undergraduates had responded in astonishingly large numbers, and for many of them, the war had provided an abrupt exposure to a world that the cloistered campuses had kept at bay.

When the colleges reassembled in the aftermath, it seemed certain that their nineteenth century, which had already lasted for 120 years, was finally and irrevocably over.

XVI
On Those Terms . . .

THOUGH the women's colleges changed tremendously during the half century that preceded the War to End War, most of the alterations were noncontroversial, the sort of physical improvement and curricular expansion that almost everyone could approve. Radcliffe had gradually emerged from the shadows by acquiring some essential real estate—the self-contained "acre for education" that provided students with the basic amenities of a residential college. At first the campus was hardly more than a dormitory, a few classroom buildings and some underequipped laboratories, but it seemed sheer luxury in comparison to the series of rented rooms in which the girls had been receiving visits by Harvard professors. During that phase, students had sometimes felt rather more like demimondaines than respectable women scholars. For several years Harvard had quietly been extending its course offerings to women, though there was still a tough and woody core of professors who remained aloof from the whole endeavor. Even those who accepted the "Radcliffe markup" and willingly taught the ladies preferred to repeat their lectures rather than have the sacrosanct paving of the Yard swept by petticoats. The illusion of an all-male college was carefully preserved, and Radcliffe students, always sensitive to the precariousness of their position, voluntarily agreed neither to enter the Yard nor to cross the square. At commencement in 1886 Mrs. Agassiz reminded them, "We had nothing to offer you except the education which Harvard provides," and for several decades, that was to suffice.

In 1899, after the Annex had been operating for almost twenty years and had acquired both a name and an enviable reputation, Professor Barrett Wendell of the Harvard English Department warned his colleagues against lowering the barriers any further. Harvard, he wrote, could "suddenly find itself committed to coeducation somewhat as unwary men lay themselves open to actions for breach of promise," an analogy that may have occurred to him as he watched members of his staff rush off to their Radcliffe assignations. Harvard's atmosphere, he maintained, should remain "purely virile," and he saw a real "danger of infatuation" threatening the faculty. It was, of course, the more junior men who were tempted by the extra income that Radcliffe offered, and they would naturally be most susceptible to the charms of the ladies. More venerable professors and those with private incomes were relatively safe, though by no means immune.

Radcliffe students didn't really achieve unrestricted access to Harvard classrooms until 1943, when teaching them abruptly ceased to be a personal option and became a wartime necessity. So many Harvard professors had been called up that there were no spares for Radcliffe. The only solution was to permit the girls to hear the remaining faculty on its home ground. They filled the empty chairs until the veterans returned, and by then they were too firmly entrenched ever to be dislodged. After that, eluding the ladies became somewhat harder, but it isn't completely impossible even now for anyone clever enough to be appointed to Harvard in the first place. The university has always provided a choice of legitimate and traditional excuses: "by invitation of the professor," "open to upperclassmen with the necessary prerequisites," "given only in alternate years" and that reliable workhorse "enrollment limited."

Men determined to keep their purlieus "purely virile" have in past years rarely had much trouble. The late great Bliss Perry, for instance, never had a Radcliffe girl in class, explaining, "There were always more Harvard applicants for work in English than we could handle effectively." Professor Copeland refused to give his famous Argument course to Radcliffe girls, explaining that it would be "deplorable" for women to become apt in argument: "We can't obliterate a natural tendency, but why cultivate it?" Barrett Wendell made no concessions, and lectured as profanely to his girl's classes as he did to the men. It may have been his way of guaranteeing that there would be no dilution of "virility," as well as preventing the infatuation that he feared. These and other vignettes of the titans appear in an essay written for the *Radcliffe Quarterly* in 1933 by Grace Hollingsworth Tucker, '03, and rather grandly titled "The Gods

154

Serve Hebe." Mrs. Tucker remembers those years most fondly, from the "philosophical hunger that should not be appeased" inspired by Josiah Royce, right down to the "moral stability we gained from gymnasium bloomers."

The original Radcliffe faculty was composed entirely of volunteers—hired mercenaries or liberal humanitarians, depending on one's point of view. Fortunately, there were always enough such men to provide the women's college with all the fundamentals and many of the glories from the Catalogue of Catalogues. Radcliffe shared George Lyman Kittredge, Charles Townsend Copeland, Chester Noyes Greenough and John L. Lowes of the English Department; Samuel Eliot Morison, Edward Channing, Arthur M. Schlesinger, Sr., and Charles H. Haskins in history; E. K. Rand in Classics; Alfred North Whitehead and Josiah Royce in philosophy; James B. Conant in chemistry; Earnest A. Hooton in anthropology; Harlow Shapley in astronomy; and most of the other giants.

There were a few capricious deprivations, but in general, Radcliffe received full value. The Olympians who taught inevitably attracted some extraordinary students, and Radcliffe somehow managed to accommodate them. Gertrude Stein, for instance, wrote in the *Autobiography of Alice B. Toklas* that "she had a very good time. The important person in Gertrude Stein's Radcliffe life was William James. She enjoyed her life and herself. She was the secretary of the philosophical club and amused herself with all sorts of people . . . she liked it all. But the really lasting impression of her Radcliffe life came through William James." Gertrude Stein was class of '97. Helen Keller, perhaps Radcliffe's best-known alumna, graduated in 1904, and her association with the college is so celebrated that it is something of a surprise to discover that the dean of Radcliffe, Agnes Irwin, had attempted to persuade Miss Keller and Annie Sullivan to attend Wellesley instead, feeling that the protected atmosphere there would make the many necessary adjustments easier. Eventually Helen Keller's pleas so moved the dean that she relented, but the unusual circumstances worried her until Miss Keller's triumphant graduation.

Harvard's ambivalence to Radcliffe persisted long after the students had demonstrated their intellectual competence and really had very little to do with it. A small part of the uneasiness may have been a sentimental desire to keep things as they were, but there is a chilly rationale that explains why full integration was so slow in arriving. "Radcliffe had no money worth mentioning," wrote Dr. Le Baron Russell Briggs, who served as president of the college until 1923. "Her unrestricted income from investments was between seventeen and eighteen thousand dollars a year. She had nothing to offer Harvard but girls, which Harvard did not want." Dr. Briggs was tactful. Harvard might have felt differently about *rich* girls, though there's no way to be sure. Now that Radcliffe has all but melted into Harvard and every facility is open to women, it seems bizarre that as late as 1948 the eminent professor of English constitutional history Dr. Helen Cam was instructed to sit behind a screen at morning chapel services. All other women in the Harvard community had apparently accepted this restriction as a small price to pay for being There. Dr. Cam, however, astonished the college community by refusing to be kept in purdah and succeeded in having the screen removed. It has never reappeared. The impact of this victory was pyrrhic even then since both Radcliffe and Harvard students have lost the habit of attending chapel, but it was regarded as crucial nevertheless.

Barnard students endured in much the same sort of limbo, though they were even easier to ignore. From 1889 to 1898 the entire college was crammed into the brownstone at 343 Madison Avenue. There were fourteen freshmen in the original class, exactly the same mystic number that had turned up for Smith's first year. Barnard, however, was soon augmented by twenty-two special science students who were not candidates for the degree, and all thirty-six were packed into the extremely cramped space, which was reduced even more by the necessity of leaving two fourth-floor rooms for the use of the landlord. The spacious second-floor front was leased to the new Women's University Club. With an annual operating budget of only $7,500, Barnard could not afford to lose any chance for extra income. The secretary of the college, Miss Elisabeth Abbot, and the dean, Miss Ella Weed, each needed an office, and these ladies settled for quarters so tiny that they were virtually closets. Every cubic foot counted, and paying tenants had first choice. There was a large dark basement in the house, but that was occupied by the janitress, Mrs. Kelly, who also functioned as cook

156

and chaperone, providing soup, sandwiches and moral supervision. "Let any girl linger unduly for an afternoon conference with some attractive young instructor," wrote an alumna quoted in *Barnard College, the First Years,* "and Mrs. Kelly was likely to be found standing on the stairs, expressing disapproval in every line of her solid figure." It was Mrs. Kelly who defined "unduly," not the faculty member or the student. Barnard's apartment—no one could call it a campus—would have been claustrophobic for a single family, and in what might have been an ingenious space-saving effort, the college engaged a thirteen-year-old boy as doorman and general factotum. He took up the least amount of room possible, much less than any grown man, and made a proportionately smaller dent in the budget.

At the beginning only six subjects were offered: Latin, mathematics, Greek, English and a choice of French or German. All these disciplines could be pursued with minimal equipment. Within a year, however, the number of courses and instructors was rashly doubled. A nearby flat was rented, and botany and chemistry laboratories were somewhat surreptitiously installed. Students in these apartment-departments soon learned to be most circumspect about discussing their work and even more careful about performing experiments, especially those that involved volatile mixtures. The botanists managed nicely, but the chemists were seriously restricted and obliged to concentrate almost entirely on theory. That same autumn the Columbia faculty of philosophy finally allowed women graduate students to audit its courses. They were not graded for their work, but they were permitted to listen before taking the examination. This attendance dispensation, limited as it was, seemed generous. While the students still had no way of knowing how they were doing in comparison to the men, they at least were familiar with the material covered in class. By Barnard's fourth year Columbia extended classroom privileges to women seniors, and Barnard jubilantly declared itself a full-fledged college, though still a rather impoverished one.

The entire endowment was $2,000, augmented by a $5,000 "foundership" given by J. Pierpont Morgan. The banker Jacob Schiff, who had been serving as treasurer to the financially shaky venture, resigned, stating regretfully in his letter that he

felt it "undignified to carry on an educational institute of such
high aims by begging from door to door, and I can see the time
coming in the near future when even this device will no longer
avail." Columbia itself, quite flush and prosperous in the 1890s,
was planning to move from Forty-ninth Street to the new
Morningside Heights campus, and it was inevitable that Barnard would either have to find the funds to follow or perish.
Mr. Schiff was known to prefer more solidly based investments,
and his resignation was regarded as ominous.

After considerable persuasion, Mr. George A. Plimpton,
then a young Barnard trustee, agreed to serve as treasurer of
the college's minuscule assets and lost no time in initiating an
intense campaign. By the end of 1893 he had charmed Mrs.
Van Wyck Brinckerhoff into offering $100,000 for a new build-
ing on condition that an appropriate site would be found at
Morningside Heights. Mr. Plimpton quickly assembled an acre
at Broadway and 119th Street, and within three years the board
had raised enough money to buy it. The price was $160,000,
and the transaction offers a splendid lesson in the advantages of
locating colleges in remote and inaccessible New England villages. This sophisticated real estate deal, however, impressed
and reassured Columbia enough so that the university officially
recognized Barnard and lent its power and prestige to supervis-
ing all instruction and examination at the women's college.

The back street days seemed over, though Barnard continued to be a poor relation, more like a second cousin once removed than a sister institution. Moreover, undergraduates still
occasionally found themselves in serious difficulties at the Columbia examinations. Those who had university instructors did
creditably, but girls who took analogous courses from Barnard
faculty members never knew when they might be tested on
completely unfamiliar material, just as Miss Nathan had been
years before. Columbia professors could not always be relied on
to share their syllabi with their Barnard colleagues, and even
those who did often digressed from their outlines.

After enough A students at Barnard had flunked finals that
were based on such digressions, Miss Emily James Smith, Barnard's young and attractive dean, succeeded in cajoling Columbia into a fairer method. Not only were Barnard faculty
members to be told exactly what their counterparts at Columbia

were doing, but the teaching schedules would be drafted coop-
eratively. Until then Columbia had made what was virtually a
master schedule and Barnard had been obliged to coax the
professors to teach in their off-hours. It was a rather lopsided
plan and one that resulted in truncated classes and serious
course conflicts for the women.

Matters improved greatly as soon as Barnard moved to
Morningside Heights. The two new classroom buildings were
much more convenient for the lend-lease faculty, who no longer felt they had to teach with one eye on the clock and their
hats in hand. With these facilities to serve as a sort of psychological collateral, money was raised for a dormitory to house almost a hundred girls. That meant that the college could accept
students from outside the city and move beyond the limitations
of a day school.

Edna St. Vincent Millay attended Barnard before going to
Vassar and liked it so much that she wished she had stayed.
There was, she felt, no comparison between the relative freedom of New York City and the "Alice in Wonderland" atmosphere of Poughkeepsie, which she found exactly like an orphanage. "Every morning when I awake," she wrote in helpless
rage to Arthur Ficke in 1914, "I swear I say damn this pink and
gray college. . . . It *isn't* on the Hudson. They lied to me. Every path in Poughkeepsie ends in a heap of cans and rubbish."
When she entered Vassar at the age of twenty-one, Edna St.
Vincent Millay was already a published poet and a veteran of an
independent season in Greenwich Village, at that time the very
synonym for bohemian nonconformity. Millay must have been
the first person—and perhaps the only one—ever to go *from* the
Village *to* Vassar, though eager hordes of alumnae were to reverse the order. If Vassar's still Victorian rules and regulations
often seemed anachronistic and intolerable to independent sev-
enteen-year-olds, they were absolute anathema to Miss Millay
and drove her to frequent tantrums and deliberate outrages.

After her first appalled year, however, she actually came to
enjoy the college, writing and acting in her own plays, basking
in the awed admiration of her dazzled classmates and delight-
ing almost as much in the discomfiture of the faculty. Henry
Noble MacCracken, Vassar's young and progressive president,
seems to have been willing to make occasional exceptions where

Miss Millay was concerned, loosening some of the rigid course requirements and even allowing her a few extra measures of personal freedom. Urged to expel her by the more conservative faculty, he is reported to have said, "I know all about poets at college, and I don't want a banished Shelley on my doorstep." Jean Gould, in her recent biography *The Poet and Her Book,* says that Edna St. Vincent Millay's answer was: "On those terms, I think I can continue to live in this hell-hole."

The limits were stretched, but even a celebrated poet could push Vassar just so far, and when Millay took an unauthorized overnight trip shortly before graduation, lunching in a nearby inn and deliberately signing her name under that of a man in the hotel's guest book, the college found itself with a perfect excuse to bar her from commencement. The more reactionary elements had waited for four years for such an opportunity, and they made the most of it. Although Edna St. Vincent Millay had written a major part of the commencement exercises and was to be the star of the program, it was decided that she could not be allowed to appear on the campus ever again. Her diploma would be mailed to her in exile—"like a codfish" in her own phrase. All she had done at the inn was have a ladylike lunch with two other girls, but the faculty chose to believe otherwise.

Vassar's adamancy aroused one of the first recorded cases of real student rebellion at a women's college, and a sizable portion of the class petitioned to have their heroine reinstated. Though the obvious idea of boycotting graduation did not seem to have occurred to them (it was only 1917, and the era of nonnegotiable demands had not dawned), the petitions and letters were effective enough. On the night before commencement Miss Millay was finally and grudgingly given permission to appear at the ceremony. MacCracken had interceded, jeopardizing his own position by doing so. "I was ashamed not to have acted earlier," he admitted long afterward, "for there were few students who had done more for their college than this young poet." And he was right. Edna St. Vincent Millay shed reflected fame on Vassar for years to come.

Barnard may have lost that glory, but it did have the Hudson. In those years, Morningside Heights was still suburban, if not precisely bucolic, and though the campus was tiny, it was surrounded by open space. By craning their necks only slightly,

students could easily glimpse the river. Better still, the charms
of downtown New York were readily accessible. Barnard's academic growth during the prewar years was typical of the progress elsewhere. Greek and Latin continued to be the *sine qua
non* of the BA, but by 1900 Greek was no longer required for
entrance. That small concession, already tried and proved at
Smith, was almost as good for the college's financial position as
an outright bequest. It immediately made the institution seem
less intimidating and enabled many more students to qualify.

The four-year course at Barnard closely paralleled the curricula at Smith, Wellesley, Vassar, Bryn Mawr and Mount Holyoke—with a few interesting and attractive exceptions. A
semester each of economics and psychology was required for
the Barnard degree, and though economics was a well-estab-
lished discipline, psychology was brand-new, and only the most
avant-garde educators considered it a discipline at all. The fact
that they were obliged to study it helped give Barnard girls
their cherished reputation for worldliness. When the idea of a
"major" replaced the random electives, the stipulations remained flexible. Graduates were expected merely "to know one
subject well"—a casual definition, but one that provided both
freedom and direction.

Though Union Theological Seminary supervised Barnard's
instruction in Biblical literature and religion, the college never
labored under the heavy Scriptural burdens that oppressed the
other women's colleges. There were a mere two chapels a week,
an academic meeting and a religious service, and while attendance was strongly urged, it wasn't forced. By 1914, very early
for such liberality, Barnard students were asked only to be
present for "college exercises" once a month. That deemphasis
on sectarian religion produced a not altogether unexpected
side benefit. In 1915 Jacob Schiff, who should hardly have been
expected to donate money to an evangelical Christian venture,
gave Barnard a desperately needed new building to celebrate
the fiftieth anniversary of his arrival in America. By then, of
course, Barnard seemed to be a much better risk than it had
been when Mr. Schiff resigned as treasurer. The Schiff building
contained space for undergraduate study rooms (important to
a college that still had a majority of day students), offices for
student activities, a lunchroom, a library and headquarters for

a physical education department. Just inside the entrance, a large brass plaque commemorating the donor quickly became Barnard's favorite meeting place. It was instantly known as Jake and lent Barnard a special cachet. The Sister colleges shared Rockefellers, Carnegies and Morgans, but only one of them had a Jake among their early benefactors.

A young woman named Virginia Crocheron entered Barnard in 1895, when the college was still wedged into the brownstone house at 343 Madison Avenue. In her autobiography, *Many a Good Crusade,* published in 1954, she describes herself as a "shy snobbish freshman" and admits that the "shabby crowded old house" was not exactly her idea of what a college could be. All twenty-one freshmen spent the entire academic-day in a single, small room on the fourth floor, rather more like first graders than university undergraduates. Miss Crocheron had visited Bryn Mawr, and that campus seemed much closer to her notion of a real campus. Her mother, however, had said, "Send her to Bryn Mawr? Certainly not. There is a perfectly good college here in New York," and it was to that one that Virginia reluctantly went. Another and even more blasé New Yorker, Alice Duer, entered in that same year as a junior. She had been "out" in New York society for four years and had already collaborated with her sister, Caroline, on a volume of published poems. At Barnard, however, Alice Duer majored in math. The poems and stories were merely a ladylike and acceptable way of earning extra income, since postdebutantes did not work as waitresses no matter how straitened their family's circumstances.

Though neither Miss Duer not Miss Crocheron cared particularly for Barnard, Miss Duer (later Mrs. Miller) was to be the author of Barnard's official history, and Miss Crocheron, later Mrs. Gildersleeve, became dean of the college and served it with great distinction from 1911 until her retirement in 1947. Eventually, Virginia Gildersleeve was to become well acquainted with Carey Thomas, and her regrets at not attending Bryn Mawr vanished forever. The two women were shipmates on a 1919 trip to England, a voyage that seems to have demonstrated that Barnard was, after all, the best choice for Virginia Crocheron. "Carey Thomas kept the staff of the ship in a state of panic," reports Mrs. Gildersleeve with amazement undiminished by the passage of thirty-five years. Her Bryn Mawr colleague and traveling companion demanded that "five shawls had to be laid upon her berth at different angles and different lengths in a very special way," and Mrs. Gildersleeve remembered that any steward who misaligned one or another was "severely chastised." Virginia Crocheron was already a distinguished educator, and she did her best to evade Miss Thomas while on board that ship. "She rather despised me," Mrs. Gildersleeve admitted, "because I lived with my parents. To her, as an ardent feminist, that seemed a feeble thing to do."

Mount Holyoke was hurried into the twentieth century by a fire that destroyed the original seminary building in 1896. It was an unfortunate and inconvenient event, but by no means tragic. Even the most sentimental alumnae were finally ready to admit that the sixty-year-old red-brick pile that had served as seminary headquarters didn't really make up in historical charm what it lacked in comfort and style. After Mount Holyoke became a college in 1888, few students had taken much pride or delight in that austere and drafty memento of the missionary era. The structure had been immortalized in a famous Currier print that showed a tall, bare building, rather like an abandoned mill, standing in a barren landscape. That surrealistic illustration, complete with the dated and embarrassing caption "Mount Holyoke Female Seminary," was invariably unearthed and printed whenever the subject of women's colleges arose. It was not an inviting picture, and it made the girls of the nineties cringe since their college was no longer even incidentally in the business of converting Hottentots and saving Sandwich Islanders. They were always explaining, apologizing, and trying to live the legend down—usually in vain. After the fire miraculously relieved them of that image, even the official histories of the college soon referred to the event, tritely but truthfully, as a "blessing in disguise." A campaign to replace the old hall with new and modern dormitories and classrooms had been meandering along for several years, progressing slowly and unsurely. As soon as the building was irrevocably gone, the response to appeals for funds was rapid and rewarding. Within a remarkably short time, Mount Holyoke had a contemporary and pleasant residential quadrangle and some impressive new academic facilities. After the inauguration in 1900 of Mary

Emma Woolley, a young and vigorous new president, college life immediately changed for the better. With a manageable complement of 50 to 100 girls in each house, the last vestiges of the restrictive social rules could be abandoned. The modern laboratories and lecture halls made it possible to revise and enlarge the curriculum to keep pace with innovations elsewhere. The new houses even had wider chairs on the verandas—a wonderful symbol of how times had changed since Mary Lyon's day, when the mere appearance of a young lady's head at the window of Seminary Hall was a cause for consternation and reprimand. Few natural disasters were ever less romanticized than the Holyoke fire.

Wellesley's fire came later, and not so opportunely. At four thirty in the morning of March 17, 1914, smoke drifted into the bedrooms opposite the zoology laboratory, and two alert students roused the entire college. Two hundred and sixteen well-drilled Wellesley girls were out of that building within ten minutes, and the rest of the residents were soon shivering in the cold New England dawn, watching in horror as their palace was reduced to rubble. Many girls were still in their nightgowns when they filed into the chapel for the regular eight-thirty service. That day's program was rather unorthodox, and after a brief prayer of thanksgiving that no lives had been lost, President Ellen Fitz Pendleton announced that spring vacation would begin at once. She added that college would reopen on schedule on April 7. When she calmly instructed the students to return to their dormitories and pack, an uncharacteristic wave of giggles swept through the church. Many girls had lost all their clothing in the fire, and their remaining possessions wouldn't have filled a change purse. The more fortunate shared their wardrobes, and the throngs that boarded the trains for Boston were modestly dressed in assorted motley. For many, it was their first trip to town without hats or gloves, and several young women were even obliged to step off the platform in unmatching shoes, though there had been some hasty swaps on the branch line into Boston. The damage to the college was appraised at $900,000, and even that seemed conservative. Twenty-eight classrooms had been destroyed, the zoology, geology, physics and psychology laboratories were in ruins, and most academic records had vanished with the administration offices. The classical plaster statues lay blackened and smoldering in the ashes of the Great Hall, reminding some spectators of the sack of Rome. The once-envied inhabitants of the main building were assigned on their return to cots in other dormitories, where they adjusted to their reduced circumstances as best they could. During the weeks that the students had been away, regaling their families and friends with dramatic accounts of the disaster, contractors had managed to produce a serviceable but undistinguished structure to serve as temporary classrooms and offices. It was quickly and appropriately named the Hencoop, and it gave the fabled campus a new and very democratic look. Though the contrived quarters were hopelessly inadequate, academic standards remained as lofty as ever. There is, after all, no place like eastern Massachusetts for spare university parts.

Mount Holyoke immediately responded with advice, condolences and cash. The other women's colleges took up collections, and Wellesley alumnae all over the world pledged assistance. Remittances poured in from everywhere, and though the individual contributions were usually small, there were no refusals. Wellesley women had been so imbued with the ideal of service that few of them had accumulated any great wealth, but they were willing to make sacrifices, and the notes and letters were often quite touching. Spinster schoolteachers, parsons' relicts and retired missionaries gave up long-awaited holidays and new clothes to buy desks and textbooks for their alma mater.

Students ran their own campaign, pressing each other's dresses (twenty cents for ball gowns, extra for ruching, ruffles and pleats), shining shoes (ten cents for buttoned boots), swatting flies (two for a penny and a bargain in May), darning stockings (five cents a hole) and giving shampoos, the cost of which varied with the quantity of hair involved. (Since the bob and the shingle had not yet caught on very widely, shampooing was still lucrative.) During vacation, girls raked leaves, sold jam and jelly, scrubbed floors and made angel cakes. In that pre-mixer era, making angel cake required considerable muscle, and there was a steady, if limited, demand for assistance. A particularly imaginative member of the class of 1916 hired herself out to count knotholes in the roof of a summer camp and turned the proceeds over to the fire fund. Unfortunately there is no record of how much this curious specialty paid or who commissioned it. Whole classes cooperated on group projects. The class of 1915 taught dancing and peddled vacuum cleaners, and one of its members, apparently a gifted raconteuse, charged a dime for each time she retold the story of the fire. She was able to contribute an extra $10, most of which was collected from freshman and impatient gentlemen callers. The worldlier alumnae organized musicales, staged pageants, concerts and masquerades and even held card parties and tea dances. They must have drawn on skills and talents acquired since graduation, since hardly any of these activities had been permitted them as students.

If the more conservative trustees and administrators had any misgivings about accepting such tainted funds, they successfully stifled them. By 1915, with the help of a nice round $750,000 from the Rockefeller Foundation, an angular $95,446 and change from Andrew Carnegie, $200,000 from the General Education Board, $250,000 from an anonymous donor and $300,000 in insurance payments, Wellesley had not only exceeded its original quota, but made up the entire amount needed for thorough restoration of the palace. It was decided, however, not to attempt to duplicate the original fairyland. Instead of the palms and statuary, future Wellesely classes got shower baths, full-length mirrors and, in 1917, the right to attend the theater in Boston. Some alumnae assessed the balance sheet and thought that Wellesley, too, might have come out ahead, though they kept their seditious thoughts to themselves.

166

XVII
The Enfranchised

ACCORDING to Scott Fitzgerald, who was constantly asked for his opinion, the Jazz Age began about the time of the May Day Riots of 1919. By seven o'clock in the evening of October 29, 1929, the last optimist was ready to concede that it was all over. The era, however, was never so neatly rounded as the dates imply, and Fitzgerald would have been the first to admit it. His own personal jazz age had obviously got off to a flying start long before the armistice was even signed, during his undergraduate days at Princeton. *This Side of Paradise* was published in 1920, full of events that had taken place throughout the preceding years. The book was fiction, but even so, it was obvious that campus life had undergone a number of drastic changes somewhat in advance of the rest of the country. A jazz age is not something that anyone enjoys in solitude, and Fitzgerald had plenty of company.

Those at the women's colleges seem to have been a bit slower off the mark. When *This Side of Paradise* appeared, hundreds of students at the Seven Sisters realized, more or less simultaneously, that they had a lot of catching up ahead of them. While they had been doggedly digging potatoes, rolling bandages and studying wireless telegraphy, much younger girls at the fashionable new preparatory schools had metamorphosed, in Fitzgerald's phrase, from "belles" to "flirts" to "baby vamps." Mere sixteen-year-olds had been out joyriding in Stutz Bearcats (red was the status color), had traded their modest middies for the sleeveless jerseys that Amory Blaine flippantly called "petting shirts" and had learned to drink smoothly from hip flasks. They were really the age group that had the loveliest war, better even than Barnard's.

The generation that had spent the years from 1914 to 1918 in Poughkeepsie, South Hadley, Bryn Mawr or Wellesley felt deprived, aggrieved and isolated, and by September, 1920, they were eager to do something about it. The Nineteenth Amendment had been ratified just in time to let thousands of newly enfranchised citizens loose on the cloistered campuses, and even those girls who wouldn't be able to vote for three or four more years were exhilarated by the victory and infuriated to discover that the colleges seemed to be ignoring the whole thing. Students arrived for the fall semester with their hair radically shingled, their skirts shortened almost to the knee and a new and startling vocabulary that included words like "libido," "repression" and "carburetor." They all were ready for a changed world, but once inside the Victorian iron gates of their colleges they were handed copies of rulebooks that hadn't had a thorough overhaul for half a century. Chapel was still mandatory, curfew remained ten o'clock on weekdays, "motoring," as the administration insisted on calling it, was permissible only in groups of three or more, and smoking continued to be strictly forbidden. The thrilling new names in fiction—James Joyce, Virginia Woolf, Sherwood Anderson and Eugene O'Neill—were not even on the library shelves. English lit stopped with Henry James. Young women who had served overseas or even worked in the local officers' canteens had been transformed by their experiences and were eager to share their knowledge and sophistication with less worldly underclassmen. Almost everyone seemed to have had at least one wartime romance, and these relationships had not always been conducted entirely in the colleges' stiffly furnished reception rooms. Within weeks the women's colleges were in turmoil, and newspapers all over the country were editorializing about Flaming, Gilded, and otherwise sadly altered Youth. It was obvious to fascinated readers that American campuses were no longer functioning as rigorous training grounds for the nation's future leaders but had mysteriously turned into mere amusement parks for "flappers" and "parlor snakes." The indications were unmistakable.

There wasn't a single Vassar alumna who couldn't quote at least a few of Edna St. Vincent Millay's poems, and most of her admirers seemed determined to follow her example and set off for Greenwich Village as soon as commencement was over. Many, in fact, began burning the candle at both ends as mere freshmen and would return to Poughkeepsie wan and hollow-eyed on Monday morning, with thrilling accounts of entire nights spent on the Staten Island ferry.

Even now Vassar students are fascinated by the Millay mystique, and apparently with good reason. No less a personage than Edmund Wilson himself was dazzled by her charm and talent and said that "she had an intoxicating effect upon people." Her effect on *him* was so profound that he proposed to her, and when she declined and married Eugen Boissevain instead, Wilson consoled himself in classic literary style by making Millay the heroine of his novel *I Thought of Daisy*. Eugen Boissevain had previously been married to the fabulous Inez Milholland, a Vassar legend in her own right and a heroine of Edna St. Vincent Millay's own undergraduate days. Boissevain therefore had the unique distinction of successively marrying Vassar's two most glittering alumnae, and he was, by all accounts, worthy of them both.

A poll taker who visited the Vassar campus in the autumn of 1920 to assess the postwar college mood found that it was much more advanced than he had expected or hoped. Students had changed not only in appearance and vocabulary, but character, morals and ambition. Those who planned careers intended to seek fame and fortune in journalism, publishing and advertising. Scores of young women were determined to go into the Theater and seemed not only unperturbed by the pitfalls of life on the wicked stage, but actually attracted by the risks. Hallie Flanagan (Davis), the remarkable and gifted director who came to Vassar in 1925, was personally responsible for many of these conversions, and her productions often drew a full set of New York critics to Poughkeepsie. Hallie Flanagan's courses were so much in demand that Vassar soon became the place to go for dramatic training, and the intense young actresses who applied there gave the campus an added fillip. Theater majors favored dangling marquis earrings and velvet "headache bands," embroidered shawls and low, throbbing voices, and they made splendid copy. "We all wanted to be vivid," said an alumna of that era, "and we loved to shock visitors. Our ideal was Isadora Duncan, and for a while everyone trailed around in long scarves and bare feet, being free. The college kept reminding us of the influenza epidemic, but that belonged to the Dark Ages as far as we were concerned. I wore a piano shawl to class for one whole winter."

Young women suddenly seemed to be going to college for all the wrong reasons—because it was the "thing to do" or simply to get away from home. A few admitted that they were there just to be closer to the action at the men's schools, and there was a lot to be had. The twenties were the heyday of football weekends and fraternity parties, and even the most blasé flapper managed some genuine enthusiasm for that sort of thing. The more serious scholars—when the journalists and pollsters could find them—coolly said that they had gone to college to broaden their interests, widen their horizons or learn about life. Many of these activities seemed quite extracurricular, often pursued on the divans of fraternity houses or at intimate tables in off-campus roadhouses. Students laughed disdainfully when they were asked if they planned to teach school after graduation. Teaching had dropped so far down on their list of professional choices that by 1921 it couldn't even be expressed as a percentage. Some particularly outspoken girls explained that "voluntary motherhood," as advocated by Margaret Sanger, would make teachers all but obsolete within a few years anyway. Undergraduates talked of the subtle differences between companionate marriage and free love and stayed up until dawn speculating about whether four years at a women's college could ruin one's future sex life. The consensus was that it could and often did. One had only to look at the faculties, which were still largely composed of dedicated women who had chosen between marriage and a career at a point in time when, despite Carey Thomas' hopes, a combination of the two was unthinkable.

There was a brief flurry of interest in studying Latin, a subject that seemed an odd choice for a college generation so determined to flout tradition, but the trend was not as quixotic as it appeared. "We took Latin so that we could read and translate the best parts of Havelock Ellis," said one member of the class of '24, back at Smith for her glorious fiftieth. "We also took chemistry and wasted a great deal of time trying to distill pure alcohol. You know, the government allowed only wood alcohol to be sold during Prohibition, and that was poisonous. We were determined to defeat them, though I don't remember that we were very successful at Smith." Laboratory experiments at the men's colleges seem to have been more productive, and there were lashings of French Seventy-fives, Big Berthas and Bronx cocktails at every fraternity party. Workable, though rudimentary, stills could be bought by mail order for $6 or $7 each, and those were common fixtures in the men's closets and wash-rooms. Drinking arrangements at the eating clubs and dormitories were often far more sophisticated than that, and one aging Princeton Tiger said flatly, "Bathtub gin is a myth. We mixed our drinks in silver shakers. That was when colleges were off limits for town police and we never worried about getting caught. I remember a bootlegger coming every Friday to Cottage Club, as regularly as the milkman. Everything we ordered would be there by three o'clock Saturday, and he even had charge accounts."

Aside from turning a previously law-abiding population into a nation of co-conspirators and accessories after the fact, Prohibition effectively finished off the last vestiges of Victorian social customs. Instead of amusing themselves at well-lighted and adequately chaperoned college proms, young people all over the country went underground for their social life. In the speakeasies they encountered a wide assortment of unsavory characters whom they would never have met otherwise, drank increasingly dubious and powerful concoctions and invented a great many new dances, all of which were described by the press as either "suggestive" or "risqué." Within a few months these two words became the most overworked adjectives in English, applied to movies, plays, books, dances and language. The speakeasies turned out to be ideal for enlarging one's horizons and doing the necessary research on life. The Prohibition years, of course, had an appropriate musical accompaniment, and the new bands were among its most delightful by-products. The invention of the saxophone coincided with the Volstead Act, and it proved to be the perfect speakeasy instrument. Unlike a piano or string section, it could be easily tucked away in case of a raid, and it produced a marvelous new sound, described by disapproving elders as barbaric, savage and certain to arouse animal passions. When those became unendurable, they were slaked in parked cars. "*Our* revolution had class," said the silver-shaker Princetonian. "Woodstock was public and vulgar."

Not everyone could repair to a red Stutz between dances, not even at the height of the bull market, but Henry Ford's flivvers were within reach of millions, and they provided a degree of privacy that earlier generations had enjoyed only on their hon-

171

eymoons. Ford's popularity had reached such a pinnacle by 1924 that there was a concerted movement to nominate him for the Presidency of the United States, and if eighteen-year-olds had been able to vote, he would have been swept into office on a wave of gratitude. Fortunately, Ford was too busy developing the Model A to have time to campaign, but the plan to draft him shows the extent of his influence much more dramatically than the cold statistics on car ownership. Those, however, can't be ignored, because there would have been no Jazz Age without the $600 Ford. Music and gin were just optional extras. The car was the real liberator. In 1920 there were 9,000,000 automobiles registered in the country; by 1925 there were nearly 20,000,000.

The numbers, however, only partly explain why cars had so colossal and irreversible an effect on behavior. The open roadster hadn't really been much more conducive to romance than the horse and buggy. The driver was constantly plagued by breakdowns and flats, buffeted by wind and drenched by rain, too distracted by mechanical problems to be concerned with seduction. The closed car changed all that: morning, noon and overnight. According to Frederick Lewis Allen in *Only Yesterday*, in 1916 a mere 2 percent of the cars manufactured in the United States were closed, but by 1926, 72 percent of them were. College administrators, of course, had heard about the endemic evils of petting and necking that were said to take place in those cramped interiors, but it was all beyond their control. Young ladies, who previously had sat primly muffled in dusters and veils on the front seats of open cars, felt much less inhibited in a sedan and saw no reason to remain stiffly upright at a proper distance from the driver. No one was watching.

As late as 1922 the colleges were still frantically trying to limit excursions in automobiles to family emergencies and insisting that their students venture out driving only with special permission and for specific destinations which had to be announced in advance. There was, however, no way that the rules could be enforced, short of hiring a private constabulary to peer into car windows, and eventually the deans simply stopped trying. The trivial limitations that remained were universally disregarded and served merely to challenge and entertain the scofflaws. "We were not supposed to drive after dark," recalled a member of the Wellesley class of 1922, "but that was nonsense. It was wonderfully easy to run out of gas in those days, and we used to dazzle the college with stories about spark plugs, radiator cracks and blowouts. I knew more about cars then than I do now after driving for fifty years. I had a list, given to me by a beau, of thirty or forty things that could go wrong. We got away with everything and never used the same excuse twice." The automobile also demolished the sticky all-girl social life that had prevailed at the colleges before the war. The dozens of clubs and organizations that had thrived when there were no alternatives suddenly found themselves holding their meetings to four echoing walls. The rejection was nearly total, and it extended to some hallowed college traditions as well as to the intramural fun and games. No one mourned the end of societies like the Nightly Nibblers or the Merry Munchers, which had owed their existence to boredom, tedium and hunger, but it was rather sad to see the same wholesale rejection of venerable customs like Tree Days, Step Sings, Junior-Senior picnics and Barnard's Greek games. Even the college publications suffered from neglect, and the weekend flight from campus seemed to be the only tradition that would survive the Jazz Age. For the first time the students had a choice, and they usually chose not to spend one unnecessary moment in each other's company. The disaffection was so marked that the colleges' very existence as single-sex institutions seemed threatened, and for a while coeducation was seriously considered. These talks had begun to make considerable headway before the stock market crash put an abrupt end to them. Resident men on campus were a luxury none of the Seven could afford.

Though a few girls seemed willing to campaign for drastic revisions of archaic social codes, most were happier just evading the rules. The job of reeducating the administrators seemed overwhelming, and the crusaders wouldn't be on campus long enough to benefit from their own efforts. When Mary Emma Woolley, the enlightened and well-loved president of Mount Holyoke, showed no signs of relaxing her stern position on smoking, girls simply strolled off into the trees with their Murads and Fatimas. "No one wanted to offend Mrs. Woolley," said one alumna. "She was a marvelous woman in all other respects." It wasn't difficult to find cover for forbidden activities on any of the spacious and wooded campuses, and smoking was the easiest of all transgressions to arrange. By the time the ban was reluctantly modified at Mount Holyoke the old college graveyard had become a four-acre ashtray, and tobacco plants, which do very well in the Connecticut Valley, were thriving all around Mary Lyon's tombstone.

Miss Woolley became president of Mount Holyoke in 1901. From 1895 to 1900 she had been at Wellesley, where she taught Biblical history, introduced new electives in the religion department and served as department chairman and head of one of the largest houses. In the course of fulfilling these obligations, she demonstrated remarkable amounts of piety, imagination and tact—a rare combination and precisely the qualifications needed by a future president of Mount Holyoke. (The amount of intercollege transference is always surprising and accounts at least in part for the similarities among all seven schools. The sister colleges seemed continually involved in training and trading each other's leaders.) It was soon obvious, however, that Miss Woolley was not gong to be the perfect traditionalist that she may have seemed. At her inauguration in 1900 she talked reassuringly of preparing Mount Holyoke women for lives of service and mentioned the great Christian foundation and the importance of character as well as intellect, but once in office, she lost no time in divesting the college of the tattered vestiges of its seminary image. Elderly women faculty members were replaced upon their retirement by the most dynamic young men Miss Wooley could find—an innovation that first seemed refreshing and then ominous. The new president made not only replacements but additions and changes, and by 1911 Mount Holyoke had a faculty of ninety, exactly twice the number that had been there when she arrived. Moreover, thirty-four of the new staff had PhDs, and there were definite indications that the doctorate was soon to be an essential requirement for a post there. The era of lady teachers—Holyoke-educated and Holyoke-saturated—which had lasted for sixty-three years was over in less than a decade.

The girls who entered during the Woolley administration found the college an altogether different place from the one their mothers and grandmothers had attended. Miss Woolley introduced an honors program in 1923 and made sweeping reforms in the curriculum. She created free electives and new majors while the men's colleges were still clinging to the academic guidelines established by Puritan clergymen for the training of their successors. The religious narrowness that had limited Mount Holyoke's appeal was dramatically relaxed. Ministers of major and minor denominations began turning up on campus as guest speakers, and the college YWCA chapter was quietly replaced by a Fellowship of Faiths.

These changes did not pass unnoticed. Priests and rabbis were an exotic sight in the village of South Hadley, and they could not escape attention. Miss Woolley's own chapel talks tended to deal with current social problems, a revolution that students found intriguing and older faculty members rather astounding. Those who remembered the college from its seminary phase (the changeover had taken place only in 1888) had never imagined that they would be hearing about minimum wages and the graduated income tax between "Rock of Ages" and "Abide with Me," and not everyone approved. Miss Woolley, who had abolished the troublesome secret societies in 1910, also did away (somewhat inopportunely) with the last of the dreary household chores in 1914 and devised an honor code for social as well as academic matters in 1916.

Though Mount Holyoke acquired sixteen major new buildings and increased its endowment from $500,000 to $5,000,000 during her administration, Mary Woolley often said that she disliked this aspect of her job. Fund drives, she felt, wasted the president's energy and diverted the faculty from its proper concerns. She preferred to devote her time (none of it was exactly spare) to causes that seem advanced even today, and she worked for the Civil Liberties Union, opposed the teachers' loyalty oaths that were a smoldering issue during the politically tense 1920s and fought for the defense of Sacco and Vanzetti so energetically that she managed to get herself blacklisted by the Massachusetts DAR. She was a passionate and committed pacifist until 1940, when she regretfully conceded that Hitler should be stopped even if that meant the use of force.

By then Miss Woolley had retired from the presidency of Mount Holyoke, but only reluctantly. She had remained in office until after the 1937 centennial and her own seventieth birthday. Impressive as her accomplishments had been, there

175

were those who thought that even the greatest woman was not indispensable, and her last years were blighted by complaints, rumors and bitterness. When Miss Woolley finally left Mount Holyoke, she was succeeded by a man—Roswell Gray Ham—and no president since has been a woman. To her, that choice seemed vindictive and unjust, and Mary Woolley never returned to the college she had led for almost four decades. Her personal papers were not made available to scholars until very recently, and until now the only biography was that written by her closest friend and housemate Jeanette Marks. *The Life and Letters of Mary Emma Woolley*, published in 1955, is a laudatory and sentimental book, and it presents the subject as a St. Joan of Women's Rights, which is overstating the case. The more ardent feminist of that duo was Miss Marks herself, and it was she who persuaded Mary Woolley to join the National Women's Party and endorse the brand-new and very questionable Equal Rights Amendment to the Constitution. These gestures gratified Miss Marks, but distressed old-line Holyoke supporters, many of whom still seemed to feel that the leaders of the college should truckle to "benevolent gentlemen" as they had in the past. Rumors of undue influence, mismanagement of investments and departmental favoritism were circulated, and only the imminence of war seems to have distracted Miss Woolley's opponents from outright slander.

The impact of reformers like Mary Woolley reached its height during the 1920s, and while an undergraduate might be obliged to slow her pace during the week at South Hadley or Northampton, she could easily make up for all her Monday to Friday deprivations and the nominal curfews made very little difference. "We used to say that there wasn't anything you could do after six o'clock that you couldn't do before," recalled one woman who had survived Smith during the twenties. "Amherst fraternities all had tea dances in those days, and the parties were held from three to six, so that we could all get back to our dorms on time. Most of the time the tea was bootleg whiskey, in which we kept a lemon floating for show. Now that everything is allowed, I can't believe that life is as much fun. We had to use our ingenuity."

Some of the old college rules, however, simply had to go not because they couldn't be flouted, but because they were humiliating and demeaning even to the least rebellious. At Mount Holyoke, where the student body had always been considered sweetly tractable and reassuringly conservative, sarcastic student editorials reminded the administration that since the government of the United States was willing to let women vote on the League of Nations issue, the college should at least allow them to choose their own bedtimes.

Curfew hours varied from one college to another, but not much. In general, undergraduates were expected to be back in their halls by eleven at the latest during the week, and then only if they were doing something approved and edifying, like attending a Philharmonic concert or a lecture by the phenomenal French sensation Émile Coué, who was still packing the auditoriums of Boston and New York by reciting his magic all-purpose formula "Day by day, in every way, I am getting better and better." Students signed out of their houses for such events, telling exactly where they were going, with whom, by what means of transportation and giving their time of return to the nearest round number. The slips were impaled upon a spike at the front desk, and the heads of houses, at least in theory, did not close any eye until the last straggler reported back. Housemothers could vary in age, marital status, degree of gullibility and general strictness, but no one ever seemed to be awarded the job unless she knew the New York, New Haven and the Hartford timetables by heart and was reasonably familiar with the Boston MTA, the New York Central and the Main Line schedules as well. Housemothers always seemed to know exactly when the curtain fell on the last act of any play, which conductors played encores and how long it took to get from the Met or the Shubert to the station. (Traffic was lighter in those days, and train service more dependable.) Girls were naturally expected to take the express and to share a taxi to the campus.

"When I consider the ten o'clock rule," raged one Mount Holyoke polemicist, "I want to mount a soapbox and wave a red flag." That was a much more provocative statement than it seems, because red flags, symbol of the Bolshevik menace, had been outlawed in several large cities, including New York. One didn't joke about red flags in 1921. Anti-communist hysteria had reached such a pitch that when a Radcliffe debating team took the unexceptionable position that "The recognition of labor unions by employers is essential to successful collective bargaining" (and won the debate), no less a personage than the Vice President of the United States mentioned the event as proof that the women's colleges had been inundated by leftist organizers.

He was overreacting, of course, as Vice Presidents often do, but the result was that all seven schools suddenly found themselves in the tabloids almost daily. Students had seemed indifferent to politics, but when the red scare grew to such proportions that it threatened academic freedom, highly vocal contingents from the women's colleges picketed the state legislatures, opposing the pending faculty loyalty oaths with admirable vehemence. The reporters who were assigned to the various statehouses quickly labeled the protesters "Daisy Chain Radicals," regardless of whether their particular college had that dainty tradition or not. The loyalty oath proposals were generally defeated, and they didn't become a serious issue again until the 1950s. "That was just about the only public issue that really excited us," said a woman who had led one group to Albany from Vassar. "We sympathized with Sacco and Vanzetti, but few of us realized what had really happened until it was too late. After it was all over, we concentrated on free love again. When Margaret Sanger was sent to jail, there was some talk of picketing the prison, but she was released before we had the opportunity."

By the mid-twenties the colleges had begun to recognize the fact that their students were, just as Scott Fitzgerald had said, "a new generation, grown up to find all gods dead, all wars fought, all faiths in men shaken." The first sign of that attitude was a simple refusal to roll out of bed and chant the doxology six days a week before breakfast. Compulsory chapel was abolished at Vassar in 1926, but the other colleges made much less heroic adjustments, pleading that empty churches would insult eminent speakers and turn the campuses into weekend wastelands, hardly different from the one in T. S. Eliot's bewildering new poem. To drop the religious requirements entirely seemed to violate the express wishes of the founders, and mandatory attendance was continued, in only slightly diluted forms, at Wellesley and Mount Holyoke for several more decades. Girls might pull their cloche hats down over their eyes and sleep through the sermons, but they were physically present. From the pulpit, fatigue and piety looked very much alike. As the religious affiliations of the students slowly became more varied, the colleges compromised by encouraging attendance at the church of one's choice, sanctimoniously mentioning in their literature that all houses of worship could be found in the immediate vicinity. Atheists and agnostics, however, were expected to attend Protestant services on campus. Only Barnard really left religion entirely to the students themselves perhaps because the wishes of the benefactors and founders of that college could hardly be cited as a reason to keep girls in church. Annie Nathan Meyer, Jacob Schiff and several other important figures in the early history of Barnard had been Jewish, and that college had abandoned the idea that a "Christian spirit" was essential to the well-rounded woman.

These small and often grudging concessions, traumatic as they were to the traditionalists, seemed insignificant to many potential students, and the colleges found themselves almost advertising opportunities for a more normal social life. They did it discreetly, of course, hinting at the fine train service and good roads to New Haven and Boston, emphasizing convenience to cultural attractions and recreational facilities, but it all added up to parties, dances and a heady new freedom. The old concept of a cloistered academic environment had become obsolete, if not actually repellent, and a great many girls who might have chosen one of the Seven before the war were busily filling out applications for Cornell, Penn or Michigan, where one stood a better chance of enjoying the sort of undergraduate life illustrated in the pages of *College Humor* and described by Scott Fitzgerald.

Inevitably, the colleges tried to lure back the defectors with new courses, some of which were surprisingly trendy and lightweight. The purists on the faculties feared that electives like Theater Arts, Marriage and the Family and Conversational Languages would lead straight to a revival of all the Woman's Sphere nonsense and to an inevitable abandonment of rigor and excellence. Carey Thomas of Bryn Mawr, naturally, was particularly distraught at this possibility and tried valiantly to hold the strict classical line at Bryn Mawr. She said bitterly that "Japanese Geisha schools are springing up on all sides. Practical vocational courses are to be given. . . . Now is the time for us to fight for our lives, for our educational convictions, and save, if we can, at least the girls of the East by refusing to give up our present college curriculum. It is," Miss Thomas continued, "our highest duty as educated women to pass on unimpaired . . . this precious intellectual heritage . . . so hardly won." Miss Thomas had seen the whole dangerous trend building before the war was quite over, and she composed those remarks in 1917 for the *Journal of the Association of College Alumnae*, alerting them to all the perils ahead. (It is still not possible to learn to play the samisen at Bryn Mawr, though the curriculum has expanded tremendously since the twenties. There are, however, fewer confections listed in that catalogue than elsewhere, and a girl of the East can still be saved in Pennsylvania.)

Though it was certainly true that more women were going to college during the prosperous 1920s, those who opted for one of the Seven represented what can only be called a narrow cross section of American society. These colleges did tend to remain socially and religiously homogeneous long after the universities had begun to reflect the changing composition of the population at large. With the exception of Barnard and Radcliffe, each of which had large proportions of day students from New York and Boston, the others seemed to acquire an increasing reputation for nonacademic exclusivity.

It's not easy to be sure if this was inadvertent or deliberate because the subject of ethnic and religious quotas is not one that the colleges care to discuss, even in retrospect. Administrators still change the subject as soon as they decently can, but there are some illuminating statistics, and it's a matter of record that by 1926 an overwhelming percentage of girls at the women's colleges were distinctly upper middle class and predominantly Episcopalian. The fundamentalist religious convictions of founders like Vassar and Durant had become decidedly unchic, and there's one fact that shows how far from their origins the colleges had strayed. In the 1920s the Episcopal Church was one of the smallest denominations in America. The *Methodist* Episcopal was by far the largest, and its tenets and usages were an entirely different basket of loaves and kettle of fish. Not one single solitary Vassar student, however, claimed membership in that huge group, and the figures were about the same at the other six. Worship may not have been very important to the girls, but the right connections were, and one needed an impeccable religious background to reject. In that same year (for which a particularly full set of figures are available) a negligible 2 percent of the Vassar student body was Roman Catholic, and the number of Jewish girls still had to be counted one by one. "There weren't enough of any minority to *be* a minority," says one of these pioneers. "We were simply a curiosity. Wellesley had the Soong sisters, but of course, there weren't enough of them to go around."

The underside of the Jazz Age, after all, was an untidy tangle of Klu Klux Klan activity, repressive immigration laws, "restricted" country clubs and suburbs and casual offhand ethnic slurs tossed around unthinkingly. ("Indiscriminately" hardly seems the proper word.) Alumnae who were asked about the benefits of attending one of the Seven during this period often mentioned "social advantages" and "the right people"— answers that would have appalled Mary Lyon and particularly disappointed Henry Durant, whose elegant college had somehow come to be first choice for the most glamorous debs in America. All in all, the twenties seem to have been a paradoxical decade for all of them. Though far from liberal in any true social and religious sense, they were definitely liberated, which is quite a different matter.

Great numbers of students seemed more than content with ladylike Cs for their course work—not too surprising in a decade when the shrug was the typical undergraduate gesture and to be offhand and sophisticated everyone's goal. "I should worry" and "So what?" were the catchphrases, and to be a grub or a grind was far worse than to be a virgin. *That* condition, at least, could be kept secret. Girls who were determined to excel academically did their studying as covertly as possible and carefully feigned indifference. Some subjects, like psychology and literature, actually helped one pose as a woman of the world, but most of the requirements were no use at all. The Scopes trial spurred a temporary interest in zoology, but not for long. To be able to talk knowingly about Freud and Joyce was a social asset, but one couldn't make much of a weekend splash with references to centrifugal force and vector analysis. Hemingway, Lewis, Anderson and, of course, Scott Fitzgerald all had a

181

tremendous influence on that generation, and smuggled copies of *Ulysses* were highly prized and conspicuously displayed. Each issue of Mencken's *American Mercury* was devoured and discussed on every campus, and students quickly got his message. Even the dilettantes knew that a vast and perilous bog of grubby materialism stretched all across the country, ready to swallow them up, degrees and all.

Europe offered the only sure chance of escape, particularly for those who fancied themselves creative. It was blindingly clear to the art and literature majors that there was no high ground west of the Boul' Mich', and they flocked there by the dozens. They left on every sailing of the Hamburg-America Line and Cunard, financed by the skyrocketing shares of Union Carbide and Electric Bond and Share, in showers of confetti and fountains of champagne. The less fortunate (but no one who went to one of the celestial Seven during the twenties was really deprived) descended on New York in groups of twos and threes to share the rent of a Village apartment and the cost of the studio couches and batik throws needed to furnish it properly. It was second best, but it beat Council Bluffs or Muncie.

Scorning teaching more than ever, graduates signed up for Macy's new training squad and registered for the secretarial course given at Katharine Gibbs. Gibbs was a rather elegant variation of the usual dreary business school, and it had been designed especially for graduates of the Eastern women's colleges. A Smith graduate, Grace Cheney of the class of 1930, became vice-president of the venture, and she ran it with the needs of her classmates very much in mind. No one who attended Katie Gibbs really intended to take dictation for very long, but the course was an effective argument for a year on one's own in New York, and concerned parents accepted it as a sign that their daughters were finally settling down and taking life seriously.

The list of actual actresses, artists and writers turned out by the colleges during the twenties may be somewhat shorter than one would have guessed from all the undergraduate interest in these fields, but all of the Seven did manage to produce several of each. Edna St. Vincent Millay's name leads the list of Vassar alumnae, but there was also Lois Long, Vassar '22, who signed her *New Yorker* fashion column "Lipstick" and often cabled it directly from Paris. Mary McCarthy didn't graduate until 1933, but she was a freshman in 1929, dining out on artichokes and mushrooms under glass, convinced that the messy business of politics was incompatible with art. After the market crash she revised her views drastically, but in a memoir of Vassar published in *Holiday* magazine in 1951, she says, "We of the aesthetic camp considered the socialists jejune and naïve. We aesthetes did not believe in politics but slightly favored the Democrats." (Eventually, the socialists and the aesthetes were to find a lot more in common with each other, and McCarthy's own fascination with politics almost overpowered her other interests.) During their first two years at college, however, the group that was to become *The Group* disdained all that and left placard carrying and union sympathizing to the tiny minority that worried about such matters.

Cheryl Crawford, Smith '25, became one of the first women theatrical producers. Smith was as proud of her as Bryn Mawr was of Katharine Hepburn. Anne Morrow, Smith '28, concentrated on lyric poetry in those days, though her professors and friends encouraged her to experiment with other forms. A Wellesley alumna, Ruth Nichols, of the class of 1923, was to become one of the original licensed women pilots in America, a distinction that was hers by default since Miss Morrow's undergraduate interests did not extend to aviation.

The first college generation to feel itself released from the old occupational stereotypes did achieve a considerable amount of literary and artistic distinction, though not always in the avant-garde areas they had hoped to explore. They were journalists and biographers, writers and illustrators of children's books and the authors of novels that sold respectably, if not sensationally. Many of those who did become teachers in spite of their youthful protestations often found posts at colleges, leaving the job of drilling tots in arithmetic to graduates of less exalted institutions. The apathy had only been an affectation, a sort of intellectual "debutante slouch," abandoned after graduation along with floppy galoshes, letter sweaters and sophomoric slang. Beginning with the classes of the twenties, the names of the seven women's colleges turn up with gratifying frequency in American biographical dictionaries.

The idea of "doing something" had somehow impressed

even the most frivolous. Those women who had lapsed, after commencement, into merely domestic routine tended to apologize when they wrote to their class secretaries, deploring the fact that they weren't "typical," but mentioning in passing that they were serving as presidents and officers of various civic organizations. The fields that they chose for their volunteer activities tended to be "worthwhile" in a Victorian sense—prisons, hospitals and the boards of schools and colleges. Few devoted their energy to the purely cultural organizations that might have seemed most likely to attract them. As the data for those years accumulated during the next few decades, it became increasingly clear that the image of the spinster schoolmarm had also gone under in 1929, along with the flapper and Electric Bond and Share. The postgraduate marriage rate for the Jazz Age classes reached 70 percent and has been rising steadily ever since. The first moral revolution had lasted for exactly ten years, five months and twenty-eight days and had been brought off with fewer casualties and less damage than anyone expected.

The first graduating class at Radcliffe.
William James at $10 an hour.

Radcliffe

Mrs. Agassiz hung the curtains, Carret House.

Quietly pursuing their occupations—Radcliffe
hockey, 1910.

Fay House.
No danger of infatuation.

Radcliffe Archives

The 1906 basketball team.

Radcliffe Archives

Smith

"Dreamy rows on Paradise Pond"—much later.

Northampton.
Ecology.

Smith College

The New Smith.

Dance class in Mendenhall Center for the Performing Arts.

Smith College

Vassar

Matthew Vassar, Noble
Emancipationist.
Portrait by J. H. Wright, 1861.

The Resolutes
Vassar baseball team.
The First, in 1876.

Tree Day at Vassar, 1921.

Maria Mitchell, role model, in her observatory with a scholar.

"Like playing the piano."
Vassar farmerettes, World War I.

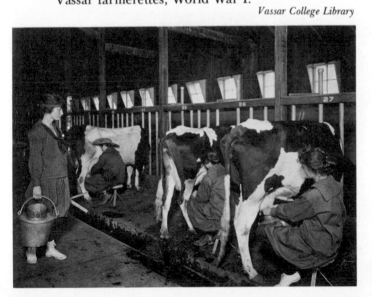

The vision merely shimmered.
College Hall, Wellesley, 1875.

Wellesley

Freshmen crew, 1878, on Lake Waban.

Calico girls, Wellesley chemistry class about 1890.

The Hoops of May, 1889.

XVIII
"An Upper Class Phenomenon"

IN an essay called "My Confession" and collected in *On the Contrary,* Mary McCarthy wrote that "to most of us at Vassar, I think, the depression was chiefly an upper class phenomenon," and extraordinary as that statement sounds, it was apparently true enough at the beginning. Students at the women's colleges did seem to get their trends a bit later than anyone else, and after a delayed Jazz Age they were to have a tardy Depression. In both cases, however, the lag was short. Girls who had raced to overtake the vanishing twenties were engulfed by the looming thirties before they could lengthen their skirts.

For a month or two the immediate effects of the market crash seemed trivial enough—reduced allowances from home, fewer trips to the city and, in rare hardship cases, postponement of that graduation trip to Europe until the market settled down. Wellesley, which had established a pioneering Students' Aid Society during the war, seriously considered abandoning the program in the flush academic year of 1929. The office was receiving so few requests for assistance that it hardly seemed worth the trouble to administer it. The society's treasurer had suggested that the fund vote itself out of existence as a quaint, unnecessary anachronism, and the matter was virtually settled a week or so after college opened in September of that year. Those students who had been gently asked by their fathers to economize for a while went to Hayes-Bickford for after-theater supper instead of to the Copley and experimented cheerfully with the Boston MTA. Over their pancakes and coffee, they discussed the possibility of a repeal of Prohibition and wondered if that would mean the end of the speakeasies. The crash was exciting, a real-life lesson in economics, and Hayes-Bickford was full of Harvard students who didn't seem particularly worried either. On the surface, college life proceeded very much as before. There were unused and generous loan funds available to

185

the daughters of temporarily embarrassed bankers and brokers (all the schools had followed Wellesley's early example in making some provision for emergencies), and those who accepted a reduction in tuition for a semester were positive that they would return it before the term ended.

Then, unexpectedly, the changes began to be a bit more obvious. Commuting Barnard girls saw breadlines and apple sellers on the street corners and wondered if Mr. Hoover might have benefited from their elective course in basic economics. Smith, Radcliffe and Wellesley students, changing trains in New York, were astonished to be approached by well-dressed panhandlers as they boarded the Merchants' Limited. By the autumn of 1930 there were a few absences in their classes, and by 1931 college enrollment was undeniably smaller. The freshmen who entered Vassar in 1929 were told by the dean in her first address that their numbers were reduced because Vassar's academic standards had been raised to new heights, but there were some girls who suspected, even then, that that might not be the whole explanation. There had been a great many short-tempered fathers that summer and some disturbing conversations overheard at country clubs and fashionable resorts.

By Christmas almost everyone knew a few students who had been forced to leave because they had to help support their families, and a Smith or Wellesley girl shopping in Boston might find one of her former classmates on the wrong side of the counter in Filene's, struggling with the pneumatic change tubes and bravely keeping up appearances. It was soon obvious that the Depression was neither upper class nor a phenomenon anymore, but general and chronic. The rumors that a friend's uncle or father had suffered a nervous breakdown or even committed suicide were turning out to be true, and people one knew very well had given up not only the cook and the chauffeur but sometimes also the house and the car. The scholarship loans of $100 or $200 were no longer adequate to keep girls in college, and all the pretenses seemed to collapse at once. By 1932 there were none left.

During the boom years loyal alumnae and their prosperous husbands had pledged bonds and shares to the colleges, and elaborate plans had been drawn for new classrooms, dormitories and athletic facilities. Virtually nothing had been earmarked for scholarships, but it would hardly have mattered in any case. The portfolios of elaborately decorated certificates were worthless except as art history. (Classic engravings of Greek goddesses had been the most popular design, closely followed by mountain peaks in borders of laurel leaves.) Alumnae benefactors had been just as likely as everyone else to believe in Samuel Insull, and the colleges that had received gifts of choice stocks like Radio Corporation, General Motors Common or even U.S. Steel were not much happier with their holdings. Radio Corporation had dropped from 101 at its peak to 2½ by 1932, General Motors had fallen from 72¾ to 7⅜, and U.S. Steel was down from 261¾ to 21¾. Outstanding pledges could not be collected, bequests of life savings often turned out to be no more than kind thoughts, and those faculty members whose meager salaries had been supplemented by private incomes or small inheritances were often reduced to bare sustenance levels.

Undergraduates, trustees, faculty and alumnae found themselves involved in a frantic struggle to keep the colleges alive, while bravely insisting that matters were not nearly so serious as they looked. The presidents of the various institutions were obliged to plead for funds without destroying the confidence of potential donors. It was a difficult position, and they managed it with varying degrees of success. The balance was extremely delicate. If the colleges were presented as tottering on the edge of bankruptcy, they could expect nothing, since there wasn't a dime available for lost causes. If, on the other hand, the fund raisers were too sanguine, they would be sent on their way with congratulations and good wishes. There were, as a result, some strange circumlocutions. President Ellen Fitz Pendleton of Wellesley wrote an article in 1933 for a Massachusetts newspaper in which she said, "Wellesley College, in spite of reduced income from funds, closed the fiscal year 1931–32 with a small but actual surplus . . . the college has reduced no salaries and has retained the entire staff. It is practising economy in maintenance and overhead expenses, but is making no reduction affecting the integrity of the academic work and does not contemplate any such reduction at present." During the same period the college had been publishing a series of "Service Fund Extras" and leading off its articles with banner headlines asking

HOW MUCH CAN YOU GIVE? Straitened as the circumstances of the colleges themselves were, they seemed islands of luxury in comparison to the surrounding communities, and in spite of their own uneasy financial situation, students did what they could. If some of their efforts, like distributing teddy bears to the children of unemployed mill hands and mailing their worn prom dresses off to the Dust Bowl, seem girlishly ingenuous, it should be remembered that the federal government's earliest efforts at relief were not much more sophisticated.

The first real Depression novelty on the campuses were cooperative houses, patterned loosely on the old domestic work system that had held costs down at Mount Holyoke in the nineteenth century. Wellesley, never pinched for funds, had used it to teach humility and build character. The colleges revived the plan, presenting it as a grand old tradition that had also happened to be very practical. All seven soon adopted some variation of the idea, and by the mid-thirties, hundreds of students had discovered that they could survive without the corps of maids, cleaningwomen and waitresses who had become fixtures during the Stutz Bearcat and raccoon coat days. A few cynics pointed out that the discharged employees immediately became objects of the relief drives, but that was just one more irony of the era. The co-ops were so desperately needed that the colleges were soon obliged to limit the numbers of students who could participate in the plan to those with particularly good grades. Scholarship seemed to improve as the market slipped, and by 1936 or so there were hardly any girls who would have flippantly admitted to a reporter that they were in college because they had nothing else to do. Even those whose families had escaped ruin had been solemnized by the general aura of misery, and when *Fortune* magazine did a survey of American college students in 1936, they found the Depression generation to be "cautious, subdued and unadventurous." The girls at the Seven were no exception.

The administrators had been concerned that discrepancies in financial circumstances might cause a real have and have-not schism, and they were right. The colleges were in no position to refuse a student who could pay her bills, and they found themselves accepting solvent candidates they might have refused in happier years. In order to continue to operate for the benefit of the deserving new poor, they had to be tolerant of a few of the imperious old rich, and alumnae who remember the thirties usually have some very distinct sense of contrasts. Those who lived in the cooperative houses were somewhat insulated, but the newly created paid jobs in the regular dormitories did occasionally create tensions. Some girls simply forgot that the waitresses were now their classmates and behaved as if they were in a hotel. "I remember one girl who used to leave tips in the leftovers on her dinner plate," said a woman who had been in the Barnard class of 1936. "I've always suspected that she was a bootlegger's daughter, but I never could prove it."

Outside jobs were virtually impossible to find in the small towns or villages like Northampton, Bryn Mawr or South Hadley, and even Barnard and Radcliffe students were not much better off. There was no equal opportunity law in those days, and hundreds of desperate men stood in line for the rare part-time openings that occurred. Ex-stockbrokers competed for work as typists and salespeople, and girls from the women's colleges were laughed out of the waiting rooms. The names of their schools had become so synonomous with wealth and privilege during the previous decade that a kind of reverse discrimination developed, and Smith, Vassar and Wellesley graduates found themselves at a distinct disadvantage when they tried to find work after commencement. "I did get a job as a French governess in 1933 in return for room and board," said a Radcliffe alumna, "but I was fired as soon as they overhead me speaking English to my mother. I had a definite Boston accent—though it wasn't so noticeable in another language."

On the campuses themselves, girls not only worked to defray their own expenses, but struggled with all sorts of fund-raising schemes to provide help for even less fortunate classmates. Little cottage industries flourished in the dormitories as students sewed and ironed for one another, made and sold candy and rarebits (there wasn't much else that one could cook in a chafing dish), typed and, in some deplorable cases, actually wrote other people's term papers and themes. "We called it tutoring," said one graduate, "but occasionally it was a bit more than that. The college was full of debutantes in those years, surprising as that seems, and they were always rushing off to parties in New York. A few of us were poor enough to help keep them in school for the year or two that they wanted to stay." The stores that clustered around the colleges and depended on undergraduate trade were sometimes persuaded to give the girls special discounts, and at Mount Holyoke a determined committee actually convinced the shopkeepers of Holyoke, Springfield and South Hadley to contribute 10 percent of their total sales on three successive days to an emergency scholarship fund. No donation was ever too small, and the colleges found themselves accepting gifts of furniture, food and tiny, odd amounts of money just as they had in the early nineteenth century. The constant white elephant sales, shows, pageants and masquerade dances gave the campuses something of a carnival atmosphere, but it all looked considerably more festive than it actually was. "We had hobo parties instead of proms," said a Vassar graduate. "A lot of people couldn't afford evening dresses and even those who could didn't want to flaunt their luck."

Eventually, the Depression years were to politicize thousands and radicalize hundreds. "During our junior year [1932]," Mary McCarthy writes, "the word 'Communist' first assumed an active reality; a plain girl who was a science major openly admitted to being one. But most of our radicals were socialists, and throughout that election year they campaigned for Norman Thomas." Elizabeth Bentley, Vassar '30, was a notorious exception, and while she seems to have been the only women's college alumna actually to have achieved Communist spydom, she was by no means unique in her membership or sympathies. Undergraduate organizations with "Peace," "Freedom" and "Labor" in their names flourished on the campuses, and Marxist study and discussion groups appeared all over, attracting girls who in more prosperous times might have spent their leisure off campus. In her confessional essay, Mary McCarthy says that she shrank, in her Vassar days, "from the sloppily dressed Socialist girls at college who paraded for Norman Thomas and tirelessly argued over 'Cokes'; their eager fellowship and scrawled placards and heavy personalities bored me—there was something, to my mind, deeply athletic about this socialism. It was a kind of political hockey played by big, gaunt, dyspeptic girls in pants." A Smith graduate remembers the activists even less sympathetically. "They never shaved their legs," she said.

190

"YCL [Young Communist League] gave them a place to go on Saturday nights. The Depression was their element, and I think they loved it and were actually sorry when it was over."

One of the side effects (or fringe benefits) of the Depression was to make the moral revolution of the 1920s permanent. "As for sex," said the *Fortune* team in their 1936 article on college life, "it's, of course, still with us. But the campus takes it much more casually than it did ten years ago. Sex is no longer news. And the fact that it is no longer news is news." That, however, is a rather cursory description of an interesting situation. What actually happened was that poverty made it so difficult for students to marry that many young women found themselves living in unsanctified liaisons with their fiancés. Poverty was a very persuasive argument. Statistically, the decade appears to have been exceptionally chaste, but the figures can be deceptive. The divorce rate, which had risen shockingly during the twenties, declined abruptly after the crash, but in many cases that meant only that people could not afford to get divorced legally. As soon as there was some economic recovery, the number of divorces reached a new peak. Miserable people had simply been waiting it out.

A sociological study made in forty-six colleges and universities from coast to coast by Dorothy Dunbar Bromley and Florence Haxton Britten during the mid-thirties showed that 25 percent of all college girls they interviewed admitted to premarital sex, and that was long before the time when inquiring pollsters could expect total candor about so personal a subject. The Crash had obviously consolidated the sexual revolution of the Jazz Age. Young people, according to the *Fortune* editors, seemed more "restrained" in their behavior, but that may have been just because the Depression had swept away so many flamboyant possessions. The red Bearcats were dented, the raccoon coats threadbare, and repeal had made the speakeasies obsolete. The flash was gone, but "there was no measurable increase in abstinence, continence or modesty," *Fortune* concluded rather wistfully.

There was, however, apparently a genuine renewal of interest in intramural activities on the college campuses. Undergraduate magazines and newspapers flourished, partly because there was a lot happening that inspired young writers and part-

191

ly because shrunken allowances didn't always stretch to cover outside excursions. Clubs and sports boomed, and girls who were obliged by financial circumstances to spend frozen weekends on their New England hillsides amused themselves skiing and skating. The Depression looked wholesome from afar.

By 1933 student writing had taken a sharp left turn, and undergraduate publications at all seven colleges were full of stories about the hardships endured by coal miners, farmers and mill workers. A course in "proletarian literature" was actually given at Vassar during the thirties, and if the echoes of Steinbeck, Odets and Saroyan that resound through the magazines are an accurate gauge of interest, most composition majors must have elected it. Hopeful young writers all over let their subscriptions to *Vanity Fair* and the *New Yorker* lapse and signed up for *New Masses,* the *Nation,* and the *New Republic* instead. The gap between the aesthetes and the politicals became less noticeable as aesthetes turned *into* politicals. The strenuous efforts of the new radicals to produce socially significant stories of their own resulted in a great many gloomy allusions to tuberculosis, black lung and the various vitamin deficiency diseases, with pellagra a special favorite of undergraduate writers. (It had recently been recognized among the children of Southern tenant farmers, and the symptoms were both dramatic and varied.) Families in these cautionary tales were invariably too large for unemployed fathers to feed, a device which permitted the authors to make an incidental brief for the complete legalization of birth control. Stark woodcuts and drawings of breadlines often illustrate these effusions, and the artists were so deeply influenced by Mexican muralists like Orozco, Rivera, and Siquieros that they occasionally forgot themselves and equipped a Dust Bowl farmer with a sombrero and a poncho.

Students who might otherwise have drifted through college with the unfocused intention of becoming "well-rounded women" were suddenly showing a great determination to study subjects that would give them marketable skills, and even the "art for art's sake" types eagerly learned typing and shorthand as a sort of job insurance. The Katharine Gibbs School had been founded just in time to receive these alumnae and was one of the great financial successes of an era that didn't have many others. Katharine Gibbs' waiting lists, in fact, were so long that many Vassar, Holyoke and Barnard girls were obliged to settle for less elegant establishments in inferior neighborhoods. It was widely believed, though without any definite proof, that all Smith girls were accommodated first at Katie Gibbs, regardless of their need to earn a living.

Secretarial school was no longer just a cover for a delightful postgraduate season in New York, but a real necessity. Fifty words a minute became an end in itself. The idea, of course, was to be nothing less than an executive secretary, but with the abrupt decimation of the executive class the designation didn't mean very much. During the worst years of the Depression, typing pools were full of overqualified Smithies and Cliffies, whose knowledge of the more exquisite nuances of English prose atrophied as they hammered out communications beginning "Yours of the inst. received. . . ." "I lost three jobs before I learned not to use descriptive adjectives in a business letter," recalled one woman who found her Bryn Mawr background something of a negative asset in her unchosen career of secretary to a hardware wholesaler.

The Depression, however, did direct a great many students into new fields, and for the first time, significant numbers of alumnae went on to graduate professional schools. During this period the list of occupations entered by alumnae expanded tremendously. Young women who might have passively taken no for an answer in more prosperous times kept knocking on doors until they found some sort of paid work, remote as it may have been from their undergraduate ideals. "When I first began at Macy's," a Smith graduate said, "all of the college girls would go out to lunch together. I didn't feel like a regular employee until I ate the twenty-five-cent special in the upstairs cafeteria. I was an English major, working in the advertising department, and the lunch was hash. The symbol was very clear to me. I remember thinking that I was now a member of the working class."

But if many alumnae were turned into career women by the Depression, hundreds of others found their ambitions thwarted by simple lack of opportunity. When the biographies of those years are sorted out, it's plain that one of the side effects of the thirties was to sideline thousands of intelligent and well-educated women into a lifetime of unpaid volunteer activities.

Ironically, compassion makes one of the most vicious circles of all, and once established, the pattern is hard to break. Throughout those years and for two decades thereafter the glorious liberal arts backgrounds seem to have been sadly underutilized. The alumnae worked at a huge number of worthwhile projects, but too many worked for psychic rewards alone.

Moreover, these activities tended to become dynastic, as alumnae recruited and succeeded each other in prestigious but unpaid positions. In scores of cities across the United States, volunteer projects show distinct traces of an old girl network, virtually the only evidence that anything of the kind exists. Smith graduates for instance, seem to favor health causes, and they can be found as gray, pink or turquoise ladies in every hospital in America, pushing the library carts, spreading tuna fish sandwiches in the aid shops, energetically and efficiently organizing fairs and benefit dances. There's hardly a mysterious or little-known disease that doesn't have a Smith alumna or two on its foundation letterhead. Known as the most healthy and athletic of all undergraduates, they become the most diligent workers for incapacitating conditions.

Vassar and Holyoke women, traditionally political, seem to draw each other into the League of Women Voters and the back rooms of campaign headquarters. After thirty dim years of stuffing envelopes and raising funds for male candidates they have emerged as a significant political force themselves. Frances Farenthold, Vassar '46, was the first woman to be mentioned as a Vice Presidential nominee, and she was one of the most conspicuous political alumnae until a Mount Holyoke woman, Ella Grasso, actually became the governor of Connecticut in 1974. So far Mrs. Grasso is the only woman to have been elected to a governorship entirely on her own, though the trend is building rapidly, and every one of the women's colleges can boast at least a few state legislators as well as an intriguing assortment of municipal officials. (Cook County, Illinois, has a Mount Holyoke alumna as a sanitation commissioner, a post of considerably more clout and status than one might think.)

Barnard and Bryn Mawr alumnae are disproportionately conspicuous in all sorts of social and family service agencies, while Wellesley and Radcliffe altruism seems to benefit art museums and cultural centers. Until their collective consciousness was raised by the new feminism of the late 1960s, college women donated their services, though now that they have been persuaded that virtue should not always be its own sole reward, they are often found in related fields as paid professionals.

The graduates of the Depression years, however, seem to have been uniquely generous with their talents and abilities, giving away far more than they leased. In the grim years that immediately followed their graduation, there was just not enough lucrative work to go around, and it was extraordinarily difficult for even the most ambitious to buck the pervasive American feeling that a woman should not "take a job away" from a qualified man. The work ethic tolerates idle women while it rejects unemployed men. Current feminist writing, berating women for decades of professional apathy, tends to ignore the profound effects of simple economics on American attitudes. The willing volunteers, satirized in Helen Hokinson's cartoons, exposed in all their diffuse restlessness by Betty Friedan in *The Feminine Mystique* and put down ever since by the militants who find these ladies a natural target, were often true casualties of the Depression. That phenomenon was *not,* by any stretch of a feminist's overheated imagination, just another sexist plot. The thirty-year epidemic of volunteerism has been variously attributed to fear of success, fear of failure, insidious Freudianism, lack of confidence and blatant discrimination, and though the attributors are partly right, these factors altogether were not as powerful an inhibiting force as the lack of jobs. That's what sent thousands of able young women into involuntary domesticity, reversing a promising trend toward worldly success that had been gaining momentum for half a century. Until the Second World War, the so-called nurturing professions—teaching, social work, public health and that most disparaged nurturing profession of all, housewifery—seemed the only realistic possibilities for all except the uniquely gifted and powerfully motivated. Men got the franchises for apple selling, and when the WPA came along, they got the picks and shovels. In that sense, the Depression was discriminatory.

XIX
Far From the Worst Place to Be

INDIVIDUAL recollections of undergraduate life at the women's colleges during World War II tend to be dominated by gloomy adjectives, with "lost," "forgotten" and "ignored" leading the list. The war coincided so closely with the academic calendar that the Smith class of 1945 actually graduated on May 13, VE day itself, upstaged to the very last. The cheering was not for the new BAs, but for Eisenhower. The college newspaper, in its final issue of the year, called that a natural coincidence and barely managed to offer a few ironic shreds of consolation to the alumnae. Instead of the usual sentimental allusions to golden college years, hallowed traditions and eternal loyalties, the graduates were enjoined to "make themselves more intelligent members of a world ready to convert back to peace, too, by using the knowledge and experience gained here through four war years." The pageants, the proms, the field days and the candlelight ceremonies had been suspended for the duration, and students graduated whenever they happened to fulfill their credit requirements—in May, August or December. Some of the orphans came back for their diplomas, but most just packed their bags and scattered without any of the classic fanfare or damp farewells. But even so, the women's colleges were far from the worst places to be during wartime. "Knowledge" and "experience" were readily available, and an ambitious girl could acquire more than the usual variety of both. In some ways, the colleges actually benefited from the general disruption. At each of the Seven, the faculties were enriched and enlivened by academic refugees from all over the world. A few luminaries like Simone de Beauvoir, Thomas Mann, and Anna Freud merely stopped to lecture, but others found regular posts and became permanent assets. In her American diary, *America Day by Day,* published in 1952, Simone de Beauvoir describes her visits to Vassar, Smith, and Wellesley

196

in marvelously ambivalent terms. Of Vassar, first on her itinerary, she writes:

> The car had stopped before a sumptuous villa; it was the guest house. Hall, drawing rooms, library, dining room, spacious rooms, in a more or less medieval style, recalled at one and the same time a luxurious "hostelry" and a monastery. My room had the whiteness and peace of the snow covered countryside; it invited one to be ill, one longed for a gentle fever to taste this silence the better, the freshness of the walls and sheets. . . . I ran into college girls in skiing clothes with skis on their shoulders; here were some who were gliding uncertainly down a little slope which would not worry a beginner at home. . . . In the blue water of the swimming pool others were swimming rhythmically under the eye of a teacher who watched them, knitting. In the library, how free and comfortable they appeared to be; they read, sunk in armchairs, or sitting cross-legged on the floor, scattered in little isolated rooms or gathered together in great halls; through the bay windows one saw the trees and snow. How I envied them. . . . How pretty they seemed. But looking at them more closely one saw there was nothing out of the ordinary about their faces. But their hair was lovely just like the shampoo advertisements, and their features, sharply accentuated by make-up, were exaggerated like those of women in their thirties, in default of nature, this mixture of freshness and artificiality, these lips thick with paint opening to reveal the flashing white teeth of youth, the sixteen-year-old smile in their eyes under long painted lashes, all appeared most attractive. . . . Others were dressed in a style that is vainly censured by the older teachers but is almost uniform at Vassar; blue jeans rolled up above the ankle, and a man's shirt which is either white or chequered with violent colored squares, and hanging out of the trouser tops; the shirt tails are tied together in front with studied negligence. The shirts are bright, but the jeans must be worn and dirty; for that purpose they are rolled in the dust, sewn with incongruous patches, and mended with darker thread where they are torn. Dressed like boys, and painted like street-walkers, many of the girls knitted as they listened to me. I was told that the taste for knitting had caught on during the war. . . . I suppose that

knitting implies an anticipation of marriage and maternity in many of the students.

At Smith and Wellesley, still dazzled and sounding as *If Today Is Tuesday, This Must Be Massachusetts,* de Beauvoir reports that she:

> slept in white rooms which reminded me of clinics. The atmosphere at Smith is gay and intimate. Wellesley is more splendid with its slate blue lake, medieval keeps and trees. As at Vassar, here too students are serious (even though the French scholars think them very superficial, and the American girls are worried when they come to Paris by the difficult examinations in law, letters or political science). They admit only young girls well thought of in their high schools. For those who don't want to work, but whose social standing demands that they pass through college, there are milder establishments. . . . At Wellesley I saw upper-class students who seemed to me as deep and serious as others appeared frivolous. "Even those who appear frivolous are not always so," they said. "You must understand that with us frivolity has a certain snob value; you would be afraid of being taken for a blue-stocking if one took your ideas and your studies too seriously; but many of the students are interested in important questions; they only hide it because it is looked down upon. No, we are not primarily interested in finding a husband; and we shall not be content with a job that will only keep us busy for a year or two. We want to take up work which is of use. We want to see the world and to enrich ourselves intellectually." Many of them repeated the words convincingly: "We want to make ourselves useful." They are preoccupied with social and economic questions, and specialize in these fields to base careers on them.

Though she spoke at other universities, the students at the women's colleges particularly fascinated de Beauvoir, and her curiosity about them was never entirely satisfied.

> One evening, while talking to an elderly French spinster. . . . I asked her about the sexual life of the students; was it true they were so free, and their life was so disorderly, that

one found the shreds of preventatives in certain parts of the campus? [de Beauvoir had heard rumors to that effect and had not had the opportunity to verify them personally.] The other French woman smiled, "On the campus, I don't know; sometimes in books. . . ." According to some statistics, about fifty percent of the college girls are virgins. But how is this established? de Beauvoir asked. "It is possible," her informant said, "that in recent years the virgins were numerous enough; some are so frightened of being caught in the marriage trap that they exonerate their lovers."

As for this exchange, de Beauvoir concludes with glorious sangfroid and terrible finality, "It is not healthy as a mode of life and most of these girls are neurotic."

Few of the Continental lecturers were as observant or as articulate as Simone de Beauvoir, but almost all were amazed by their audiences and often confused and disconcerted by their first impressions.

The men's colleges and large coeducational universities, forced by the exigencies of war to concentrate on teaching navigation, radar technology and basic Japanese to future officers, had little room for the German novelists, Czech historians, French philosophers and Italian artists who fled to America in the early forties, and some extraordinary and unexpected intellectual prizes went by default to the women's schools. The Ivy League, of course, managed to accommodate most of the mathematicians, physicists and chemists, but the humanists were a bit harder to place. Young men were not signing up for Byzantine architecture, Flemish painting, or advanced Dante in those days, but a measure of culture was still considered all right for girls despite the war. As a result, distinguished scholars who had never faced even one woman in their classes at Heidelberg or Padua suddenly found themselves surrounded by wall-to-wall girls, notebooks ready for the highlights and knitting at hand for the duller stretches.

If some of the émigrés had heard about the comparative casualness of American educational methods, very few were adequately prepared for the actuality. The war had completely erased the decorous ladylike look that had prevailed on the campuses until then, and the famous 1944 photograph of Vassar girls in their jeans and billowing shirts that appeared in *Life* magazine only hinted at the revolution. Students found that shortages and rationing were a perfect excuse to replace hosiery, shoes, and skirts with bits and pieces of uniforms, begged or donated by servicemen. By 1942 the real status costume included paratrooper's boots and a cracked leather flier's jacket, though sailor's middies and army ponchos were also prized. Everyone seemed to revel in looking as forlorn as possible from Monday to Friday, though the transformations wrought on weekends were so total that many professors had trouble recognizing students they'd known all semester.

Most of the Europeans eventually adjusted, but not always at once and not always completely. The students were respectful and responsive, but they were women, and that in itself required a long and arduous acclimatization. Misunderstandings and difficulties multiplied along with the gratifications. Because Old World eminence was not always a guarantee of proficiency in English, a considerable amount of erudition was often lost in translation. The frustrated note takers tended to become bemused knitters when an hour of exposition resulted in a half page of cryptic subtitles, and the Europeans often found it impossible to accept the fact that American students could be so hopelessly monolingual. They were, however, quick to salt their papers with sonorous new terms. During those years, no undergraduate essay was complete without at least one mention of *Zeitgeist, Sturm und Drang,* or *Weltanschauung.* "I remember a comparative literature course with the writer Joachim Maass," said a Mount Holyoke graduate who had been there during the middle forties. "He lectured in German for the first three weeks, never doubting that we all knew it well enough to follow the discussion. Even after he switched to English, he continued to say all the key words in German. My notes for that course consisted of one sentence, which I've never forgotten. It was: 'If I were to tell you the secret of the universe, you would sit down by the riverbank and weep: Gilgamesh.'"

A clear advantage of attending a women's college during the war was the fact that the faculty was not likely to be either drafted or pressed into other government service. Coeducational colleges struggled through the crisis with skeleton staffs and truncated catalogues, but since the Seven had faculties composed predominantly of women, they could continue to offer a full and often expanded range of courses. The most powerful arguments for coeducation were temporarily stilled, and the women's colleges got a great many able and interesting students who would have gone elsewhere in peacetime.

By the summer of 1943 there were so many distinguished foreign scholars in the United States that Mount Holyoke was able to gather them together for a convocation patterned on the great French intellectual community at Pontigny. From 1910 to its abrupt end in 1939 the twelfth-century Cistercian abbey at Pontigny had been the site of an all-Europe intellectual festival, a forum where artists, writers, scientists and philosophers could meet and discuss the relationships between their varied disciplines. During its heyday the French town had attracted the likes of André Gide, Paul Valéry and André Maurois, all of whom had served as seminar leaders at one time or another. Mount Holyoke's *petit* Pontigny may have lacked a few of the amenities of the original (the wines available in wartime South Hadley, for instance, were not comparable to the best Burgundies; the world-class scholars were housed in Porter Hall, a comfortable enough dormitory but hardly *une bonne auberge;* and the closest approximation of a café in the vicinity was Glessman's drugstore), but the meeting was an immense success nevertheless. The Mount Holyoke assemblage included Henri Rolin, who had been president of the Belgian Court of Appeals before Hitler; the exiled Italian art critic Lionello Venturi; Alfredo Mendizabal, a refugee from Franco's Spain; the French surrealist André Masson; the novelist Julian Green; playwright Henri Bernstein; and the mathematician Jacques Hadamard. The international group was joined by an imposing collection of American intellectuals—the New World's finest. John Peale Bishop attended, along with Maurice Peyre of Yale and the great James Bissett Pratt of the Williams College Philosophy Department. All in all, there were at least thirteen different nationalities and more than 200 participants during the month-long session. Gustave Cohen, the Belgian-born medievalist, conducted the proceedings with the help of the philosopher Jean André Wahl, who had arrived in South Hadley almost directly from a Nazi concentration camp. The encounter between Wahl and Mount Holyoke was so mutually agreeable that Wahl was invited to stay and teach philosophy there. He filled that post with delight for two years, finding his students the equals of those he had left behind at the Sorbonne and his surroundings pleasantly pastoral.

The women's colleges became something of a haven for refugee students as well as refugee teachers during the war, but Smith undergraduates were made aware of the problem even earlier. In 1939 their compassionate president, William Allan Neilson, told them in chapel of the problems faced by Spanish, Polish and Czechoslovakian scholars, who were the first groups to suffer dislocation and hardship. Those lucky enough to escape to exile in still neutral countries were struggling to live on $50 a year, Neilson said, and the Smith editorialists went to work directly after the recessional hymn. "They would be amazed," wrote one of the sympathizers in the *Smith College News*, "to hear someone at Smith say she can't afford to help them . . . our worries seem infinitesimal compared to theirs . . . we are rich if we can buy a pack of cigarettes every few days. And yet they need pencils as much as anything; that is, after they have enough food to keep them from starving." In response to these appeals, Smith students managed to raise $2,000 for refugee scholarships, a small proportion of which was collected by smoking all cigarettes down to the last shred. By impaling the butt on a toothpick, it was possible to help a displaced European student. Smoking, in fact, seemed a very patriotic act, especially if one saved every scrap of foil and turned it into the metal drives. That way it was possible to assist the war effort and the refugees simultaneously.

The foreign students who actually came to the seven women's colleges, however, often had mixed feelings about their experiences. "The girls seemed so immature," said one woman who had landed at Wellesley at the end of an agonizing hegira that led through Eastern Europe to London and finally Shanghai. "So untouched, like convent girls in Europe. Our universities, of course, were in the major cities, and as students we were responsible for our own lives. Few women attended, but those who did were the most independent and nonconforming. To come, as I did at twenty-two, to a tiny country town, to live in so protected an atmosphere, to tell the housemother where I was going and how long I would be gone, was strange beyond belief. I felt that I had escaped into childhood. My uncle, who had been a professor of chemistry at the University of Prague, also found himself in one of the women's colleges, teaching what the American girls called Baby Language. He could not teach chemistry in German, and his English was not sufficient. Of course, he was fortunate to have a home and a job, but every time he heard that expression—Baby Language—he suffered. Professors in Europe did not correct test papers or bother with matters like attending school dances. To him, the women's college was like a kindergarten, and the pay for faculty was pitiful—perhaps a hundred dollars a month. The discipline all seemed social, not mental. We did not understand the honor system, for example. An examination without monitors was unthinkable to a foreigner, and my uncle outraged his students by asking them to name the girls who sat on either side of them. That had been the custom abroad, so that similarities in papers could be checked. In America there was no one in the room, and the girls could walk around, get drinks of water and even talk to one another. And yet they were required to be in their rooms by midnight, to sleep only at approved hotels when away from the college."

The armed forces had preempted so much space in the universities for their various training programs that there were far fewer openings for women undergraduates, and those who were accepted often felt short-changed socially as well as academically. The men were there, but they were the property of the Army or Navy, confined to their barracks and reminded constantly and forcefully that they were no longer college boys, but potential officers. "At Cornell I had a fourteen-year-old prodigy in my English class," said a woman who had transferred to Bryn Mawr in 1943, "and he seemed to be the only male with free run of the campus. I decided that if I were going to spend my college years in a cloister, I'd be better off at one run by experienced nuns. Bryn Mawr turned out to be a great improvement—it was a mecca for V–5 cadets stationed at Princeton."

The wartime classes at the women's colleges became much more diverse and cosmopolitan than they had ever been before. The war had effectively ended the Depression, and college became a realistic possibility for hundreds of girls who would never have been able to afford it in previous years. For

203

the first time, ethnic surnames began to show up in the catalogues in really significant numbers, and there was even a small, brave vanguard of black students, though that designation was at least twenty years away from being acceptable, let alone wholly descriptive. The country needed all the competence and expertise it could get, and a new spirit of purposeful careerism was evident everywhere. That was to be only a temporary state of affairs, but it was invigorating while it lasted, simultaneously raising hopes and lowering occupational barriers. The first few wartime classes, as a result, were full of precocious and early achievers. Girls who might have slipped quietly and unprotestingly into traditional feminine roles immediately upon graduation were often obliged to postpone marriage, and for once, there seemed to be no shortage of interesting alternatives. It was a tense and abnormal time, but from 1941 to 1945 women had a better chance of entering the professional schools than they would until the 1970s. Careers in law, medicine, architecture, science, and government suddenly seemed within reach, and scores of women managed to slip through war-created gaps into previously all-male bastions while the incumbents were otherwise engaged.

The integration of Radcliffe students into Harvard classrooms was a wartime exigency, accepted by the faculty with a grace that varied from good to hardly passing. Unlike shoe rationing and meatless Tuesdays, however, it was to be a permanent change. The transition was smoother than anyone expected, though a few traditionalists—nostalgically or inadvertently—continued to address their mixed classes as "gentlemen." "There were no Harvard men at all in one of my classes," said a woman who had been one of those integrated, "but the man who was teaching us never admitted that to us or himself. Each day he'd say, 'Good Morning. I see we have some guests today.'"

But if launching a career during wartime was simple, getting ahead afterward was not. "And then, the boys our age had come back from the war," Betty Friedan wrote in a recent (December 30, 1974) article for *New York* magazine, "and I was bumped from my job on a small labor newspaper by a returning veteran, and it wasn't so easy to find another job I really liked." Ms. Friedan soon joined the last holdouts of her Smith

'42 class in strenuous postwar domesticity, but the bump turned out to be more traumatic than it seemed at the time. That anonymous returning veteran may have been at least partly responsible for the simmering resentment that eventually became *The Feminine Mystique.*

By 1946 it was becoming more difficult than ever for a woman to gain entrance to graduate school, and the job market for mere BAs had shriveled to its prewar dimensions. Girls were once again being offered the same limited table d'hôte that had confronted their mothers and grandmothers—teaching, typing, social work—and this time thousands seemed to have declined these dreary options. They swallowed their disappointment and settled for much less than they had planned. "I don't think it occurred to any of us to protest," said one biologist who had hoped to enter medical school in 1948. "You just didn't argue with the GI Bill of Rights, even if it meant that you ended up as a laboratory technician instead of a doctor."

On the campuses themselves the war quickly accomplished what decades of student petitions and pleas had failed to do. The Victorian social code that had survived the First War, the twenties, and the Depression finally began to disintegrate. The curfews and sign-out lists survived, but in comparison to the Army or the Navy, a women's college was a relaxed and unrestricted place. De Beauvoir was right about that. Regular undergraduates at Smith, Mount Holyoke, and Wellesley suddenly realized how free they actually were.

By 1942 the women's colleges were sharing their facilities with platoons of Waves and Spars whose rigidly controlled lives made a few curious relics of the nineteenth century seem trivial. (Vassar even had its first male undergraduates—men for whom there was no space elsewhere.) Military regulations had no give whatsoever, though college rules could often be stretched by the magic words "overseas" or "fiancé." Each college actually became two distinct schools—one civilian and the other military. There was almost no contact between them, though at least one vestige of the war effort survived well into the 1960s. In order to make room for the women's training corps, civilian students were crammed into "temporary doubles," a euphemism for rooms that were neither. "We were still sleeping in double-decker metal bunks in 1956," said a Wellesley girl. "Dual permanent singles would have been more accurate."

Every weekend the colleges were inundated by hordes of young men stationed at nearby bases, and there was an atmosphere of feverish gaiety. Policing all this frantic activity turned out to be virtually impossible, and though the administrations did their best to enforce standards of deportment, they were overwhelmed by the job. In theory, no man could be entertained behind totally closed doors, and "Open the width of a wastebasket" became the quixotic standard of ladylike decency. Wastebaskets shrank with each passing week, until some of them were so narrow that they would hardly swallow a single sheet of paper inserted sideways. "Another rule was that one person's foot had to be on the floor at all times," recalled a Wellesley alumnae, "though I think that was an unwritten law." There is some disagreement about whether that stipulation was a joke, a fact or mere apocrypha, but the import was clear. In war or peace, college women were still expected to maintain a semivertical position in the presence of men.

Freedom without privacy became a constant challenge. Since neither the undergraduate girls nor the officers in training were permitted to have cars, most of the men's short leaves were spent in a desperate search for an unoccupied corner. The library stacks and carrels were full of affectionate couples by five o'clock every Saturday; girls who had never touched an oar or a paddle signed up for crew, a subterfuge that assured access to the college boathouse; and there were even those who cheerfully volunteered for kitchen duty, a small sacrifice to pay for exclusive rights to the pantries and storerooms. With the help of two merchant marine cadets from New London, a pair of Vassar girls succeeded in turning a capacious equipment closet in the chemistry lab into an agreeable, if somewhat stuffy, lounge. A KEEP OUT GOVERNMENT PROPERTY SECRET sign liberated from the base worked so well that the closet was still padlocked when the weekend tenants returned for their fifth reunion in 1948, its furnishings intact except for the damage done by mice to the LOOSE LIPS SINK SHIPS poster.

Before the attack on Pearl Harbor the undergraduate mood all over America had been strongly pacifist, and it took somewhat longer than is generally recognized for the college generation to accept the fact of war. A Smith editorialist wrote in a widely reprinted and admired essay:

> All of our lives we have been indoctrinated with absolute pacifism. Our parents, filled with horror at the last war and its outcome, imbued us with a real aversion to war. In school and college we were told that no cause, however great, was worth the sacrifice of so many human lives, and for this we were given historical proofs. The effects of twenty years of indoctrination cannot be wiped away in two months. . . . In two weeks the campus changed from firm non-intervention to a state of teary jitters, of almost hysterical uncertainty.

It was a condition that was to persist for the duration, exacerbated by the fact that students were being encouraged to accelerate their programs, as well as to volunteer for Red Cross projects, aircraft spotting and work on the reactivated college farms. A weekly schedule that included six full-credit courses, night vigils in the observatory, and a few hours of potato digging was not at all uncommon. A few students even took part-time jobs in industry. Almost everyone was in the throes of a wartime romance and struggling with the still debatable question of whether or not one should "wait for marriage." Though virginity was not unanimously considered an asset, it was not yet regarded as a burden, and the debates were intense. The findings, however, were inconclusive because those who took the negative position (how would you feel if you said no and he was wounded or killed?) were intimidated by the same fear of pregnancy that kept the opposition virtuous. Secret marriage was the only solution if that happened, and it was fraught with risk and difficulty. Officers in training were not permitted to marry, and to do so meant boot camp or the infantry instead of college and an eventual commission.

The women's colleges didn't attempt to poll their students on attitudes toward premarital sex, but there was considerable evidence that morality had undergone a radical change, and there was no reason to assume that girls at Smith, Vassar, Holyoke and the rest were an exception to a national trend. The bohemian theories of the twenties and thirties had long since been tested, approved, and widely adopted by undergraduates. The director of the Marriage Counseling Service at Pennsylvania State College, where some discreet and serious research had been done during the war years, reported that by 1946, 60 percent of American girls were "non-virgins on the day they marry" but added that college girls seemed to be "somewhat more chaste" than the population at large. They were, in any case, more cautious and so adept at argument that the ultimate decision could be almost indefinitely postponed. By the time a girl said yes the statistics could be hopelessly distorted.

Faculty members who taught at the Seven throughout the 1940s often remark on the great changes in student goals during that decade. There was a perceptible and disturbing shift that was apparent almost everywhere by 1947, a loss of direction that showed itself it several ways. Girls who had entered college with clear ideas about their abilities were suddenly switching from department to department, apparently unable to maintain their interest long enough to fulfill even the minimal requirements for a major field. The Celestial Seven had never been plagued by dropouts, but the number of students who came for a year or two and then left increased sharply. Most of the defections seemed to take place at the end of the sophomore year, with the symptoms of misery usually appearing by November. "Sophomore slump" became endemic, the subject of student editorials and concerned administrative conferences on every campus. Recovery was slow and usually only partial. Interdepartmental majors did not seem to be the answer, although less rigidity in requirements had been one expressed desire of undergraduates. Subclinical cases became acute as the deadline for selecting a major approached. More leeway, however, only seemed to cause more confusion as students flirted first with one discipline and then another, finally settling on whatever seemed to demand the smallest measure of commitment. "I had the feeling that even my brightest students were marking time," said a professor who left Smith in 1948 to take a lesser position at Williams. "I noticed it not only among the freshmen who entered after the war, but even in individual students who had begun in 1943 or 1944 with very definite goals. Even they seemed to be affected by a sort of pervasive ennui. We were really at a loss to explain it except as a sort of postwar letdown."

The slump syndrome varied widely, but its stages were distinct and progressive. The onset was most often the conviction that one had chosen the wrong college and that the boredom and sense of futility could be alleviated if only it were possible to transfer to a large coeducational university. The positive act of sending for catalogues and filling out applications was beneficial in itself, and during this brief phase the victims often did some of the best and most original work of their college careers. Once having made the decision and diagnosed their wretchedness as the consequence of being in an isolated, artificial and all-female environment, the languor disappeared. There was a tremendous amount of proselytizing, as girls who had seen the light attempted to persuade their roommates and closest friends to follow their example. Entire halls, clubs and special interest groups often declared their intentions to transfer almost simultaneously. "At one time or another during the late forties we thought we would lose the newspaper staff, the political science majors or all the acting talent on campus," recalled a Wellesley administrator who had been a graduate assistant during that phase.

The feeling of student dissatisfaction was actually palpable. The rules, the food, chapel, the distribution requirements, the climate, the marking system—all of it seemed to become unendurable at once. Eggs goldenrod, tuna wiggle, three hours of outdoor sport, two church services a month, science for poets, English for chemists, slush, and grades sent home to Father—all made splendid pegs on which to hang one's rage. Professors were deluged with requests for references and recommendations from honors students in mid-thesis and candidates for the highest campus offices. The slump seemed to hit the extremes of each class, creating an inexplicable coalition between the most serious and the most frivolous, the scholars and the butterflies, the stars and the strugglers. Only the drearily average seemed relatively resistant to the spreading restlessness, a situation that distressed the faculty most of all. Girls who had never been excited by the prospect of college weren't so likely to be disappointed by the actuality.

The crisis came when the optimistic transfers were regretfully informed that universities to which they had applied were unable to accommodate them because of the surge of returning veterans. The women's colleges suddenly found themselves in a double bind—a significant and vocal minority of malcontent upperclassmen and waves of entering freshmen who made no secret of the fact that a single-sex institution had been their last choice. Each successive class seemed less enthusiastic than the one before, fuller of girls who longed with all their hearts to be elsewhere.

The fact that they were surrounded with young men was very little consolation. The veterans had little time or money for the traditional distractions of undergraduate life. Their $65-a-month allowances from a grateful government barely stretched to cover the necessities, and most were eager to finish college and get on with something more lucrative. The war had aged them psychologically as well as chronologically. The twenty-three-, twenty-four- and twenty-five-year-old men who had returned from the battles of Europe and Asia were understandably impatient, and a women's college that still insisted on its students signing in at 1 A.M. didn't seem to offer much opportunity for mature relationships. There was no housing for married students, not even the Quonset huts and barracks that had appeared on other campuses. As soon as the war was over, all Seven attempted to return to the status quo ante as soon as possible, and it was that intransigence that undergraduates found so insensitive. Young women had also been changed by the war, and many who entered college in the years immediately after it found the atmosphere oppressive, puerile, and claustrophobic. To ask a man who had participated in the Normandy invasion to settle for an hour or so of coy chatter in the dating parlors, a stroll around the lake, a house dance at which fruit punch and cookies were the only refreshment was an embarrassment in itself. That may have been diverting to the seventeen- and eighteen-year-old cadets who had had no other choices, but it was absurdly inadequate for these same young men four years later. The colleges had responded splendidly to the war, but they seemed unwilling and unable to make further concessions to the peace.

It's apparent from interviews, from letters to the alumnae magazines, from class notes and responses to reunion questionnaires that women who attended one of the Seven during the last half of the 1940s are less enthusiastic and more critical of their colleges than any generation that preceded them. As a group they are slower to credit their education for their successes and quicker to blame it for their failures. Their lists of alumnae daughters are shorter, their contributions to development funds somewhat stingier, their commitment to the continuing idea of single-sex education weaker. They are the ones who usually answer yes to referenda on whether their alma maters should convert to coeducation. Sophomore slump is not easily outgrown.

The easiest answer to restlessness and anxiety in the forties was marriage, and the postwar classes married almost unanimously, literally standing in line to get to the altar. College chapels, so rarely attended during the academic year, were booked solidly for two weeks after graduation. (Vassar had done away with compulsory church in 1926, and the custom had never really been established at Barnard.) Even in the late forties, however, it was almost impossible to graduate from Smith, Mount Holyoke, or Wellesley without at least some exposure to organized religion, and Bryn Mawr girls of every persuasion usually emerged quite familiar with the concept of Inner Light. Norma Rosen, Holyoke '48, wrote in an April, 1972, piece for the *New York Times Magazine,* "We were all—Christians, Jews, whatever—netted into compulsory chapel service three times every two weeks and two Sundays out of four." The pretty Gothic or vaguely Romanesque chapels were there, and they did make charming settings for summer weddings. One's classmates could be persuaded to remain on hand for the ceremony, and after a wedding dinner at a historic country inn like Wiggins Tavern in Northampton, the bride could depart in an aura of double glory—sending her mortarboard and veil home in Father's station wagon. Alumnae tell of serving as bridesmaids twice or even three times in a single day, but the All-Seven Star must be a Barnard graduate who was maid of honor one morning at ten, again at noon, was married herself at four, and reappeared the following day before leaving on her honeymoon to be matron of honor for her roommate. By the time the first class notes appeared in the alumnae quarterlies, scribes were triumphantly reporting that 60 or 70 percent of the group was already married, and within two years 100 percent records seemed a distinct possibility. The statistics were similar for all seven colleges, with Bryn Mawr girls (our failures only marry) vowing to love, honor, cherish, and even obey as eagerly as anyone else.

The birthrates were equally prodigious, as college women vied with each other to produce four-, five-, six-, and seven-child families in the shortest possible time. There are no separate statistics for alumnae of the Seven, but college graduates in general were having 81 percent more children between 1941 and 1947 than ever before. This phenomenon was *limited* to the highly educated. (Grade-school graduates were having only 29 percent more children.) The figures confounded the experts, who could hardly believe that the traditional inverse ratio between years of school and size of family no longer applied. They checked and rechecked, but the facts were incontrovertible. Smithies and Cliffies, one year out, met in the laundries of garden apartments and asked each other, "If one baby takes all your time, how much more can three or four take?" stuffed another batch of diapers into the dryer and traded recipes for spaghetti sauce. The rest, of course, is feminist history. Marriage and housekeeping, in the years immediately following World War II, seemed to leave time for nothing else, as college women applied all their ingenuity and imagination to them, making them as challenging and difficult as possible, as "rewarding."

The pressures to marry seemed irresistible, exerted by parents, classmates, industry, advertising, and popular psychology, but most of all by the returning veterans who were the fiancés and beaux of alumnae and students. The sexual revolution that followed the first war had been sadly incomplete—"sleeping together" was possible; "living together" still thirty years away. Only marriage was even thinkable to the ex-serviceman eager to become an officer of IBM. They were very persuasive, those veterans, with their tales of suffering, hardship, and loneliness, and they carried an entire generation of college women off to the boondocks, where the new housing was and the jobs and graduate schools were not. The radical feminists call it sexist conspiracy. The victims, who didn't know they were victims until they were told some fifteen years later, called it love.

XX
"A Less Ambitious Direction"

ONE of Vassar's most durable legends has it that the first professor of astronomy, Maria Mitchell, took her most gifted students by their leg-o'-mutton sleeves and marched them down the halls of Old Main (then just Main) until they decided upon a future career—often one in astronomy. At that point she released her grip, and teacher and protégée returned to the observatory to stake out a corner of the universe for further investigation. The redoubtable Miss Mitchell was exactly what feminists now call a role model, and there was no shortage of them at the women's colleges during the first half century or so.

Not all could have been either as relentless or as inspiring as Miss Mitchell, but the colleges were staffed by extraordinary women who consciously set a lofty example. Even Vassar girls who seemed unlikely candidates for the Maria Mitchell career march were impressed by the ubiquitous and influential history professor Lucy Salmon. Miss Salmon was a member of one of the first coeducational classes at the University of Michigan, graduating in 1872. Her mother, who died when Lucy was seven, had attended the original Ipswich, Massachusetts, seminary run by Mary Lyon and Zilpah Grant, and that fact had apparently made Lucy Salmon's widowed father more receptive than most mid-Victorian papas to the idea of advanced education for girls. After Michigan, Miss Salmon taught at a public high school in Iowa, then returned to Ann Arbor for graduate work in history. Armed with an MA and a considerable amount of rare and specialized knowledge of English and American constitutional law, she accepted an appointment at the State Normal School in Terre Haute, Indiana, a job in which her abilities were sadly underutilized.

The intrepid Miss Salmon then spent still another pioneering year as a graduate student at Bryn Mawr before becoming Vassar's first history teacher. She was made a full professor almost immediately, and she remained at Vassar for a professional career that lasted from the late 1880s until she was well past the mandatory retirement age of seventy. She continued to teach at Vassar until the middle of the Jazz Age, and she seemed as provocative to the flappers as she had to the belles of the nineties. Almost single-handedly, she revolutionized the curriculum, brought about the partial transfer of administrative power from the president and trustees to the faculty, and altered or bypassed many of the more absurd social regulations. Miss Salmon was strongly antimonarchist by training and inclination and well versed in the uses and abuses of absolutism. Little by little, she remade the college to suit her own progressive notions. With the help of the Vassar librarian Adelaide Underhill, Lucy Salmon also succeeded in creating a superb research collection, and when the new library building was completed in 1900, a great deal of the credit for both structure and contents devolved on the history professor.

Lucy Salmon's greatest innovations, however, were within her own classrooms. Very early on, she had come to believe that learning should be a dialogue between professor and student, and she conducted her seminars as sophisticated conversations. It was a remarkably contemporary approach to college work, and Miss Salmon was one of the first faculty members anywhere to attempt it. She astonished her students still further by bringing daily newspapers into the classrooms. Until then current events had been considered outside the province of higher education, if not actually beneath it. There have been dozens of Vassar tributes to Lucy Salmon, but one of the most direct is the anonymous comment quoted in the biographical essay that appears in *Notable American Women*. "It doesn't always seem like history and sometimes it's rather dull, but you are never the same person afterwards," said one of her students, and that seems a nearly perfect summation. Much of Vassar's reputation for political and social activism is traceable to Lucy Maynard Salmon, who continued to radicalize alumnae for thirty-eight years, counteracting passivity, complacency and smugness wherever she found it. That was a demanding job in itself, but the challenge suited and delighted her.

Vassar had no monopoly on faculty movers and shakers, but it did have a head start and seemed to attract and produce them almost from the beginning. Wellesley, however, had a celebrated and nearly notorious firebrand in Vida Scudder, who taught there during the exquisitely genteel years just before and after the First World War. Miss Scudder was so genuinely and deeply involved in the labor union movement that on one occasion she seems to have actually got herself arrested. (Accounts vary—some reporters say that Miss Scudder was merely admonished by the police, but others insist that she was actually held in custody.) In any case, such activities were unthinkable for college professors in 1912 and, in fact, have only very recently become acceptable. In 1912 Miss Scudder's affiliations aroused real panic. Vida Scudder was a true pioneer—Wellesley's first agitator—and she made a practice of attending and participating in the union meetings held in various Massachusetts mill towns, rarely missing any. She was often accompanied by a sympathetic colleague, Ellen Hayes, and the two lady professors managed to cover a considerable amount of territory. They were both in great demand as speakers and much admired by spinners, dyers and weavers from Fall River west. On the particular occasion that was so grossly misunderstood and so nearly disastrous, Miss Scudder had been addressing the Professional Women's Club of Lawrence on what now seems a relatively bland topic— the safety of children during strikes. Her rhetoric was restrained and academic, but 1912 was a depressed year in the woolen industry, and there were long and bitter disruptions all over the state. The local papers made much of the fact that two Wellesley faculty members always seemed to be among the pickets and protestors—and on the wrong, or working-class, side at that. Immense pressure was applied to the college to dismiss both teachers, and telegrams, letters, and editorials flooded the Wellesley mailboxes. The kindest epithets applied to the Misses Scudder and Hayes were "rabble-rouser," "anarchist," and "Bolshevik." In those years, the fathers of Wellesley students tended to be manufacturers or millowners, and alienating these real and potential patrons for the sake of two replaceable teachers seemed unwise.

The college was inclined to capitulate to public opinion until Miss Scudder wrote a memorable and effective letter explaining the exact nature of her involvement. In it, she devoted considerable space and eloquence to her abiding faith in Wellesley's tradition of academic freedom. Her prose convinced the administrators and trustees that the press should never be allowed to influence the policies of the college, and Miss Scudder and Miss Hayes remained at Wellesley, venerated and cherished even by those they had embarrassed. "But we kept Miss Scudder on," in fact, became something of a stock reply to future charges of conservatism, and there were many of those during the twenties.

Toward the end of the nineteenth century the specter of spinsterhood seems to have lost some of its power, and young women of that era seemed more willing to take risks than ever before or since. Simply by deciding to go to college in the first place, they had separated themselves from the majority of their contemporaries and broken out of the Victorian lockstep. The second move was often the easier one. When a student *did* opt for marriage and motherhood in those days, the colleges actually rejoiced. For many years, that was the best advertisement they could have, and the class scribes greeted each birth announcement with the unrestrained delight of new grandparents. Every baby helped dispel the persistent charges and troublesome rumors that the women's colleges subverted nature by deflecting impressionable girls from their true destinies.

The weight of statistics remained right up until the 1950s. Though women from 1900 to the 1950s talked eagerly about combining marriage with a career, comparatively few actually managed to do it. Instead, they chose either one or the other. In very special circumstances, there could be a succession of roles. Spinsters, widows, and divorcées "went out to work," but most American men continued to regard a fully employed wife as an indication of the husband's improvidence, tangible proof that he had not lived up to the traditional prenuptial promise to support his bride in the manner to which she was accustomed. Alumnae of the Seven, always statistically a bit out of the mainstream, married later and less unanimously, producing fewer children than girls who had attended a coeducational institution or none at all. Although their names turned up with much greater frequency on lists of noted American women, those were often maiden names, useless for the kind of public relations the colleges always seemed to need. An embarrassment of spinsters also meant that there might not be enough alumnae daughters to carry on the tradition, and few large financial bequests because the eminent women scholars and dedicated public servants were so inadequately rewarded by society. "Benevolent gentlemen" have been essential to the survival of women's colleges ever since Mary Lyon first suggested that the idea for her seminary should be made to seem as if it had originated with them. None of the Seven could have existed or thrived without a constantly replenished supply of gratified fathers, contented husbands, proud uncles, and, more recently, favorably disposed foundations. Too many exceptional alumnae—no matter how worthy and useful—have always been a calculated risk. Americans, after all, are happiest in the presence of the average and a bit uneasy when confronted with extremes of any kind—an attitude that is most obvious when one is trying to raise money.

There have been times in our history when our national romance with the average has reached particular peaks of intensity, and the Eisenhower years seem to have been one of those periods. The whole country was obsessed with normality—perhaps understandably enough after twenty consecutive years of economic depression and war—and it didn't take long for undergraduate attitudes to reflect the majority mood. It was an era when very few people seemed interested in taking chances, possibly because they had already inadvertently taken too many. Whole senior classes at the Ivy League colleges lined up to be interviewed by companies that promised the greatest security and the most generous pension plans. Boys of twenty asked prospective employers sophisticated questions about medical insurance and loan funds. They compared fringe benefits and chose jobs with the corporation that offered the longest list of perks. To be a vice-president by the age of thirty-five seemed to be almost every young man's goal, and most seemed eager and willing to tailor themselves to fit the house image. The sociological literature on this period is extensive and now somewhat dated, but the notes in the men's college quarterlies still make entertaining reading. Just two decades later, the degree of conformity that young people would tolerate seems amazing—column after column of virtually interchangeable middle-management jobs in sales, development, research and marketing, the conservative pattern broken only by the mention of a doctor, lawyer, or clergyman. Medical, law, or divinity school, however, was not the place to look for rebels during the early 1950s. That was where you found the most security-minded young men of all, and, very often, the least adventurous.

And once a young man had his future neatly arranged, usually by Christmas of his senior year, he discussed it all with his Smith, Wellesley, or Vassar girl. (It was the era of togetherness as well as of normality.) Strolling around Paradise Pond, the Bird Sanctuary or Lake Waban, the couples talked things over. Chances are the corporation would be moving them around a bit at first, so perhaps the best thing would be for the bride to take a temporary sort of job, just something to keep herself busy. If the suitor happened to be one of the PhD candidates or planning on law or medical school, the girl's options would be even more restricted. Once he had his degree, she could start work on hers. They might take turns in school, but with a crucial 1950s difference. Ladies were last. With appalling docility, the women undergraduates accepted all these conditions. Half the seniors at the women's colleges were usually engaged by the opening of second semester, and professors braced themselves for a novel January ritual. For the first few weeks after vacation they would be confronted by a roomful of girls with arms outstretched, palms down. It was ring-admiring season, and the form was strict. Little groups would go from desk to desk, comparing, exclaiming and handing around the plastic-laminated newspaper announcements that the fiancées had brought to class. On sunny days, the betrothed would take care to sit near a window, to that they could catch beams of light in their rings and flash them on the blackboards and ceilings. Academically, nothing much would be accomplished until the second or third week of the term.

From 1944 on the alumnae of the women's colleges seemed to show markedly less interest in careers of their own. Most girls expected "to work for a while," but they shied away from anything that would mean a long-term commitment. Fewer students applied to graduate school, and the attrition rate of those who did go on for advanced degrees was higher than before. The colleges suspected, not without some justification, that the dropouts had had an ulterior motive all along. If one was not engaged by Tree Day, or Lantern Night, or in time for the Spring Step Sing, then graduate school was the intelligent woman's last resort.

Girls who went to work as *Time-Life* researchers or junior assistants in publishing houses were rumored to live a dreary life, sharing walk-up apartments and drifting into unhappy love affairs with married men. The all-purpose alumnae note for the mid-fifties seemed to begin, "While Tom is studying for his orals—or finishing the training program, or interning—I am working in the dean's office part time. We expect more thrilling news in time for the next issue." The role models were still teaching in the women's colleges, but undergraduates seemed to be rejecting them right and left.

According to the Mellon survey of Vassar women assembled by Donald Brown and published in 1956 in the *Journal of Social Studies,* the alumnae of that era were overwhelmingly "future family oriented." The indomitable Maria Mitchell could have marched that entire generation all the way down to New York and back without getting a single commitment to a career in astronomy, even though related fields, like astrophysics, were attracting thousands of young men. Women students, however, were majoring in psychology, sociology, English, art, and languages, choosing these subjects because they felt that they would "enrich family life." They studied conscientiously, but their goals were often not the sort to gladden the heart of a dedicated teacher. What the majority wanted was a normal, well-rounded life, and it seemed impossible to live one of those, 1950s style, in a hospital emergency room, a laboratory, or even a studio.

The best index of the craving for normality may be the colleges' own registers of "distinguished alumnae" for those years. All Seven show noticeably fewer prominent professional women for the decade between 1949 and 1959 than for any other period in their history. Since the older women (before 1945) faced greater obstacles, and the younger women (after 1959) may still have their greatest achievements ahead of them, the drop is even more striking than mere numbers indicate. Smith, for instance, claims ten "distinguished alumnae" for 1895 to 1905, when classes where tiny and most fields still closed to women or simply nonexistent. From 1950 to 1960, when Smith graduated about 450 each June, only seven alumnae names made the postgraduate honor role of achievement. (The Smith list has since become much longer.) Similar discrepancies are apparent everywhere, suggesting that college women may have been the chief casualties of the feminine mystique, with less resistance to its blandishments than many less advantaged groups. The vast majority of contributors to Betty Friedan's 1963 book, in fact, seem to be either Smith women like herself or products of other equally illustrious institutions. Most of the poignant and bitter quotations on which she based her manifesto were provided by women who had voluntarily withdrawn from the business or professional world—lapsed liberal arts majors, for the most part, who thought wistfully of Sartre and Caravaggio as they wrote notes to the milkman and tacked up nursery-school drawings on their bulletin boards. The only encouraging news to emerge from the fifties is that these same alumnae now say, almost to a woman, that they are active in the women's liberation movement and deeply committed to its goals. Hundreds of them are reporting that they're back in graduate school or working at salaried jobs, some because inflation has galvanized them into action, but most because that well-rounded life turned out to have its jagged edges after all.

Few subjects have been as thoroughly and as tiresomely explored as the cult of femininity that suffocated so many capable young women during the fifties, and every feminist has her favorite team of scapegoats. The choice is wide, but one of the sounder and more logical explanations is the enormous influence of a group of post-Freudian psychologists who carried the "anatomy is destiny" notion to its ultimate extremes. One of the leaders of this school of thought was Marynia Farnham, a Bryn Mawr alumna and psychiatrist who published *Modern Woman—The Lost Sex* in 1947, collaborating with Ferdinand Lundberg, a newspaper reporter and biographer. Lundberg's contribution was a turgid but authoritative prose style, sharpened by his own unregenerate masculine bias. The book was widely read and passionately discussed on college campuses (everybody was studying psychology in that decade, and the lecture halls could hardly hold the crowds signed up for the introductory courses).

The Farnham-Lundberg thrust was straight to the heart, and the message was simplistic. Women could achieve tranquillity and a sense of personal worth by applying all their abilities to childbearing, child rearing, and the household arts. Double-handedly, Farnham and Lundberg attempted to elevate domesticity to an economic and social status lost since the machine age. They reasoned that technology had made housework too quick and easy to be satisfying and that women unconsciously longed to regain the sense of worth enjoyed by every colonial dame who carded her own wool, stoked her own wood fires, kneaded and baked her own bread and bore six living children out of ten pregnancies. Sears, Roebuck, General Foods, General Electric, and Margaret Sanger had deprived the contemporary woman of these basic satisfactions, thereby creating a vacuum in their lives and producing a sex that was not only "lost" but neurotic and miserable.

Lundberg and Farnham proposed to bring back almost everything but diphtheria, childbed fever, and outdoor plumbing. They actually advocated a "government supervisory agency devoted to women who live as women—that is women as mothers." The "first general task of this agency," they maintained, "should be one of propaganda, with a view to restoring woman's sense of prestige and self-esteem as actual or potential mothers. The first step would be to revise, completely, by the dissemination in popular channels, of scientific data, present public misconceptions about the nature, deeds, and capacities of women." That done, the text continued, "the agency might well set about procuring for women solid public honors for activities as women. Such public honors would be accorded to women like Florence Nightingale. But they would also be accorded to women who had raised children who turned out to be well-rounded citizens, valuable community leaders. We do not mean here, achievers per se. Foreign countries," Lundberg and Farnham admitted, "Soviet Russia, the Third Reich, Fascist Italy worked out methods of issuing medals to mothers on the basis of the quantity of children they brought into the world." That policy, the authors agreed, left some room for improvement. America was probably not ready for anything so exactly analagous a mere twenty-four months after the end of the war with the Axis. The Farnham-Lundberg plan would, instead, reward mothers for the *quality* of their children and would be a "Policy designed to produce fewer child behavior problems and delinquents, fewer criminals and socially maladjusted, fewer alcoholics, fewer neurotics in general and fewer men unfit to defend the society they live in." (The differences between these proposals and those outlined in *Mein Kampf* are less significant than they seem. Hitler was also concerned with eugenics and very generous with medals and decorations.)

Most of the text of *Modern Woman* is devoted to chronicles of social ills brought about by women's headlong pursuit of goals beyond the hearth, a trend that seems to have coincided with the movement for higher education. Lundberg and Farnham did not want to abolish the colleges, but they did suggest that more attention be paid to domestic science and child psychology, even if that meant short shrift for the Renaissance or James Joyce.

Instead of racketing around the workaday world, college-trained women (Bryn Mawr girls included, though Farnham's large psychiatric practice seems to have kept her away from the stove a good deal of the time) should stay at home and concentrate on the mental and physical fitness of their children. If they did a good job and their offspring were up to the rigid standards set by the authors (no extra points for achievers per se), the women would get an unspecified public honor—perhaps World Class Mother for the best, all-American for the runners-up, honorable mention for the merely diligent. Though it now seems inconceivable that a whole generation could have swallowed such twaddle, complete with its acknowledged Fascist overtones, it did happen. The evidence is thoroughly documented in every feminist anthology.

All by themselves, Farnham and Lundberg could hardly have brainwashed an entire decade of young women, but they had considerable help. Their message was quickly seized on by popular magazines; by industry eager to retool for peace (sewing machines instead of tanks); by young men (the girl of their dreams was as soft and as sweet as a nursery, not as tough and as sour as the president of their corporation); and, saddest to say, by quite a few college administrators and social science professors. Revised definitions of womanhood poured forth from every medium. Girls who strayed from the new parameters were damned as hard, cold, and, worst of all, "emasculating." The giant national corporations which wielded so much power during those years actually issued guidelines for the wives of their employees based on these theories. The ideal corporate wife selflessly volunteered her services to the community in which she found herself, made no objections when her husband was transferred from one city to another and was always home when he returned from the rough day at the office, ready to listen and soothe. Her contact with politics and business was vicarious. Men made the world go round, and their wives kept them from getting dizzy.

Women even dressed for this nineteenth-century part in the long sweeping skirts and needle-heeled shoes that fashion designers promptly provided. Even the hourglass figure, which had been abandoned with such relief by the liberated women of the 1920s, was revived. The Warner Lingerie Company marketed a nasty and confining arrangements of hooks, bones, and garters known as the Merry Widow Corselet, and it completely remolded the body to mid-Victorian measurements.

Girls who longed for success in the larger world (or even for a *chance* at success) were regarded as selfish and perverse, while those who actually persisted felt guilty and alienated. To many women, the life of a doctor, lawyer or scientist, of an opera singer, actress, dancer, writer, or painter seemed irreconcilable with the social climate in which they lived. The struggle to fulfill the insistent demands of a considerable talent while simultaneously trying to live up to the elaborate fifties pattern of wifehood and motherhood could actually lead to madness and death. Sylvia Plath, Smith '54, the gifted poet who committed suicide in 1963, may be an extreme case, but extremes prove points. Thousands of other women, less driven or more "stable," just became neurotic and miserable. The abilities and gifts that they had struggled to develop and perfect were donated to charity, along with the duplicate wedding presents, the rickety Bathinettes, and the college textbooks. The annual Bryn Mawr book sales could always count upon a nice assortment of French classics, a basic library of Great Western philosophers from Descartes to Sartre and a mixed bag of social scientists— Keynes, Sabine, Samuelson and Comte, with a bit of Engels and Marx often included. In the fifties, even intellectual young couples were cautious about what they displayed on suburban bookshelves.

The less brilliant or gifted found it was easier to fit into the Merry Widow straitjacket—another child, three more hours a week of volunteer service, a course in French or Oriental cooking and, very often, a few years of psychoanalysis to get rid of the hostilities and aggressions that seemed to be ruining their lives. Female ambition was regarded as a curable disorder, to be treated by an analyst or alienist, which is the more precise form of the word. Alienists' offices were jammed during the late fifties and early sixties, and the names on their calendars came right off the dean's lists of a few years before. Some of the analysands emerged from therapy persuaded, at least temporarily, that a nice even-textured loaf of bread for dinner was just as fine an achievement as a sonnet in the *New Yorker*. Other, more difficult cases were sent out to have their flings at a career, just to prove to themselves that it "hardly paid" to work. Scores of magazine and newspaper articles were written to convince the skeptics that the cost of household help, taxes, clothing, and commutation far exceeded the amount of money a woman could earn and that their work was actually a form of self-indulgent extravagance. The damage to the workingwoman's children, of course, was incalculable in terms of dollars and cents. Even so, some married women worked anyway, stoically enduring the patronizing cliché "My wife's job is cheaper than a shrink."

Throughout this decade women were constantly bombarded with elegies to the "free self-determined day" of the housewife, so different from the dreary routine of a nine-to-five job, so much more challenging and varied. (The age of conformity attached a special virtue to the homemade, which of course, was never to *look* homemade. "I made it myself"—the boast of the kindergartener—became the cliché of the well-adjusted grownup woman, as guests admired her needlepoint, her clothing, her exquisite Gâteau St.-Honoré, her garden and even her vinyl tile floors.) No one noticed that these homilies to the domestic arts increased in enthusiasm with the distance of their authors from the concerns of kitchen and nursery. Unbearably pressured, women finally capitulated. It's enervating to be constantly defensive, to resist and reject the life-style adopted by almost all of one's contemporaries. There is a great relief in failure under such circumstances. Women actually welcomed it as peace with honor.

224

Within a very few years an even more ominous trend was to become apparent. Women had come to terms with failure and had actually begun to fear and dread *success*. Matina Horner, now the president of Radcliffe College, based her doctoral thesis and several later studies on this new and disturbing phenomenon. Although she had first observed it among alumnae of a "large midwestern university [most probably Michigan, where she earned her degree], "the syndrome seemed endemic. The early warnings had first sounded in the late 1950s, and by the time she began investigating *Sex Differences in Achievement Motivations and Performance in Competitive and Non-Competitive Situations* for her dissertation, there was no lack of evidence. Women students everywhere in America had been so profoundly affected by the cult of femininity that they were denying their own abilities, refusing to utilize them. The tag line "Nobody loves a Phi Beta Kappa" was no longer a joke, but a genuine threat. No one would love a doctor, a financial analyst, an architect or an attorney, unless the lover were a woman and the professional a man. When Mrs. Horner tested groups of Radcliffe girls in 1969, she discovered that a full 75 percent of them showed "evidence of high fears of success," a finding which was particularly distressing since Radcliffe students are selected for their records of "high ability, achievement, motivation and previous success."

Many girls arrived at college with great hopes for careers, but after a semester or two at Harvard they "changed their plans toward a less ambitious, more traditionally feminine direction." Young women who had been babies in the 1950s obviously were desperately in need of rehabilitation as much as, if not more than, their mothers. Though the liberation movement had reached its height in 1969, it was clearly not powerful enough in itself to undo the psychological damage that these girls had already absorbed. If the mothers had been exposed to Farnham and Lundberg, the daughters grew up afraid to win fellowships, promotions, or elections. The new president of Radcliffe seems the ideal person to remedy matters. Her theory about the fear of success is now regarded as almost indisputably correct, and college administrators are doing everything possible to restore confidence among their students. The women's college may be the ideal setting for this project. Many of the victims improve rapidly when they are not subjected to the constant judgment and dominance of men, many of whom still regard the outstanding woman as a threat, and only the mediocre as lovable.

In a July, 1949, article for *The American Mercury,* Carolyn Bird, Vassar '35 and now one of the most enlightened feminist writers, noted that the most popular members of the college faculty at that time were the anthropologist Dorothy Hail, who "glorified maternity," and the psychologist Mary Langmuir of the Child Study Department, whose vision of the good society was child-centered. It had taken only two years for the insidious Farnham-Lundberg influence to spread upward as well as outward and down. The president of Vassar in those years, Sarah Blanding, impressed Ms. Bird as "more concerned about the alumna who marries and finds homemaking dull than about the professional who has a hard row to hoe in a man's world." Good Vassar graduate that she was, Carolyn Bird refrained from making any value judgment upon that priority. The Blanding attitude was not unique in any case. The presidents of the other women's colleges also seemed far more attentive to the needs of the many average and well-adjusted girls than the few extraordinary ones. Both Smith and Mount Holyoke had male presidents during this era, and feminism, on campus and off, was in total eclipse.

There were, of course, remarkable exceptions at each of the colleges. Even in the 1950s not everyone hoped to be supermom and president of the hospital auxiliary. Every campus had its political activists (you could be against Richard Nixon as early as 1952), artists, dancers, actresses, writers, and young women who were excited by the possibilities of new majors in Russian, Far Eastern Affairs, Urban Problems, and the like. According to the survey made by Donald Brown and published in the *Journal of Social Studies* in 1956, the "high achievers" were not only out of step as students, but destined for later trouble. In his study of Vassar women he found the "talent elite" to be low on "peer-group oriented activity while in college but high in orientation toward professional role and identification with faculty values . . . rarely marry and even more rarely have children . . . rather they attain advanced degrees and hold responsible professional positions . . . problems arise both out of their personal backgrounds and from the dominant cultural

226

situation of women, which they are to some extent flouting."

A clear note of disapproval is apparent even through the sociological jargon of the Mellon report. Bright and gifted girls have few friends, though they may be teachers' pets. They get doctorates instead of husbands and babies. In the end, they may be sorry. The prevailing psychology seemed to offer an alternative to thousands of girls, and they accepted it gratefully. For someone who had doubts about her own chances of success (and who, at twenty, has not), the Freud-Farnham coalition was a godsend. If you weren't absolutely sure that you could write that novel, survive the third year of medical school or cope with Blackstone on torts, there were other approved paths to self-respect and happiness. Straight paths. Almost every pundit in the 1950s was saying so, and the arguments were seductive and stereophonic.

The "high achievers" were not the only students to find themselves low on social peer-group activities during those years. It was a bad decade to be a member of any minority. When the Los Angeles Wellesley Club recently assembled forty-five memoirs for a centennial booklet, the lone black alumna of the class of 1950 could only say that "my experience as the only Negro for my first two years at Wellesley and one of no more than six anytime I was there actually confirmed my identity as a black person."

She would not have had significantly more company at any of the other colleges. Until the beginning of the sixties, six sisters at a Seven Sister college were about par. The commendable efforts to recruit, accommodate and cater to the needs of black students were to be a phenomenon of the next decade, and nonwhites who braved the chill of a women's college campus before then had to be remarkably resilient, prepared to have their "identity confirmed" in negative as well as positive ways. The colleges had not yet learned how to cope with pluralism, and individual experiences tended to be both traumatic and funny, often revealing an almost incredible naïveté on the part of well-meaning administrators. A black Mount Holyoke student of that era recalls being awakened late one night and asked to dress and come to a dormitory where a dance was being held. A solitary black undergraduate from one of the nearby men's colleges had appeared on the stag line, and those in

227

charge of the party were viewing the situation with great trepidation. The boy was tapping his foot and obviously planning to cut in. The housemother wanted to be sure that a suitable partner would be there before the band switched to a slow number. So far only fast sets had been played, and the dancers were showing signs of fatigue and impatience.

Throughout that decade roommates were still assigned on the basis of national origins and religious background, insofar as those could be determined. Even after questions about church affiliation were dropped from the application forms, the assistant deans continued to match up incoming students according to the old guidelines. The applicant's picture was usually enough of a clue, but "mother's maiden name" helped sort out the dubious cases. Race was obvious. Girls whose names ended with a vowel usually found themselves living together, so that, in the words of one veteran administrator "they wouldn't disturb anyone else when they went to seven o'clock mass." Eventually the colleges were to prepare elaborate questionnaires designed to reveal preferences that might be more indicative of congeniality, asking new students about their musical tastes (rock or classical), their special interests (science, modern dance, transcendental meditation, jogging, other) and even their sexual attitudes (liberal or conservative), but during the 1950s the system was much less sophisticated. "Fellow nationals" and "coreligionists" were paired, regardless (often *very* regardless) of anything else.

There had always been a certain degree of cliqueishness at the colleges, but it seemed more marked during the fifties than at any period since the abandonment of secret societies decades before. The fifties were the heyday of the preppie or, as the colleges preferred to call her, "the community-oriented girl from an independent school." Fresh from Foxcroft or Madeira, Farmington or Brearley, they came to Smith, Vassar, Wellesley and Bryn Mawr in presorted batches, to Barnard, Radcliffe and Mount Holyoke in smaller numbers but equally distinct groups. Although they may not have been a numerical majority, they did set the tone and the style—circle pins, kilt skirts, the cool emphasized speech that was almost a patois of its own. The Ivy League was still all male, and by 1950 most of the motley crew of war veterans had finished up and left the campuses to their rightful heirs.

Everything was back to normal—house parties, final clubs, fraternities, the gentleman's C, letter sweaters and football weekends. College was more fun than it had been since the 1920s. The boys (and they were boys again, not tired twenty-five-year-olds struggling along on government pittances) had cars, generous allowances, job offers, and no coeds on their own campuses. "The community oriented," says Carolyn Bird in an analysis done for the *Vassar Alumnae Magazine* in 1968, "came to Vassar because it was the thing for the daughter and future wife of a distinguished citizen to do." These women, Ms. Bird continues, "have put over school bond issues, built the League of Women Voters, and kept art museums and symphonies going. As wives they have contributed to the productivity of some of the country's leading men. Mary Lindsay, the wife of the [then] mayor of New York, is one of the few whose names are widely known. These girls dominated Vassar just before and after World War II." Another, whose name is even more widely know, was Jacqueline Bouvier Kennedy Onassis, who left Vassar without graduating.

That was a typical pattern of the time. The alumnae notes of the fifties are very heavily sprinkled with the parenthetical notation "ex-member of the class." The preppies didn't always stay, but they had a considerable impact while they were there. When outsiders thought of Vassar, Wellesley, and Smith in those days, they did not envision the group that Ms. Bird calls "the dedicated . . . who came to nourish a talent or make the world better"—the girls in baggy sweat shirts who stayed over weekends to finish the scenery for little-theater productions or to organize a protest against Senator Joseph McCarthy. There were more of the "dedicated" than anyone would have known, but they maintained a low profile and, like any other minority, tended to keep—and be kept—to themselves. The image makers were outfitted by Peck and Peck, majored in French and psychology, came out at the Plaza and never missed a Senior Spread or Green Key weekend. Twenty years later they still often are known by their undergraduate nicknames—Pooh, Emjay, or Petey. They are remarkably loyal to their colleges, and tend to sign the letter that begins "Now more than ever. . . ."

The third major campus subculture Ms. Bird cited was "the professionals," who came "to find a place in the world by succeeding in well-paid, well-respected occupations." They were the least conspicuous of all, and according to the Bird survey, the majority of Vassar professionals have served as teachers and educational administrators, although Vassar did manage to produce an impressive number of doctors, lawyers, public officials, authors and business executives even during the period when the more social types outnumbered and overwhelmed them. It's now these professionals—once the smallest and least assimilable group of all—who are the best argument for the future. An All-Seven list of women who seemed the mavericks of the forties, fifties and early sixties has become a veritable Who's Who of the arts, sciences and professions.,

Many of the most conspicuous and articulate of the new feminists were students or teachers at one or another of the colleges during this era or just after. Gloria Steinem was a product of Smith, Nora Ephron of Wellesley, Erica Jong of Barnard, and Liz Schneider, a writer and leader of the women's rights and educational reform movement, graduated from Bryn Mawr. Others, like Linda Nochlin, who contributed the essay "Why There Are No Great Women Artists" to *Woman in Sexist Society*, has been a member of the Vassar faculty; Catherine Stimpson, the biographer of J. R. R. Tolkien, also writes feminist articles and has taught English at Barnard; and Patricia Meyer Spacks, whose newest book is *The Female Imagination*, has been in the English Department at Wellesley since 1959.

The writers include Meg Greenfield, Smith '52, and Elizabeth Brenner Drew, Wellesley '57, whose political and literary interests range far beyond feminism. The poet Maxine Kumin is a Radcliffe alumna; the late Sylvia Plath graduated from Smith. Patricia Black, author and editor of many Russian translations, is now at work on a biography of Solzhenitsyn. She was one of the first students in Bryn Mawr's innovative Russian language and culture program during the 1950s.

Betsy Ancker-Johnston, Wellesley '49, served as U.S. Assistant Secretary of Commerce for Science and Technology. Both Phyllis Curtin, Wellesley '43, and Judith Resnick, Smith '49, are opera stars. The theatrical costume designs of Patricia Zipprodt, Wellesley '46, enliven hits and make even turkeys palatable. Terry Kovel, Wellesley '50, has written or collaborated with her husband on at least a dozen art and antique books, and her newspaper column is nationally syndicated. Matina Horner, president of Radcliffe, did her undergraduate work at Bryn Mawr, and Patricia Newell, president of Wellesley, is a graduate of Vassar.

But such lists, however gratifying, must necessarily be specious and incomplete. They inevitably slight quiet greatness in favor of bonus strokes for the already famous. Some of the most remarkable women, working in law, medicine or scientific research, rarely make headlines, and many of the most prolific writers publish only in professional journals. They're not celebrities—just notables. The only purpose served by such a roll call is to illustrate the extent of the reversal in attitude that has taken place during the last twenty years and to show that the women who made it happen have miraculously recovered from the apathy that once seemed so characteristic of their undergraduate years. The alumnae of these decades, so many of whom seemed destined for lives of placid domesticity and parochial narrowness, have matured into the role models of the seventies. Hundreds of the "future family-oriented" have joined the "flouters" and the "professionals." Donald Brown's categories, so sadly valid for 1956, are happily obsolete, the percentages a mere historical curiosity.

The colleges are now busily tracking down these alumnae in their studios, laboratories and offices. The letters ask if they'll please come back for student-alumnae career workshops or return as commencement speakers. Their photographs are in great demand by the news offices. They are, after all, the women who can justify, better than anyone else, the continuing existence and support of the "peculiar institutions." It has been a thoroughgoing revolution, and those who once seemed to be "flouting the dominant cultural situation" now exemplify it. Others who sweetly accepted the propaganda of the postwar era have apparently rejected it forever, a turnabout that is even more heartening. The best news of all is that these developments have occurred so fast that most of the new heroines are still young enough to enjoy every delectable irony of their new position.

XXI
To the Barricades

DURING their nearly 700 years of collective history, equal to an entire Roman Empire, two Dark Ages or a triple Renaissance, the women's colleges had survived natural catastrophe, palace rebellion, religious reformation and financial crisis. They endured assorted minor scandals, several kidnappings, a few tragic suicides and romances of varying degrees of mentionability, but complete knowledge of these events seemed to be limited to a very few. The twenties may have been a bit flashy, but after that, mentions in the newspapers were rare and discreet.

Though most of the colleges published institutional biographies at one time or another, these were enlivened by only the most impeccably bland anecdotes. The writers of such books were usually devoted alumnae or professors emeriti, and they concentrated heavily on neutral subjects like new buildings, revised curricula, modernized rules and the orderly succession of leadership. Miscreants were seldom named, though there are many tantalizing allusions to retirements and withdrawals for reasons of health and family obligation. Until very recently, these two fuzzy euphemisms seemed to blanket almost everything from plagiarism to promiscuity, and they protected administrators, faculty members and students alike. In the official histories, professors are either inspiring or anonymous, college officers capable and beloved, trustees dedicated and hardworking, and students ultimately reasonable and cooperative. Even in fiction, the Seven were treated as a kind of Open City, and Gertrude Stein's voluntary suppression of her *roman à clef* about "Fernhurst" is a perfect example of the genteel convention at work. There were strong family loyalties among the colleges, and Radcliffe just didn't calumniate Bryn Mawr for personal gain. This tacit, but powerful, inhibition persisted until Mary McCarthy wrote the first of *The Group* stories in 1954,

232

and when the entire book finally appeared in 1963, there were many loyalists even then who believed that she had let down the side. Some have still not forgiven her for exposing and satirizing Vassar so explicitly. "At least she didn't make Lakey a real lesbian until after graduation," said one Vassar contemporary of McCarthy's. "I suppose we should be grateful for that."

Once every five years or so an ephemeral headline like HEIRESS ABDUCTED FROM WELLESLEY, COMMUNISTS INFILTRATE SMITH, or RADCLIFFE LOVE NEST DISCOVERED might show up in the tabloids, but the stories rarely delivered as much as they seemed to promise. Subsequent editions of the papers would reveal that the heiress had been called for by a new chauffeur, the party cell at Smith had consisted of six sophomores protesting sweatshop conditions in the Massachusetts mills, and the Radcliffe love nest had been nothing more than a case of mistaken identity on the banks of the Charles. Except for the obligatory announcements of commencements, honorary degrees and the occasional mention of a Nobel laureate or a particularly impressive bequest, colleges in general received little national publicity, and the Eastern women's colleges least of all.

That tranquil and essentially satisfactory situation came to an abrupt and final end in the early 1960s, when undergraduate life in America received more media coverage than in the entire previous century. On campuses all over the country, TV cameras became almost as familiar as stately elms. Colleges and universities were suddenly generating hard news, and on the quieter days the newscasters began appearing in Poughkeepsie, South Hadley and Bryn Mawr. Since they were in the vicinity anyway or passing through on their way to the bigger stories, they stopped by to ask the young women for their opinions on Vietnam, drugs, sex, racial tensions, the death of God, the feminist revolution and other sizzling topics of the day. Had any bras been burned? What percentage of the students smoked pot? Did men stay overnight? When were they going coed? The reporters put 1960s questions, and they got 1960s answers. There was free-floating unrest everywhere, and the slightest show of interest aroused it. The women's angle was acute and honed to a sharp edge.

The colleges soon turned out to be that journalist's dream—the feature story that hasn't been done in living memory. There was a forty-year backlog of information, and the feminist surge gave it all a particular relevance. The first impulse of the activists had been to call for the dissolution of all single-sex institutions, and the effects of that demand were felt almost immediately. There were hints at the very beginning of the sixties that Vassar was considering a merger with Yale, and eager reporters converged on every women's college campus, hoping to be on hand for the ensuing dramas. While they waited, they speculated. Would the new college be Yassar or Vale? Was Wellesley about to betroth herself to MIT, and which sounded better, Techley or Wellesmass? How could Smith and Mount Holyoke, with nearly 4,000 women between them, manage to share Amherst's 1,500 men? It was, of course, widely assumed that the entire structure of separate colleges would topple within weeks, and the reorganizations promised to be a kind of academic *La Ronde*, with appealing elements of romance and intrigue.

Vassar students responded to the earliest rumors of a merger by hanging bedsheet banners welcoming Yale from their dormitory windows. Most seemed jubilantly in favor of coeducation and only mildly disturbed about abandoning their delightful rural campus to the first commercial bidder. The possibility of a coordinate arrangement had long been a topic of conjecture, and each succeeding class of Vassar freshmen had higher expectations that they would be the elect. For some optimists, Poughkeepsie was just a detour on the road to New Haven. The president of the college, Sarah Gibson Blanding, was thought to be in favor of coeducation or at least receptive to the idea. Most of the college community knew that she had been visited by the president of Yale, then A. Whitney Griswold, on several separate occasions. What other reason could there be? If matters had gone that far, students reasoned, then they would inevitably go farther. Miss Blanding, who had alienated a considerable portion of the student body in 1962 by some rather inflexible pronouncements about drinking and promiscuity, was briefly restored to popular esteem. If Vassar moved to Yale, all would be forgiven, even the statement she had made in assembly that any student who felt that she could not be both temperate and chaste should leave Vassar before the college was obliged to expel her.

That lecture would have been quickly forgotten if the Yale merger rumors had seemed promising, but when the hopes evaporated, the sex and drinking talk was revived and remembered. Vassar students, disappointed at being deprived of a great new educational adventure, were restive and aggrieved. America was right in the midst of a social revolution, but students felt that they were living in the "Poughkeepsie Victorian Seminary for Young Virgins" and seemed likely to stay there for the foreseeable future. The full text of Miss Blanding's assembly speech was delivered to the New York *Herald Tribune* (Who Says a Good Newspaper Has to Be Dull?), and despite the fact that the story was already a month old by the time it crossed the city desk, the *Tribune* devoted front-page space to it. The women's liberation movement was just beginning, and the Vassar ultimatum seemed symbolic of much that was wrong with the whole system. An incident that had caused only a mild stir on the Vassar campus soon became a major issue. "We are no worse than any other college," Miss Blanding had said. "This is a problem all over the country." The *Ladies' Home Journal* found this statement so titillating that Miss Blanding was asked to discuss the matter at greater length in the magazine, and she eventually did. Her attitude continued to be unequivocal. Vassar stood for an "innate" standard of behavior, and those who could not conform to it should apply elsewhere or arrange to transfer to a place with a less elevated moral code. The new militants chose to interpret these words to mean that chastity and temperance were entrance requirements, like languages and math.

Students (and some faculty) who had taken the original statement very lightly now felt intellectually obliged to react more strongly. A poll was taken, and the campus was found to be deeply divided. Fifty-two percent supported their president's position, 40 percent opposed her, and 8 percent were "undecided." Vassar in 1962 was obviously no exception to the ancient rule that there are girls who do, girls who don't and girls who can't make up their minds. That in itself would not have been news to the American public, but the concept soon acquired some interesting ramifications. Did a college have any right to regulate personal behavior? Could education be denied to the intemperate and unchaste? Was the notion of *loco parentis*

235

still valid and workable in an age when actual parental attitudes varied so widely? Repercussions from the Vassar story sounded up and down the Eastern seaboard, and it was quickly obvious that the moral revolution not only was well under way, but had won converts in Northampton, Cambridge, South Hadley, Wellesley, Bryn Mawr, on Morningside Heights.

Although no other women's college president had yet said that students whose academic potential exceeded their moral discretion would be expelled, there was reason to believe that it could happen at any moment. Almost every college, it seemed, had a clause in the catalogue alluding to deportment, and all of them were rather vague and poorly defined. Wellesley could expel those "who in the opinion of the college authorities should not remain," Bryn Mawr could eject a student for "unsatisfactory" conduct, Mount Holyoke was not bound to keep anyone "not in sympathy with its ideals and standards," and Radcliffe could dismiss girls "felt not to be desirable members of the student body." Vassar's stated policy was to discharge those whose "presence is deemed detrimental" and who did not "uphold the highest standards." "Detrimental" and "highest standards" were the words that had caused all the trouble in the first place. The student government had asked Miss Blanding to be more specific, and she had obliged with her literal definitions. There was, however, an equal amount of confusion on the other campuses about the exact meanings and applications of the behavior codes and a pervasive feeling that they all were relics of a bygone era. Most of the students seemed to agree that what they did "privately and discreetly" was no concern of their college, some felt that "social mores affected everyone in the community," and one outspoken Vassar cynic said that if Miss Blanding's pronouncement were taken seriously, two-thirds of the girls would be obliged to withdraw by nightfall.

Within weeks of the Vassar publicity, parietal rules became topics of passionate interest and debate on all the college campuses. Virtually everyone felt that she had to take sides since there seemed a good chance that civil rights were at stake. Teetotaling virgins became ardent advocates of alcohol and free love as a matter of principle. The skirmishes continued throughout the entire decade, and college newspapers and alumnae magazines were turned into forums for parietal filibusters. The nuances grew increasingly subtle, obscure and tangential as letters came in from parents, alumnae, trustees and other interested parties. Husbands, fiancés and fathers wrote to the editors, and the arguments began to take on an almost metaphysical tone. Since the majority of college rooms were designed for two or more, wouldn't the rights of one person be abrogated if the other were given exclusive rights for the evening? Where would the dispossessed go?

The fact that these questions had been settled years before by the men's colleges only aggravated the situation. The double standard was obviously alive and well all over New England and the Middle Atlantic states. Men had learned to circumvent and ignore their parietal rules, and an offense had to be truly outrageous before a Yale, Harvard or Princeton man would be suspended for ungentlemanly conduct. (Just about the time that women were battling for the modest privilege of dormitory keys, a group of Princeton students was temporarily rusticated for their part in a particularly unsavory incident. At the height of some dubious festivities in a university-owned house, several women of peccable reputation apparently jumped from a second-story window. The incident would probably have passed unnoticed if one of the jumpers had not gone to the police and claimed that she had not only been deprived of a promised fee, but deliberately pushed by one of her hosts when she demanded it. After a short interval and some complex negotiations, the men were allowed to return, and the escapade became a treasured Princeton legend.) In 1962, however, women were not being given any such second chances, though they were beginning to think that they should be.

As soon as the debates on parietals started, it became clear that girls were not nearly as open-minded as they pretended. Since total freedom seemed to be the only worthwhile long-range goal, students concealed their doubts and presented a united front, keeping their misgivings and apprehensions to themselves. College spokeswomen insisted that parietal rules "infantalized" them and were a perfect example of "lingering paternalism." Undergraduate reformers demanded the right to live in off-campus housing, to entertain men in their rooms behind firmly closed doors and to be given house keys so that they could come and go at their own discretion. The idea of a duty officer—one of their own generation—checking them in and out of their halls had come to seem particularly odious. The administrations countered by emphasizing the threadbare maxim that a residential college could not be run for the exclusive benefit of individuals but was obliged to function for the good of all.

Various compromises were offered—visiting hours from six to ten, appointed hall monitors and polite voices over the public address systems calling "Time, gentlemen, time." The signals were ignored, the monitors became instant pariahs, and the keys, when finally granted, were often lost. Students found that they couldn't study with a party going on in the next room, that the announcements sounded more like a hospital than an English pub and that robberies were increasing as misplaced keys turned up in unauthorized hands. The colleges began to feel besieged and embattled. *In loco parentis* was becoming even more of a burden to the *locum* than it was to real parents. A father might have to deal with two or three rebels, but even the smaller women's colleges had to cope with thousands. The generation gap was a yawning canyon, and no one seemed to know where responsibility should begin or end.

To make matters worse, applications throughout this period were dropping a percentage point or so each year. The women's liberation movement had begun to affect girls who might otherwise have chosen one of the Seven, and those who did come often felt sullen and resentful at not getting to the school of their first choice, which always seemed to be Swarthmore. "We lost a great many potential candidates to coed institutions just because of the parietal issue," said a woman who had been an assistant dean at Smith in the early sixties. "We were not in the strongest bargaining position when the agitation began, and we knew it. We represented the Establishment in an era when the young were intensely against all that stood for."

Bit by bit, the colleges gave in to student demands. By the middle of the decade alcohol was generally permitted for those of legal drinking age in the state, a concession that gave Barnard and Vassar a definite (if short-lived) edge. That was the first major capitulation, and for a few months it seemed significant. The novelty of chablis with macaroni or zinfandel with New England boiled dinner, however, wore off sooner than

238

anyone would have expected. "There is nothing more deadly than six girls gulping warm beer in their bathrobes," said a Wellesley alumna of that interlude. "We didn't really care about drinking by ourselves or in the college dining rooms. Imagine sitting on your paper mattress with another girl and having cheap booze in a plastic toothbrush glass. What would be more depressing?" And by the time undergraduates had won this basic human right, drinking was out and drugs were in. All the administrative anguish had been for nothing, and students seemed to care less for alcohol than for Postum.

Since drinking was no longer even a symbol of the freedom they wanted, the crusaders moved quickly and decisively on to more important issues. The campaigns for open dormitories were vigorously pursued, with at least one quixotic result. Young women who would have been perfectly happy with co-education often found themselves advocating and defending cohabitation. The news media were much more interested in mixed housing than in mixed classes. Those, after all, had been around for 100 years. "As soon as we got male exchange students, the dorms turned into Ramada inns," said a Wellesley alumna. "You signed up for a coed house at your own risk, expecting that there would be lots of nights when you couldn't sleep in your own bed. I finally started carrying a toothbrush to class."

The confusion of the sixties was more profound than it seemed, and antagonisms and divisions among students developed along brand-new lines. For the first time, girls separated themselves into moral and ideological categories. "The college was split at least three ways," said a member of Bryn Mawr's class of '65. "There were free spirits, straights and zeros. The code words probably varied from one place to another, but we all seemed to recognize each other on sight." The free spirits, however, were the most dramatic and persuasive, and their style soon became the dominant one.

Within a very short time, an effective coalition developed between the political activists and the social revolutionaries. It was a mutually satisfactory relationship, almost symbiotic. Free spirits, often in expanded states of consciousness, could be counted on to swell the ranks of any demonstration. "They attracted the attention, and we got the dirty work done," said one crusader.

"It worked out beautifully." The evolving and multifaceted student movement seemed to have something for everyone in its early days. "Peace" and "freedom" have always been magic words, and the organizers invariably managed to work them into their exhortations. All causes seemed noble and good, and undergraduates from the women's colleges eagerly joined the protest demonstrations that were taking place on other campuses. The idealistic aspects of CORE and SNCC were powerful draws, and hundreds of girls participated in the marches through the South. Many of them were profoundly and genuinely radicalized by these experiences and returned deeply committed to change and determined to implement it.

The SDS, which had virtually ignored the women's colleges at first, soon realized that 10,000 young women represented a great untapped resource, easily activated and surprisingly receptive. When the SDS paraded in Washington in 1963, undergraduates from the Seven were conspicuously represented, with Smith alone sending a contingent of forty. For a college that had always been known for its fresh-faced athletes and provisional Junior Leaguers, that was a sizable platoon.

In 1965 a Smith editorialist wrote:

> "The student body of today is different from that of five or ten years ago. College bound, they have been pushed and pressured into greater seriousness and harder work since earliest high school days; they have been given much more independence in the family; by the time they reach college they are simply in no mood for paternalism, for the arbitrary laying down of the law without rhyme or reason. He who is forced to grow up earlier naturally expects the status of maturity as well as its demands. . . . And then there is the legacy of the civil rights movement; acceptance of extra-legal tactics, new political consciousness, and the appearance of the New Left from which come the activists and experienced organizers. Another part of the problem is that college administrators have not changed that much within the same period.

That was a remarkably restrained editorial for its time, a fact which explains why Smith selected it for inclusion in the centennial issue of the alumnae magazine. At other times and in other places the diatribes were considerably more inflammatory, often obscuring the same valid points. Through all the jargon, the clichés and the polemic, it is obvious that the reformers were often right. Administrators had really not "changed that much," though they made some valiant attempts. Still, their efforts often seemed merely palliative, designed to make students grateful for small favors. "There were a great many of us who hoped each September that the kilt skirts and circle pins would come back with the new freshmen," admitted one director of admissions, "and a very persistent feeling that 'it can't happen here,' whether *it* was drugs or sex or racial hostility. We were used to tranquillity—or apathy—and it was very hard to believe that the alterations would be permanent."

"Sure, there were improvements," said a Mount Holyoke alumna, "but it was as if the czar had increased the potato allotment for the serfs. We were still serfs, and they were still czars."

The overworked committees who devised the concessions found the disdain of the rebels almost incomprehensible. The rigid distribution requirements that had obliged all students to take math or a physical science had been loosened; pass-fail options were instituted, and grading systems revised time and time again in response to requests for more autonomy and less stress on competitiveness. Alarmed at the increasing number of dropouts and hoping that many of them were as much the result of simple claustrophobia as from any real desire to turn on and tune into the drug cult, the colleges arranged various versions of an "interim" term. This time-out period could be used for independent study, special projects, paid work, or spent on campus in an assortment of mini-courses. These innovations were perfunctorily acknowledged and then largely ignored.

A few, like the pass-fail system, turned out to be less of a boon than had been expected. Potential graduate students found themselves less pressured in college but increasingly tense thereafter. It was soon obvious that pass-fail had almost as many undesirable side effects as the Pill. University graduate schools glanced summarily at the Ps of the new grading methods and selected their incoming law and medical classes from benighted schools that still ranked their students and graded them on a sliding scale of 60 to 100. Pass-fail was fashionable, but it wasn't practical, not even for the freest of free spirits. "I started out as a history major," said a Vassar alumna. "Then I decided that history was too structured and that I wanted to be a potter. I took all my art courses pass-fail, though, and would you believe that they asked me in a dish factory what my grades had been? In a *dish* factory."

The idea of an interim or winter term seemed even more attractive when first presented, but relatively few students really took full advantage of the plan, though almost all had been in favor of the theory. The three weeks usually allocated to these breaks were seldom long enough for a meaningful job, and neither faculty nor students were universally enthusiastic about spending the slushy days of midwinter exploring some brand-new discipline. The raves generally came from those who had found a way around the whole dilemma. "I loved it," said a Smith alumna. "It was perfect for skiing, and a group of us got jobs as waitresses in New Hampshire." That had not been exactly what the college had hoped for, and after three years the interim idea was abandoned by Smith, though it has lingered elsewhere in mutant forms. At Mount Holyoke, the smorgasbord seems particularly exotic with offerings in the literary works of Baha Ullah, herbiculture, marine ecology and various feminist subjects, including women in sports, the church and literature. The response there has been gratifying, and the winter term idea continues to flourish.

The more humane application of distribution requirements has been an unqualified success everywhere, approved by both faculty and student appraisers. Professors seem glad to be relieved of the job of teaching the totally disinterested, and while a small minority of students manage to slip through college without ever venturing outside a familiar area, the privilege is not abused as often as had been expected. "We never succeeded in making a physicist out of an actress under the old system," said a Smith scientist. "The only difference is that beginning in 1965, we admitted it and graduated some less resentful actresses. As far as I know, every scientist who got a degree from Smith was literate, at least in my department. I can't promise that the drama majors can plot a vector, but they usually don't have to."

There are, however, guerrilla battles still being fought over grades, and that issue has not been entirely resolved. Mount

242

To the Barricades

Holyoke remains a veritable Vietnam of anguish and confusion, and students there seem to have found a way to give the marking system a kind of analogous significance. It makes a useful metaphor, and the activists seem unwilling to let it die. "They tell us that marks are a necessary evil," one student said. "So is war. I'm not willing to accept either idea."

The campus revolutionaries of the sixties were remarkably adept at this sort of sophistry, and they have bequeathed their technique, intact, to their successors. Though the basic causes of student dissatisfaction originally may have been parietal rules, required courses, and "control over our own lives," these quibbles seemed trivial in the context of the time. In order to lend them dignity and substance, they had to be attached to larger issues. That has always been a hallowed revolutionary gambit, and it surfaced wherever there were campus demonstrations. Free speech, people's parks and university expansion were the reasons given for riots and confrontations, but often the real issues were much more parochial. "We needed faculty support and sympathy," admitted one veteran rebel, "and we weren't going to get it by asking for more meat in the stew." One way and another, dormitory closing hours became entangled with government policy in Southeast Asia, and faculty members at the women's colleges who allied themselves with student protesters often found that they were also advocating Enovid on the college health plan, a diet dining room or the legalization of marijuana.

"We accepted what amounted to a party line," said a young male history instructor who had been at Barnard in 1968. "We became apologists, rationalizing and defending all sorts of things that we only half believed, and a few of us made fools of ourselves, going the whole route with long hair, beads, grass and, in some cases, love affairs with students. It was an extraordinary period, and professors were vulnerable to all sorts of seduction. As a class, you know, we tend to identify with students. Perhaps that's why we teach in the first place. There were so many good things about the movement that it was easy to overlook the bad. There were some follies and excesses, but nothing as evil as what was going on in the country at large."

Because a significant number of the most articulate and persuasive feminist writers were alumnae, graduate students or in-

243

structors at the women's colleges during this era, a great deal of cross-radicalization took place. Kate Millett, one of the angriest of all, was teaching philosophy and literature at Barnard while she researched and wrote *Sexual Politics* for her Columbia doctorate. After raising the consciousness of her Barnard sections to barricade heights, Millett moved on to the Bryn Mawr sociology department, where she galvanized dozens more. By then Kate Millett had become one of the most influential personalities in the movement, and students responded to her with the awe they thought due a celebrity. To all intents and purposes, Bryn Mawr emerged from the sixties as a coeducational college, connected to Haverford by one of the most heavily traveled miles in Pennsylvania.

As the fundamental idea of a women's college came to seem increasingly counterrevolutionary, student attitudes turned hypercritical. There were few defenders of a single-sex education in the early sixties, and the abolitionists seemed to have all the heavy artillery. When Gloria Steinem, Smith '56, announced publicly that the best women's college was necessarily inferior to the worst coeducational school, scores of dazzled and disgruntled Smithies were immediately transformed into militants, and Smith College became their natural target. Though it was a tactless statement, the general atmosphere was conducive to this sort of extravagance, and Steinem's chance remark was widely quoted. To undergraduates it seemed far more relevant than the tedious feminist arguments of that earlier Smith alumna Betty Friedan. The graduates of the sixties were already sure that they would never be suburban housewives, and Friedan's frustrated correspondents belonged to another generation. Nevertheless, the fact that Smith had educated both these activists seemed fraught with meaning, and support of the new feminism was the only appropriate response. Now, however, hairline cracks are threatening this solidarity. The emergence of still another Smith graduate, Sidney Abbott, spokesperson for the radical lesbian faction of the movement and co-author of *Sappho Was a Right-On Woman,* has caused considerable ambivalence. "She proselytizes," said a Smith senior. "And that's bad taste."

Toward the end of the sixties a more conservative feminism gradually began to supplant the earlier, unyielding versions.

The enlightened moderates on the faculty still manage to imbue their students with a sense of outrage and injustice, but there seems to be a growing feeling that the women's colleges might serve a transitional purpose and that it could be a great mistake to dissolve them in acid. In her contribution to *Woman in Sexist Society,* one of the basic anthologies of the new feminism, Linda Nochlin, professor of art at Vassar, says, "In actuality things as they are and as they have been in the arts as in a hundred other areas are stultifying, oppressive and discouraging to all who did not have the good fortune to be born white, preferably middle class or above, males." The fault, Professor Nochlin continues, "lies not in our stars, our hormones . . . but in our institutions and our education." The Vassar girls who absorbed these statements before and after they appeared in book form may not have been infused with affection for Vassar, but they did realize that within its lecture halls and studios they were judged on their merits as artists. (The admission of men to Vassar in 1970 has not yet changed that, though the risks grow with the percentages.)

The acceptance of "women's studies" as a separate academic discipline has naturally attracted a small but influential number of true believers to the campuses. Those who teach the trendy new courses in Women Novelists, the Feminine Sensibility, Sex Roles in Industrial Societies and the like have an unprecedented opportunity for feminist agitprop, and they intend to exploit it. The catalogue descriptions of these courses are marvelously varied, but the subject matter is a familiar chronicle of injustice, frustration and despair. Students are extremely responsive to this material, and most emerge from these seminars shaken and determined to avoid the tender traps that ensnared their mothers. (Missionaries have done well at the Seven since their founding.) "Hobson's choice," said one dean with rare candor. "We can go along with the feminist movement, or we can bankrupt ourselves trying to convert to a coeducational college. Since this doesn't seem to be the best time to gamble on our ability to attract first-rate male students, we're reaffirming our commitment to women." It's a shaky and precarious existence, and the colleges are buttressing their position by insisting, almost in unison, that an institution "predominantly" for the education of women "builds confidence" as no other place can, and that it is still the only educational situation in which women can be "first-class citizens."

Right now Smith, Mount Holyoke and Wellesley are functioning almost as adjuncts of the liberation movement, subject to all its vagaries and changing priorities. Such dependency, whether on the "good will of benevolent gentlemen" or the whims of contemporary feminists, is at best uncomfortable and insecure. Though the relationship is cordial, it seems particularly subject to strain and fatigue. The women's movement is self-limiting, and once its objectives are gained, the question of single-sex institutions will be reopened to even crueler scrutiny. In a speech to the 1974 Mount Holyoke Alumnae Council, Landonia Gettell (wife of Richard Gettell, president of that college throughout the sixties) acknowledged that "women of accomplishment" are beginning to say, "Talk of feminism is beside the point; just go do it."

The fact that black students were actively recruited throughout this era aggravated already tense relationships. The transition to heterogeneity was considerably more traumatic than the optimists had hoped. "We should have done an environmental impact study," admitted a Smith administrator. "Our attitude was pathetically naïve. At the time, many of us thought that the problems were financial and that generous scholarship funds would be the answer to everything. We were wrong." As the percentage of black students neared 15 or 20 percent of each student body, it became excruciatingly clear that the Seven were unprepared for the role they had so confidently assumed. They were Second World establishments with good intentions, and that was not enough to prevent the sit-ins, walk-outs and protests that continually erupted.

Inner-city students had not known what to expect in places like South Hadley and Northampton, and they were rarely content or at ease with what they found. Bewilderment and frustration solidified into resentment and often contempt. "How could anyone honestly and effectively encourage someone to come into a community or institution which will either make you a dedicated Smithie or wonder 'what next'; an institution in which you daily hear complaints by both black and white students; an institution which makes drastic changes in established policy in social and academic areas simply to draw in more students, rather than a sincere effort at progressive change?" asked one of these girls in a letter to the *Sophian* in 1969. "My fellow black undergraduates have had to countenance insensitivity, unconscious racism and all but hostility," said a young woman who had been elected president of the Smith senior class but who had resigned without taking office. (That was to be a familiar pattern—enthusiastic, popular acclaim followed by icy rejection by the acclaimee—and it was repeated on other campuses time and again.)

The colleges responded by assembling informative literature designed expressly for prospective minority students, but these well-meaning efforts seem to have missed the mark. "Their booklets were patronizing and phony," said a girl who had come to Wellesley from Roxbury. "Full of sister this and right on that, the way they imagined we talked. No matter what they said or even if they got one of us to say it for them, the place itself was all wrong. They never understood why we needed a clubhouse or a dorm or even a dinner table of our own, at Wellesley or at any of the other ones. We were always in a foreign country, like tourists. That's how it was, though I suppose there were some exceptions." The demands for "black studies" and Afro-American majors often seemed to deepen the schisms. By the time the colleges persuaded themselves of the need for such programs, their academic and vocational value was already being disputed by educators. "The advisers tried to talk you out of the black courses," said a Mount Holyoke graduate. "A student would want to learn Swahili, and they would tell us how much more useful French would be. Maybe they didn't mean it as a put-down, but that's what it felt like."

The financial setbacks of the seventies have alleviated these strains in a quixotic and embarrassing way. There are now fewer black students on the campuses because there is less scholarship money available. The recession has turned out to be a great leveler, and the colleges have inadvertently begun to regain some of their old middle-class feeling. (The recent history of the Seven often seems to be an anthology of just such ironies.) Now that the most critical phase of campus disruption has subsided, the firebrands seem preoccupied with more personal goals. The reformers are themselves reformed, absorbed into a temporary limbo of graduate schools or the permanent limbo of careers. That, in any case, seems to be true of the men, as James Kunen pointed out in a recent article for the *New York Times Magazine*. Kunen's first book was *The Strawberry Statement*, an insider's view of the Columbia uprising, but his current efforts are anything but incendiary—cool analyses of films for *Esquire*, ironic end papers for *New Times* magazine, and recollections in tranquillity for that showcase of mature responsibility, the New York *Times* itself.

The women who were involved in the turmoil of the sixties, however, seem to have been much more permanently affected, whether they were perpetrators, participators or merely spectators. The alumnae notes of the sixties and the first few years of the seventies reflect a profound change in life-styles. The columns of engagement and wedding announcements that made such redundant reading in the quarterlies are shrinking—the space they once occupied usurped by detailed and enthusiastic job news. The endless parade to the altar that wound through the forties and fifties seems delayed, if not completely stalled. If anyone still classifies herself as a housewife now, she doesn't admit it to her class secretary, and only her husband knows for sure.

Alumnae questionnaires show a remarkable increase in commitment to work, and lifework at that. The choice of occupation is astonishingly varied, with more and more graduates choosing independence over security. In addition to the new wave of women architects, bankers, brokers and politicians, there are jobs which defy any attempt at classification. Recent classes include tapestry weavers, hydroponic farmers, Sinologists, truck drivers, Arabists, feminist historians (not all of whom are able to resist calling their projects "herstory"), cooks on sailing ships, sex researchers and at least two out-and-out felons. One of those, Diana Oughton, Bryn Mawr '63, died in the 1970 explosion of a Greenwich Village town house where she had been assembling bombs for the Weathermen. She had considered herself a soldier in the Red Army and admitted to one of the survivors that she still "had a lot to learn."

The other and more appealing radical is Bridget Rose Dugdale, who is now in an Irish prison, serving a nine-year sentence for the $10,000,000 art robbery that she masterminded for a group of Irish terrorists. Ms. Dugdale, who received her master of arts degree (there can be no more appropriate one) from Mount Holyoke in 1965, had become deeply involved in the civil rights struggle while in this country and returned to England determined to put all her acquired knowledge and abilities to effective use. Four members of her organization were in British jails charged with planting bombs about London, and Ms. Dugdale intended to use the art treasures to force the British to release the men to Irish authorities. When her own capture thwarted that plan, she announced that she would go on a six-week hunger strike while awaiting trial. That, however, was also foiled, and she was tried and sentenced on schedule.

The disordered and sometimes tragic record of the sixties seems to prove that although it takes longer to radicalize a woman, the results can be dramatic and lasting, usually, if not invariably, constructive. It seems safe to say that the old stereotypes are finally inoperative. As these alumnae reach and pass the critical age of thirty, their chances of relapsing into earlier patterns becomes increasingly remote. They wouldn't have admitted it as contentious undergraduates, but these women seem to have been in the right places at exactly the right times.

XXII
Valedictory

FROM the outside, the conversion of a single-sex college to a coeducational institution looks easy enough—a matter of informing Cass and Birnbaum, Lovejoy and Barron, who prepare the popular guides; then a few expensive and untidy weeks while the plumbers, carpenters and steamfitters make the necessary alterations to dormitories and gyms; the appointment of a new dean of appropriate sex; and finally, a dignified announcement to the press. Ideally, that should all be managed over the summer, so that the college can be ready to receive its first mixed classes in September. Yale, Harvard, Wesleyan, Princeton, Williams and Dartmouth have all done it within the last four years. Amherst will do it, after more than a century of vacillation. And although the process was never as quick, as simple or as thoroughgoing as it seemed, the Ivy League has survived. The alumni who threatened to withhold all contributions if Old Macho ever admitted women have begun to honor their pledges again. The recalcitrant professors who stubbornly addressed their classes as "gentlemen" are nearing retirement age, and the wiring in the older buildings has finally been adjusted to accommodate hair dryers. Each year a few more women are being appointed to the faculties, and while the percentage is still too small to be wholly satisfactory, the ratio is improving. It seems that although men will resist an idea whose time has come, they are more reasonable the second time around.

The arguments for all-male colleges have become hard to remember and almost impossible to justify. America isn't training a Puritan clergy anymore, and there has been a great deal of occupational diversification since 1632. Coeducation is a known quantity, tested and proved all over the world. The data on that has been accumulating for 150 years, and there's no longer much doubt that the plan is sensible, economical and natural.

Its opposite is none of these things. And even if the recently reorganized men's colleges haven't yet produced their first Presidents or Cabinet members, all other criteria of success are being met. (The class of '74 is still underage for high office.) There has been no erosion of academic standards or lessening of postgraduate achievement. The quality of undergraduate life has improved noticeably and on all levels. If there ever was a young man who withdrew his application to an Ivy League college or a professor who refused a teaching appointment because of the presence of women on campus, their cases are not on record. The service academies have not been besieged by defectors from the Big and Little Three. Annapolis, West Point, and the Air Corps and Merchant Marine academies would provide only a temporary shelter in any case since Congress voted in June, 1975, to end sex discrimination in these institutions. (The resolution did not include the words "with all deliberate speed," but that was the implication.)

The pioneering women undergraduates at Ivy League schools may have had rather a thin time of it for a semester or two, but their complaints have diminished as the male-female balance approaches an equitable 50-50. Civilization has come to the frontier, though inversely from West to East. Women are no longer regarded as intruders in New Haven, undesirable aliens in Princeton, strangers in paradise. They are now generally treated as first-class citizens, lovers and friends. It hasn't taken long, and it hasn't hurt much. A brand-new college generation appears every year, and there's a complete turnover every four. By 1976 girls can expect fewer automatic requests to type papers, launder Shetlands or sew on buttons. In the world at large, prejudices and stereotypes tend to linger for twenty years or so, but universities are delightfully different. Patterns of behavior come and go between June and September.

The women's college that converts, however, is on shakier ground. The most desirable boys in America do not storm their high school guidance departments demanding applications to ex-girls' schools, no matter how splendid the college's reputation or how long and unbroken its tradition of excellence. Boys go where boys are, and girls go along with them, whenever they can. The candidates who once chose the Seven Sisters as a matter of course have other tempting possibilities before them. For the first time in their glorious history, the women's colleges are being forced to acknowledge the incontrovertible and painful fact that separate is never truly equal but, at best, only analogous. Now that the delicate sibling relationship between the men's and the women's colleges has been dissolved or realigned, the myth of equality has evaporated. The remaining women's colleges are vulnerable and unprotected, in danger of finding themselves a haven for the militant, the frightened and the rejected, and that's not a future they care to contemplate.

Certainly the best way for a women's college to make the transition is to ally itself with an already existing men's school, preferably one of equally impressive lineage. In the academic party game, however, there are several more players than places. Barnard and Radcliffe have simply tightened the ties that already bound them to Columbia and Harvard, and Bryn Mawr has formalized and elaborated on its reciprocal agreements with Haverford. These three were historically and geographically lucky, but four of the original Seven have been left to arrive at more imaginative and radical solutions of their own. By the end of the 1960s even the conservatives agreed that at least one aspect of the pervasive discontent at the single-sex colleges was remediable. The trustees and the administrators couldn't do much about the general malaise afflicting American society, but they could provide their students with one very important distraction. If coeducation didn't eliminate the misery entirely, it could certainly be counted on to redistribute it.

Vassar, the most remote of the Seven, admitted its first duly constituted coeducational class in 1970. The administration had some limited experience with male students after World War II, when veterans were temporarily allowed to attend courses toward degree credits elsewhere, but aside from that, Vassar had never been anything but a women's college since 1961. The postwar background soon turned out to be no help whatever. In competing with the Ivy League and a thousand other schools for those first men, Vassar was in the most difficult seller's market imaginable. Recruiters dutifully made the rounds of high schools and prep schools only to be ignored and derided. Adolescent boys are not remarkable for either tact or open-mindedness, and the Vassar representatives were not always able to field their questions. An alumna who made the rounds of West Coast high schools was unable to persuade even a single young man to take home a catalogue, and she reports that many arranged interview programs were entirely unattended. The job wasn't much easier in either the Midwest or the East. "If you went to see the Vassar rep, you kept quiet about it," said an Exeter graduate. "That was really the last resort."

As a result of this resistance, Vassar was obliged to make a number of unobtrusive but definite concessions. Scholarships helped attract men, and so did a deemphasis on SAT scores. Alumnae and faculty members openly admit that the men's credentials were rarely as dazzling as the women's and that a distinctly double academic standard prevailed for at least two years. "I'd call it *triple* standard," said a woman who graduated in 1973. "If any reasonably masculine type actually applied, they'd admit him if he could sign his name." As a numerical minority the men were faced with the classic minority dilemma. They could either resist and disrupt the female status quo, or they could allow themselves to be assimilated by it.

The first mixed classes became object lessons in both modes of behavior, and the years from 1970 to 1974 were not Vassar's most tranquil. When the student body capriciously elected a flamboyant transvestite as president, shock waves reverberated from the Hudson to the Connecticut Valley and crossed the Continental Divide. "We heard about it at Scripps," said a San Franciscan. "That September, 1974, issue of *Esquire* became a collector's item." "He wasn't even a true transvestite," one Vassar student said. "That was just a campaign costume. *Esquire* made it all sound much weirder than it was." But while the *Esquire* article alone might have been discounted as irresponsible journalism, the yearbook produced by the Vassar class of 1975 was an inside job, just as florid and not so easily explained. To many astonished readers, it seemed conspicuously lacking in taste, quality and redeeming social value. "I certainly wouldn't call it pornographic," said one graduate, "but a college yearbook shouldn't look like *More Joy* either. If the seniors wanted to protest, they could have skipped the whole thing and sent the money to Biafra. Now we're known for the only X-rated annual ever."

Such incidents seem calculated to make alumnae of Wellesley, Smith and Mount Holyoke continue to return the referenda on coeducation marked "No." Undergraduates, faculty members and even administrators may deplore their situation as segregees, but there is always the consolation of dignity—cold comfort, but not entirely expendable until there's a desirable replacement. These three continued to explore the possibility of coeducation without tears and to temporize, insisting that the system as it exists is undoubtedly flawed—still male-dominated and still imperfect. The spokespeople maintain that a women's college can be a viable alternative. It can repair the psychological damage done by centuries of second-class status, offer rare opportunities for leadership, take on a new mission, reaffirm a deep commitment to excellence and provide the matchless gift of confidence.

But constant repetition can dull the soundest arguments and turn truth into truism. Though President Alan Simpson of Vassar is right when he says that the all-female college is always in danger of sheltering its students from the realities of a world in which women must compete with men, his words do not soothe the vested interests at Smith, Wellesley and Mount Holyoke. "I do not wish to preside over the liquidation of a first-rate institution," said one Wellesley trustee. "The subject of coeducation comes up every twenty-five years or so and goes away. We can't reconstruct ourselves just to stay in fashion." There are faculty members, alumnae, administrators and even students who agree with that point of view. They are intimidated by sentiment, discretion, vanity and that mixed bag of incidents known as the Vassar Experience.

Conversion may be perilous, but the single-sex college is no more immune to the hazards of the seventies than any other place. Drugs, theft and what officials call "new sexual frontiers" are problems everywhere, and women have shown themselves to be devilishly imaginative, even in isolation. The New York *Times* recently reported that a Mount Holyoke dormitory had been New England headquarters for a cocaine dealership, and that two of the students involved had been found with $9,000 worth of the stuff. The new sexual frankness has permitted a few conspicuously vocal branches of the Radical Lesbians to emerge on the women's campuses, and they can be just as image-shattering as Vassar's showy transvestites. For one thing, there are more of them, and they represent a larger constituency. Students often confide that they feel intimidated by these groups, and several have actually left or transferred because of them. "The lesbians don't frighten me, but I hated the leers and questions I got whenever I told the name of my house," said one fifth-generation Wellesley student. "I realize that lots of people are experimenting now, but it seems less obvious in a coed school, or maybe just easier to avoid. Anyway, I'm happier at Dartmouth."

As the single-sex college becomes an increasingly quirky choice, many potential students reject it out of hand. This ambivalence, of course, was never a problem when the Ivy League was exclusively male, but within the past four years, there are definite signs that the appeal of women's college is extremely limited and growing more special every year. Those who do go, in spite of qualms, are often troubled and dismayed at what they find. A member of Smith's counseling department admitted that one of the most frequent causes of student anxiety was the appropriate attitudes toward alien sexual mores. "Girls do not want to judge their peers," said this psychologist, "so they come here and ask me what they should do. I suggest another house or, in cases of real anguish, another college. We are a very diverse community these days, and not every girl can handle that at eighteen or even twenty."

Smith and Mount Holyoke have found a way of achieving a half measure of coeducation. Their five-party agreement with Amherst, the University of Massachusetts and Hampshire College seems both practical and successful. Buses ply among the separate colleges every half hour, and permission for cross-registration is rather readily obtained. It's less chancy than Vassar's total commitment, and it provides almost as much in the way of human variety. The Connecticut Valley exchange is one way around the costly and unnecessary duplication of facilities and courses, and it helps uncloister the Smith and Holyoke students. Nevertheless, it's just school busing on a more mature and elegant level, and it's neither entirely satisfactory nor wholly equitable. Underclassmen are still expected to spend most of their time on their home campuses, and the circuit riding consumes large chunks of the schoolday. (For the last several years the women's colleges have also participated in a twelve-college resident exchange, but this program has been dwindling in popularity as the formerly all-male enclaves have acquired co-eds of their own. Smith, Wellesley and Mount Holyoke students seem as eager as ever to spend a term at Dartmouth, Williams or Amherst, but the plan is becoming more and more of a one-way brain drain, and its future at this point seems uncertain.)

Since Wellesley is too far away to join the Connecticut Valley bus quintet, it has made separate pacts. A deserving Wellesley girl (good grades and good reasons) may take courses at Harvard, MIT and other Boston institutions, but the Wellesley campus still seems not only "predominantly" but overwhelmingly female. The number of Harvard, MIT or BU males who pick up their reciprocal options to attend Wellesley is small, and as one Wellesley sophomore said, "We get the odd engineer with a passionate interest in medieval art, and that's about it." The exchanges are at best stopgap measures, and they beg the ultimate question, which can be best expressed in the single word "when."

At the moment feminism has lent the women's colleges some additional time to think and plan. The catalogues bloom with courses in women's studies—history, psychology, literature—redesigned to build the ego and replace the sense of self that has been lost or stolen over the ages. The courses are popular and well taught, but they seem to perpetuate the insidious notion that women are an alien species, so irredeemably different that they could perhaps be unassimilable. It's a fashionable idea, but one that may eventually undermine the very cause of equality that it was meant to advance. The pioneers in women's education never envisioned an age in which women would study themselves as a distinct subculture, and the trend would have distressed them profoundly.

Exactly a century ago, in 1875, just as the craftsmen were putting the finishing touches on the original Smith buildings and the members of Wellesley's first class were alighting from their carriages, the advantages of coeducation were already being debated. The concept of separate women's colleges had begun to seem dubious and redundant even then. That same August, 1875, the Reverend Edward C. Towne of North Easton, Massachusetts, an influential clergyman, something of a gadfly and the patriarch of a dynasty that has served the Connecticut

Valley colleges in one capacity or another for generations, wrote to the newly installed president of Smith, his esteemed colleague Dr. Seelye, asking why Sophia Smith's money had not been used to found a coordinate women's college at Amherst instead. The letter was widely circulated, and it aroused second thoughts not only in South Hadley and Northampton but far beyond. State universities were opening all across the country in the 1870s, and most of them admitted women from the very beginning. New England educators who traveled west to see the future returned and reported that it worked. Vested interests at the distinguished Eastern men's colleges, however, regarded their charters as Holy Writ and refused even to consider amending them. They pointed to the Union Pacific Railroad, which was operating (at a deficit, but regularly), and said that young women had several new options. They could entrain for Iowa or Michigan or stay and matriculate at one or another of the small new coeducational colleges nearer home. Those who insisted on an equivalent to Harvard, Yale or Princeton, however, had to pay for their vaulting ambition, and the price was separation. To nineteenth-century women, that did not seem either unreasonable or exorbitant. The optimists believed that separate women's colleges were but temporary detours on the way to full equality and that the route would someday be direct and coeducational. The realists counted their blessings. Single-sex education was a fine makeshift for what promised to be a long meantime.

In the last and hardest analysis of all, the predominantly women's college is a segregated institution—benign and modified, but suggesting by its continued existence that women may still need special treatment and accommodation. The confidence, security and even the freedom that a woman may enjoy in such an environment often turns out to be a four-year illusion, vanishing abruptly on the day after commencement. The Sister colleges were peculiar to another time and place, peculiar in a pure and splendid sense that no longer applies. They were a unique and remarkable educational adventure, but it's finally time for the last valedictory, the inevitable hail and farewell that is the rite of passage into the real world.

BIBLIOGRAPHY

ABBOT, EDWARD, "Wellesley College." *Harper's New Monthly Magazine* (August, 1876).

ABBOT, FRANCES M. "A Generation of College Women." *Forum,* XX, (1895).

———. "Three Decades of College Women." *Popular Science* (1904).

BARNARD., F. A. P. "Should American Colleges Be Open to Women as Well as to Men?" 20th Annual Convocation of the University of the State of New York, Albany, N.Y., 1882.

BARNARD, FREDERICK AUGUSTUS PORTER. *Memoirs of F. A. P. Barnard,* by John Fulton. New York: Macmillan and Co., 1890.

BARNARD COLLEGE. "A History of Barnard College." Published in honor of the 75th Anniversary of the college, 1964.

BEAUVOIR, SIMONE DE. *America Day by Day,* trans. by Patrick Dudley. London: Gerald Duckworth & Co. Ltd., 1952.

BEECHER, CATHARINE E. *A True Remedy for the Wrongs of Women.* Boston, 1851.

BIRD, CAROLYN. "A New Look at Vassar." *American Mercury* (July, 1949).

———. "Fifty Years of Vassar Girls." *Vassar Alumnae Magazine* (October, 1965).

BIRMINGHAM, STEPHEN. *The Grandees: America's Sephardic Elite.* New York: Harper & Row, 1971.

BLATCH, HARRIOT STANTON, and A. LUTZ. *Challenging Years: The Memoirs of Harriot Stanton Blatch.* New York: G. P. Putnam's Sons, 1940.

BOROFF, DAVID. *Campus U.S.A.: Portraits of American Colleges in Action.* New York: Harper & Brothers, 1958—61.

BRACKETT, ANNA C. "Vassar College." *Harper's Magazine* (February, 1876).

BROWN, DONALD R. *Social Changes and the College Student: A Symposium by Donald R. Brown* [and others]. Washington, D.C.: Council on American Education, 1960.

BRUCE, J. M. "The First Great College for Women." New York *Examiner* (April 22, 1897).

BYERLY, WILLIAM E. "Radcliffe College Thirty Years After." *Harvard Graduate Magazine* (December, 1909).

CARTER, C. "Vassar—The Kind of Education Girls Get." *Business Week* (May 26, 1956).

CHENEY, MAY S. "Will Nature Eliminate the College Woman?" *Journal of the Association of College Alumnae* (January, 1905).

COLE, ARTHUR C. *A Hundred Years of Mount Holyoke College, The Evolution of an Educational Ideal.* New Haven: Yale University Press, 1940.

CONANT, CHARLOTTE HOWARD. *A Girl of the Eighties at College and at Home, from the Family Letters of Charlotte Howard Conant and from Other Records.* By Martha Pike Conant and others. Cambridge, Mass.: Houghton Mifflin Co., Riverside Press, 1931.

CONVERSE, FLORENCE. *Story of Wellesley.* Boston: Little, Brown, 1915.

CORDELL, WILLIAM and K. C., "Youth in College," in *American Points of View.* New York: Doubleday, 1937.

DEXTER, ELIZABETH A. *Colonial Women of Affairs.* Boston: Houghton Mifflin, 1924.

EMERICK, C. F. "College Women and Race Suicide." *Political Science Quarterly* (June, 1909).

FINCH, EDITH. *Carey Thomas of Bryn Mawr.* New York: Harper & Brothers, 1947.

FITZGERALD, F. SCOTT. *This Side of Paradise.* New York: Charles Scribner's Sons, 1920.

FORBUSH, GABRIELLE. "How War Strikes Home to a Woman's College." *The Outlook* (November 21, 1917).

FULTON, JOHN. *Memoirs of Frederick A. P. Barnard.* New York: Macmillan and Co., 1896.

GAYNOR, J. "Men of Vassar." *Esquire* (September, 1974).

GILCHRIST, BETH BRADFORD. *The Life of Mary Lyon.* Boston: Houghton Mifflin, 1910.

GILDERSLEEVE, VIRGINIA CROCHERON. *Many a Good Crusade.* New York: Macmillan Co., 1954.

GINZBERG, ELI, and ASSOCIATES. *Life Styles of Educated Women.* New York: Columbia University Press, 1966.

Godey's Lady's Book, The Daughters of America (July, 1864).

GOODLOE, ABBE CARTER. "Undergraduate Life at Wellesley." *Scribner's Magazine,* Vol. 23, No. 5 (May, 1898).

GOODSELL, WILLYSTINE. *The Education of Women: Its Social Background and Its Problems.* New York: Macmillan Company, 1923.

GOULD, JOAN. *The Poet and Her Book: A Biography of Edna St. Vincent Millay.* New York: Dodd, Mead, 1969.

GURKO, MIRIAM. *Restless Spirit—A Biography of Edna St. Vincent Millay.* New York: Collier, 1962.

HACKETT, ALICE PAYNE. *Wellesley: Part of the American Story.* New York: E. P. Dutton & Co., 1949.

HALSTED, C. "College Life at Vassar and Wellesley." *Metropolitan Magazine* (July, 1898).

HANSCOM, ELIZABETH DEERING, and HELEN FRENCH GREENE. *Sophia Smith and the Beginnings of Smith College, Based upon the Narrative by John Morton Greene.* Northampton, Mass., 1925.

HIGGINSON, THOMAS W. "Ought Women to Learn the Alphabet?" *Atlantic Monthly,* Vol. III (1859).

HITCHCOCK, EDWARD. *The Power of Christian Benevolence Illustrated in the Life and Labors of Mary Lyon.* New York: American Tract Society, 1858.

HODGKINS, LOUISE MANNING. "Wellesley College." *New England Magazine* (November, 1892).

JORDAN, MARY A. "The College for Women." *Atlantic Monthly,* Vol. LXX (1892).

———. "The Heads of Some Women's Colleges." *Outlook* (August 2, 1902).

KAHN, E. J., JR. *Harvard—Through Change and Through Storm.* New York: W. W. Norton & Co., 1968.

Kendall, Elaine. "Miss Blanding's Dream House." *Saturday Review* (June 16, 1962).

KILPATRICK, WILLIAM H. *The Dutch Schools of New Netherlands and Colonial New York.* Washington, D. C.: Government Printing Office, 1912.

LETTERS FROM OLD-TIME VASSAR, written by a student in 1869–70. Poughkeepsie: Vassar College, 1915.

LOSSING, BENSON J. *Vassar College and Its Founder.* New York: C. A. Alvard, 1867.

MACDOUGALL, ALLAN ROSS. *Letters of Edna St. Vincent Millay.* New York: Harper & Brothers, 1952.

MARKS, JEANETTE. *The Life and Letters of Mary Emma Woolley.* Washington, D.C.: Public Affairs Press, 1955.

MARTIN, GEORGE H. "The Early Education of Girls in Massachusetts." *Education,* Vol. XX (1900).

"Matthew Vassar and the Vassar Female College." *American Journal of Education,* Vol. XI (1862.)

MCCARTHY, MARY. *On the Contrary.* New York: Farrar, Straus and Cudahy, 1961.

———. *The Group.* New York: Harcourt, Brace, 1954.

MCCORD, DAVID. *An Acre for Education: Being Notes on the History of Radcliffe College.* Cambridge, Mass.: Crimson Printing Co., 1958.

MEIGS, CORNELIA. *What Makes a College? A History of Bryn Mawr.* New York: Macmillan Co., 1956.

MEYER, ANNIE NATHAN. *Barnard Beginnings.* Boston: Houghton Mifflin, 1935.

———. *It's Been Fun.* New York: Scherwin, 1951.

MILLER, ALICE DUER, MYERS, SUSAN. *Barnard College: The First Fifty Years.* New York: Columbia University Press, 1939.

MITCHELL, MARIA. "The Collegiate Education of Girls." *Education,* Vol. I (1881).

Mount Holyoke College Memorial, 25th Anniversary of the Mount Holyoke Female

Seminary. Published for the Seminary by S. Bowles & Co., Springfield, Mass, South Hadley, Mass., 1862.

MOUNT HOLYOKE FEMALE SEMINARY. "Mary Lyon's Plan for the New England Seminary for Teachers." College Archives, 1832.

NICHOLS, DAVID C. "Perspectives on Campus Tensions." 1970 American Council on Education, Washington (papers prepared for the Special Committee on Campus Tensions).

PHELPS, ALMIRA L. *Hours with My Pupils.* New York, 1859.

PLUM, DOROTHY A., and GEORGE B. DOWELL. *The Magnificent Enterprise: A Chronicle of Vassar College,* edited and annotated with additions by Constance Dimock Ellis. New York: Poughkeepsie, 1961.

RADCLIFFE COLLEGE. *Report of Radcliffe Historian for 1903.*

RICHARDS, H. M. "The Curriculum and Equipment of Barnard College." *Columbia University Quarterly* (March, 1910).

ROGERS, AGNES. *Vassar Women: An Informal Study.* Poughkeepsie: Vassar College, 1940.

RUSH, BENJAMIN. *Essays: Literary, Moral and Philosophical Thoughts upon Female Education.* Philadelphia: 1798.

RUSSELL, BERTRAND. *The Autobiography of Bertrand Russell, 1872–1914.* Boston: Little, Brown, 1967.

SACK, SAUL. *History of Higher Education in Pennsylvania.* Harrisburg: Commonwealth of Pennsylvania, Pennsylvania Historical and Museum Commission, 1963.

SAFFORD, IRENE A. "The Decision of Columbia College." *Overland Monthly* (May, 1883).

SEELYE, L. CLARK. *The Early History of Smith College.* Boston: Houghton Mifflin, 1923.

Smith College: Celebration of the Quarter Century, Cambridge, Mass.: Riverside Press, 1900.

Smith College Prospectus, 1872, 1873, 1874 (College Library).

STEIN, GERTRUDE, *Fernhurst, Q.E.D. and Other Early Writings,* ed. Leon Katz. New York: Liveright. 1971.

———. *The Making of Americans.* New York: Something Else Press, 1965.

———. *Selected Writings of Gertrude Stein, ed.* Carl van Vechten. New York, Random House: 1946.

STOW, SARAH D. (Locke). *Class of 1859, History of Mount Holyoke Seminary, South Hadley, Mass., During its First Half Century 1837–1887,* published by the seminary, 1887.

TAYLOR, JAMES MONROE. *Before Vassar Opened—A Contribution to the History of the Higher Education of Women in America,* Cambridge, Mass.: Houghton Mifflin, 1914.

TETLOW, JOHN. "The Eastern Colleges for Women." *Education,* Vol. I (1881).

THARP, LOUISE HALL. *Adventurous Alliance: The Story of the Agassiz Family of Boston.* Boston: Little, Brown, 1959.

THOMAS, CALVIN. "Social Life at Barnard." *Columbia University Quarterly* (June, 1900).

THOMAS, M. CAREY. "The Curriculum of the Women's College." *Journal of the American College Association* (February, 1903).

———. "Should the Higher Education of Women Differ from That of Men?" *Educational Review*, Vol. XXI (1901).

THOMPSON, ELEANOR WOLF. *Education for Ladies 1830–1860.* New York: Kings Crown Press, 1947.

Traditions at Wellesley 1875–1916, compiled and edited by Executive Board of Wellesley College Alumnae Association. Chicago: 1916.

WARNER, FRANCES LESTER. *On a New England Campus.* Boston: Houghton Mifflin, 1937.

WARNER, JOSEPH B. "Radcliffe College." *Harvard Graduate Magazine* (March, 1894).

WHARTON, ANNE H. *Colonial Days and Dames.* Philadelphia: Lippincott, 1900.

WILLARD, EMMA. *Plan for the Improvement of Female Education,* quoted in Henry Barnard educational biography: *Memoirs of Teachers, Educators, Promotors and Benefactors of Education, Literature and Science.* New York: 1861.

WILLARD, J. H. (MRS.) "A Memorial of the Late Emma Willard." Procedures of the Seventh Anniversary of the University Convocation, State of New York, 1876.

———. "A Sketch of the History of Troy Seminary." Procedures of the Thirteenth Anniversary of the University Convocation, State of New York, 1876.

WINTHROP, JOHN. *The History of New England 1630–1649.* Boston: 1853. 2 vols.

WOODY, THOMAS. *A History of Women's Education in the United States.* New York: The Science Press, 1929. 2 vols.

Index

263

Black, Patricia, 230
Black students, 204, 227–28, 246–47
Black studies courses, 247
Blaine, Amory, 167
Blanding, Sarah Gibson, 226, 234–36
Blatch, Harriot Stanton, 126–27, 145, 146
Boissevain, Eugen, 169
Booth, Lydia, 42
Boston *Advocate*, 98
Boston School of Oratory, 127
Boston University, 115
Bradstreet, Anne, 11
Briggs, Dr. Le Baron Russell, 156
Brinckerhoff, Mrs. Van Wyck, 158
Britten, Florence Haxton, 191
Bromley, Dorothy Dunbar, 191
Brown, Donald, 219, 226–27, 231
Brown University, 116
Bryant, William Cullen, 59
Bryn Mawr College, 29, 35, 132 ff., 144,
    161, 162, 167, 183, 203, 213, 221, 222,
    223, 228, 232, 248
    alumnae, professional, 230–31
    alumnae volunteer projects, 194
    coeducation with Haverford, 244, 252
    curriculum, 179–80
    and the Depression, 193, 194
    expulsion clause, 236
    founding of, 82–88
    image, 30
    marriage, postwar, 212
    religious atmosphere, 211
    sixties' student unrest, 239
    and women's liberation movement, 244
Byerly, William F., 64

Cam, Dr. Helen, 156
Cambridge Public Library, 65
Career opportunities for women vs. mar-
    riage, 216–17
    post-World War II attitude toward,
        217, 223–25, 230–31
    and sixties' alumnae, 248
    World War II, and, 204–5

Carnegie, Andrew, 166
Carret, Mrs., 65
Carey Thomas of Bryn Mawr (Finch),
    136–37, 139
Carroll, Thomas, 19
Catholic finishing schools, 96
Channing, Edward, 155
Cheney, Grace, 182

Civil Liberties Union, 175
Civil War, 103, 104
Clark, Miss, 125
Clarke's Deaf and Dumb Academy, 115
Clinton, De Witt, 9
Cliqueishness, 228–29
Coeducation, 30–31, 79, 84–85, 115, 173,
    201, 234–35, 239, 250–57
    Columbia-Barnard, 157
    and Ivy League, 30, 31–32, 33–34
    at Radcliffe-Harvard, 153, 156
    and Seven College Conference, 30–34
    at Vassar, 30, 32–33, 252–55
Cohen, Gustave, 201
College Equal Suffrage League, 146
College Humor, 179
Colonial Days and Dames (Wharton), 12
Colonies, and education for women,
    10–12
Columbia University, 30, 88, 248, 252
    affiliation with Barnard, 157–59
    and founding of Barnard, 71
Columbia University Medical School, 72
Committee on the Collegiate Education
    of Women, 72
Communism, 177–78, 190–91
Comparative Guide to American Colleges
    (Cass/Birnbaum), 89
Comte, Auguste, 223
Conant, Charlotte, 121, 124, 125–26
Conant, James B., 155
Connecticut Valley exchange, 255–56
Cook, J. P., 64
Cooperative houses, 188
Copeland, Charles Townsend, 154, 155
Cornell, Ezra, 86
Cornell University, 86–87, 115, 127, 203
Coué, Émile, 177
Crabbe, George, 15, 16
Crawford, Cheryl, 183
Crocheron, Virginia. *See* Gildersleeve,
    Virginia Crocheron
Curfew hours, 168, 177
Curtin, Phyllis, 230

Dame schools, 15–16, 17, 18, 20
Dartmouth College, 30, 33, 250, 255, 256
Darwin, Charles, 110
Darwinian theory of evolution, 109–10
De Beauvoir, Simone, 196–99, 205
Democratic Club, 126
Depression, the, 185–95, 203, 205
Descartes, René, 223

265

Gould, Jean, 160
Grading systems, 241–43
Graduate schools, women and, 193, 205, 218–19, 220
Grandees, The (Birmingham), 75
Grant, Ulysses S., 104
Grant, Zilpah, 213
Grasso, Ella, 194
Gray, John C., 69–70
Gray, Mrs. John C., 69
Green, Julian, 201
Greene, John, 50–52
Greenfield, Meg, 230
Greenough, Chester Noyes, 155
Griswold, A. Whitney, 234
Group, The (McCarthy), 183, 232
Gwinn, Mamie, 88, 134–37, 140

Hadamard, Jacques, 201
Hail, Dorothy, 226
Hale, Sarah Josepha, 23
Ham, Roswell Gray, 176
Hampshire College, 255
Hankey, Mary Parsons, 74–75
Harper's New Monthly Magazine, 54, 105, 124
Hartford Seminary, 22, 23, 26
Harvard Corporation, 65, 66, 68, 69
Harvard University, 30, 55, 71, 74, 116, 153–54, 185, 225, 250, 252, 256, 257
   and founding of Radcliffe, 62–63, 64, 65–70
   integration of classes with Radcliffe, 204
   parietal rules, 237
Harvard Annex, 66–68, 153. *See also* Radcliffe College
Haskins, Charles H., 155
Haverford College, 30, 82, 84, 244, 252
Hayes, Ellen, 215–16
Hedge, F. H., 64
Hemingway, Ernest, 181
Hepburn, Katharine, 183
History of New England 1630–1649 (Winthrop), 10
Hitchcock, Edward, 36
Hitler, Adolf, 175, 201, 222
Hodder, Alfred, 134–35, 136, 137, 140
Hokinson, Helen, 195
Holiday, 183
Homer, Dr. Mary 102
Homosexuality, 142–43. *See also* Fern-

hurst; *Group, The;* Thomas, Martha Carey
Hooper, Edward, 68
Hooton, Earnest, 155
Hoover, Herbert, 186
Hopkins, Mistress, 13
Horner, Matina, 225, 231
Howard, Ada, 123, 124
Howland Institute, 86
Hoy, Helen, 145
Humphrey, Sarah, 113
Hutchinson, Anne, 10–11

I Thought of Daisy (Wilson), 169
Insull, Samuel, 187
Intellectual Philosophy (Smellie), 96
Interim term, 241–42
Intramural activities, 191–92
Irwin, Agnes, 155
It's Been Fun (Nathan), 76
Ivy League, 217, 228. *See also* specific colleges
   and academic refugees, 199
   and coeducation, 250–51, 255

James, King of England, 79
James, Henry, 168
James, William, 64, 155
Jazz Age, 167–84, 185, 191, 214
Jefferson, Thomas, 9–10, 12
Jewett, Milo P., 42–47
Johns Hopkins University, 87–88
Jong, Erica, 230
Journal of the Association of College Alumnae, 180
Journal of Social Studies, 129, 226
Joyce, James, 168, 181, 222

Katharine Gibbs secretarial school, 182, 192–93
Katz, Leon, 140
Keller, Helen, 155
Kelly, Mrs., 156–57
Keynes, John Maynard, 223
King, Bessie, 86
Kingsley, Florence Morse, 123
Kithredge, Dr., 102
Kittredge, George Lyman, 155
Kovel, Terry, 231
Ku Klux Klan, 181
Kumin, Maxine, 230
Kunen, James, 248

269

and sixties, 234 ff.
and World War II, 206, 207–8
Sexual Politics (Millett), 244
Shapley, Harlow, 155
Shattuck, Lydia, 110
Silver, Clara, 144
Simpson, Alan, 254
Siquieros, David Alfaro, 192
Sketches of the History, Genius, and Disposition of the Fair Sex (Anonymous), 24
Smith, Austin, 48–50, 51, 53
Smith, Emily James, 158
Smith, Sophia, 35, 48–53, 58, 114–15, 257
Smith College, 29, 66, 111, 120, 122, 124, 126, 156, 161, 170, 183, 204, 205, 208, 218, 228, 229, 234
  all-girl dances, 147
  alumnae, distinguished, 219–20
  alumnae, professional, 230
  alumnae volunteer projects, 194
  black students, 246
  coeducation, 31, 32, 34, 254–57
  De Beauvoir's description of, 198
  and the Depression, 186, 189, 193, 194
  distribution requirements, 242
  early years of, 113–19
  and feminist movement, 226, 244, 246
  and foreign students, 202
  founding of, 48–53
  image, 30, 48
  interim term, 242
  and Jazz Age, 176
  married graduates, 128
  and parietal rules, 238
  and political activism, 190–91
  religious exposure, 211
  and SDS, 240
  secret societies, 148–49
  sexual mores, 207
  "special students" enrollment, 118
  "unwritten code," 113, 119
  and World War II, 196, 207
Smith College News, 202
Smoking ban, 173–74, 202
Social clubs, 173
Socialism, 190
Society for the Collegiate Instruction of Women, 62–67
Society of Religious Inquiry, 110
Solzhenitsyn, Alexander, 230
Sophia Smith College, 53. *See* Smith College
Sophian, 247

"Sophomore slump," 208–11
Sororities, 148
Sorosis, 71
Spacks, Patricia Meyer, 230
Spars, 205
Speakeasies, 171
Sprague, Dr. Robert, 218–29
Springfield *Republican*, 116
Springfield *Union*, 98
Stafford, Deacon, 91
Stanton, Elizabeth Cady, 126, 127
Stanton, Harriot. *See* Blatch, Harriot Stanton
State support, for female education, 9–10
Stein, Gertrude, 134, 139–41, 142, 155, 232
Stein, Leo, 134, 140
Steinbeck, John, 192
Steinem, Gloria, 230, 244
Stillwell, Mary Elizabeth, 123
Stimpson, Catherine, 230
Stock market crash, 173, 185
Strawberry Statement, The (Kunen), 248
Students' Aid Society, 185
Student unrest, 233–49
Success, fear of, 225
Suffrage movement, 76, 78, 79, 81, 103, 126–27, 131–32, 143, 144 ff.
Sullivan, Annie, 155
Swarthmore College, 238

Taylor, Abraham, 83
Taylor, Hannah, 85
Taylor, James Monroe, 145
Taylor, Dr. Joseph, 35, 82–88
Teaching profession
  origin of, 25–28
  training for, 27
  women and, 93, 104, 144, 170, 182
Tenney, Professor, 109
Tennyson, Alfred Lord, 59
Textbooks, early, 18–19
This Side of Paradise (Fitzgerald), 167
Thomas, Helen, 141
Thomas, James, 85, 86–88
Thomas, Mrs. James, 87
Thomas, Martha Carey, 85–88, 130, 132–42, 162–63, 170, 179–80
Thomas, Norman, 190
Thoughts upon Female Education (Rush), 22
Tilden, Samuel, 127
Tolkien, J. R. R., 230
Towne, Edward C., 111, 256–57

270

272